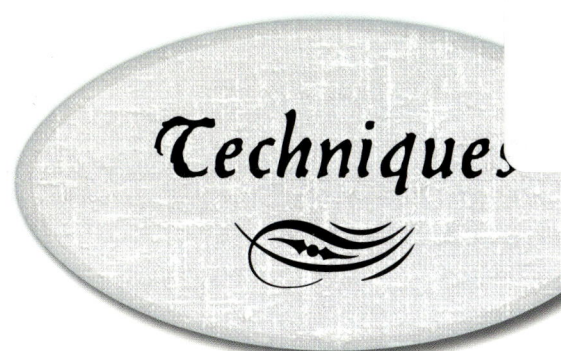

Techniques

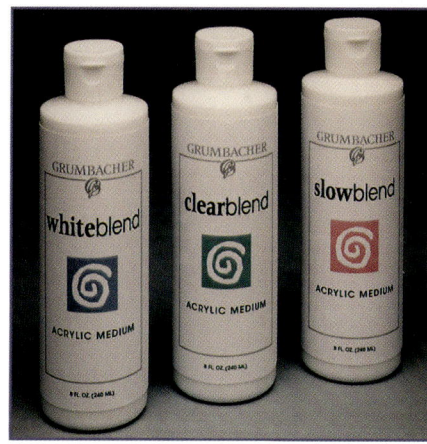

The instructions in this text depend on Grumbacher's fine acrylic colors, brushes and mediums, including extensive use of Whiteblend, Clearblend and Slowblend. These paints and mediums are water-based and non-toxic. If substitutes are used, the results will vary. Whiteblend, Clearblend and Slowblend are special mediums that slow the drying time of acrylic paints and allow even a novice to create beautiful color blends the first time. They make painting with acrylics very easy, and you will need them throughout this series. Use only cool, clean water when mixing, painting or cleaning up with these paints and mediums—not oils, thinners or turpentine.

Grumbacher Wet Palette

This is the best way to keep acrylics wet on the palette for as long as you choose, letting you use paint that was mixed hours or even days before. Saturate the sponge pad with water until it almost floats in the tray. Wet both sides of the special paper, place it on the pad and remove any puddles or wrinkles.

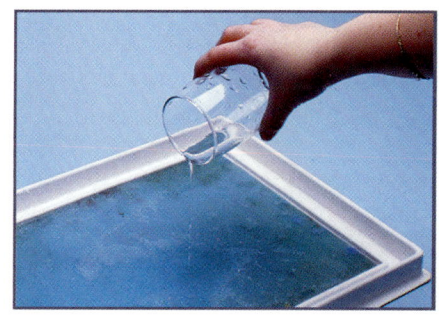

Place your paints on the palette paper and mix your colors. The paint will stay workable as long as the sponge pad remains wet. As the pad dries out around the edges, the paper will curl. When this happens, lift up a corner of the paper, pour water over the pad and press the paper back in place. Place the lid on the tray when you need to store mixed paints.

Mixing Colors

Mixing colors, like painting, is an art—not a science! It's up to you to decide exact hues; there are no precise formulas. The color mixtures in this book are based on Grumbacher Finest Artists' Acrylics. Colors are listed in order of the quantity used; some approximate proportions are given. Often it's best to mix colors directly on the brush or sponge. This is particularly useful when only a small amount is needed or when a gradual change of value or color is desired, as when highlighting an object.

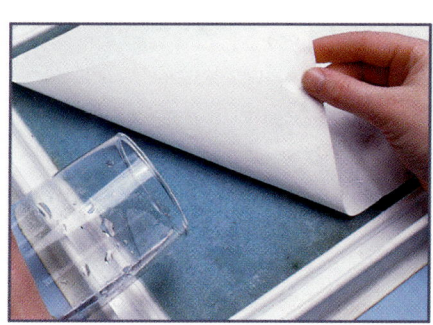

All the projects in this book require some colors to be prepared before you begin. For these mixtures, squeeze out a marble-sized dollop of each tube pigment required along the edge of your palette paper. Use a clean painting knife to pull a small amount (about the size of a pea) of the first pigment from the dollop. Add other colors in lesser amounts and mix to a uniform shade. Mix and adjust the color as needed. It is easier to add color to a mixture than to subtract it, so always start with small portions. When you have determined the right proportions, mix the amount you think you'll need. Often more paint is required than expected, and the excess is handy for touching up the painting.

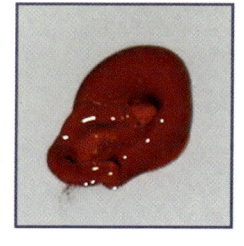

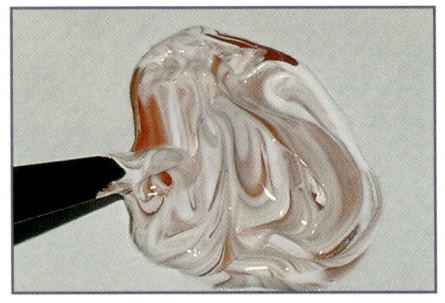

Unless the instructions state otherwise, paint mixtures should have the "creamy" consistency of Whiteblend. Occasionally the instructions will call for a *watery* consistency—add enough water to the paint to give it the density of ink. When instructed to create a *marbleized* mixture, do not mix the paints completely, but rather leave a mottled, streaky appearance as shown at left.

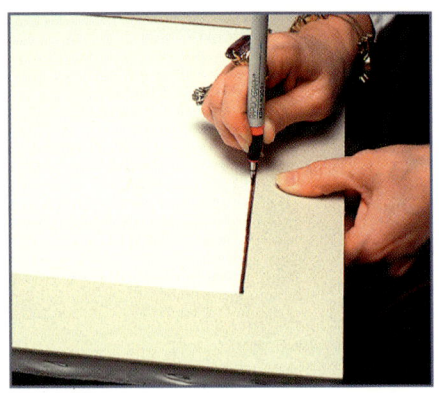

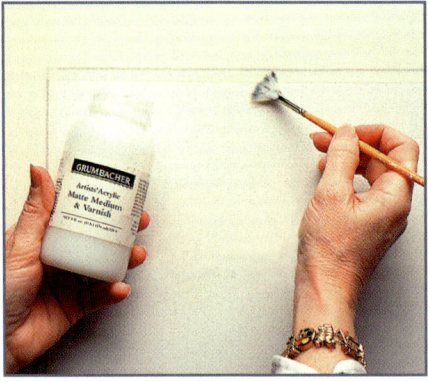

French Matting

Lay the canvas on a flat surface, then place the mat template over it. Hold the template securely and go around the inside edges with a Rapidograph pen. Remove the template and dry the ink. Cover the border with masking or shipping tape, overlapping the tape about ½" inside the ink lines. Seal the tape by applying Grumbacher Matte Medium over the inside edges of the tape, fading toward the canvas center; dry.

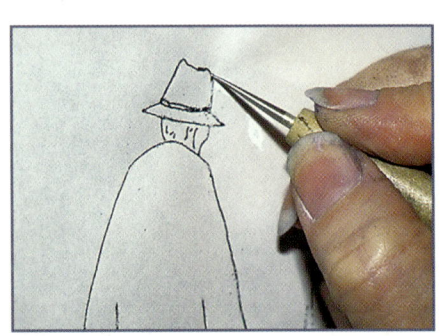

Transferring a pattern

Transferring and Protecting the Design

Select the appropriate pattern from the pullout section of this book. Lay the canvas on a flat, sturdy surface. Refer to the painting instructions to position the pattern, then tape it firmly in place. (Note: The patterns are flexible; you can move the elements around.)

Insert a piece of graphite paper between the pattern and canvas, shiny side down; trace the lines with a stylus or pencil to transfer them. Lift a corner of the graphite paper to check for missed lines.

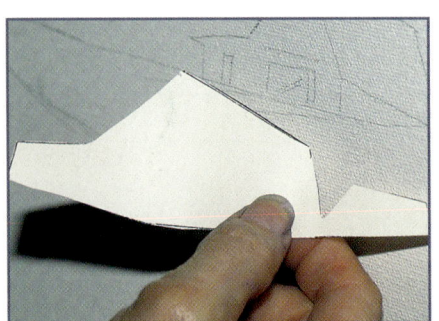

Applying an adhesive protector

When the directions require an adhesive design protector, use the same technique to trace only the outline onto adhesive paper. Cut out the image, remove the backing and press it onto the canvas.

Paint carefully around the adhesive protector. Start with the brush on the cutout area and stroke away from it. If you stroke toward the protector, you will force paint under it.

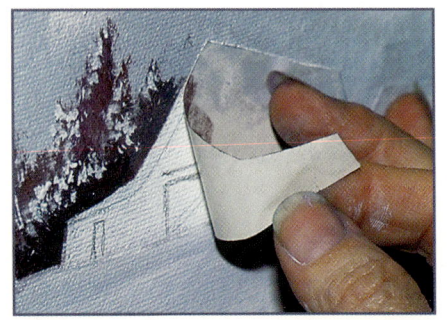

Removing the protector after painting

If transfer lines remain after the painting is finished, after the area thoroughly dries, erase the lines with a kneaded eraser or clean moist sponge.

Applying Paints

Familiarize yourself by studying the color placements of the painting. Read through the instructions, visualizing how you are going to execute each step. Have a piece of canvas or a scrap of watercolor paper handy to test your colors and strokes before applying them to the painting. Working **wet-on-wet**, wet paint over wet paint, is easy. Use a clean, towel-dried brush or sponge and work quickly. Working **wet-on-dry**, wet paint over dry paint, is easier. Use a clean, moist brush or tool. This technique allows you to work as quickly or as slowly as you desire. Working **wet-on-sticky**, wet paint over drying or sticky paint, is tricky! Add Clearblend or Slowblend to the sticky area of paint, allow the paint to dry thoroughly, then touch up with a wet-over-dry technique.

Loading the brushes: Keep a large container of clean water nearby, and always moisten your brushes before using them. Before loading them with paint, remove excess water from large brushes by squeezing the bristles. Tap smaller brushes on a clean towel. If you do not get good coverage, moisten the brush again.

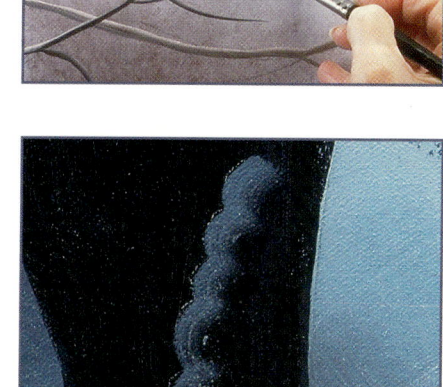

Double-loading: This refers to applying two colors to the brush at one time. It is easier for creating delicate details such as birds or tree limbs, as shown at the top right. Load the brush with the darkest color of the subject matter. Pull one side of the brush through the highlight color to create a dark and a light side. Position the brush so the stroke will be half dark and half light as you draw it along the canvas.

Side-loading: Load the angle brush with Clearblend and blot on a paper towel to remove the excess. Dip the long tip of the brush in the paint. Stroke the brush back and forth on a clean spot on your palette to move the paint from the long tip to the shorter tip. The paint should fade from solid on the long tip to very light on the short tip. Pull the brush on the canvas, reloading as necessary.

Loading a painting knife: Use the knife to spread the paint in a thin layer across the palette. Remove the paint from the knife. Hold the knife edge in the paint and pull diagonally to load a ribbon of paint on the edge. After loading the knife, follow the instructions in each painting to use it.

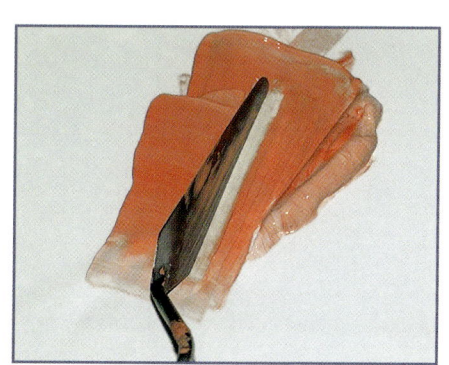

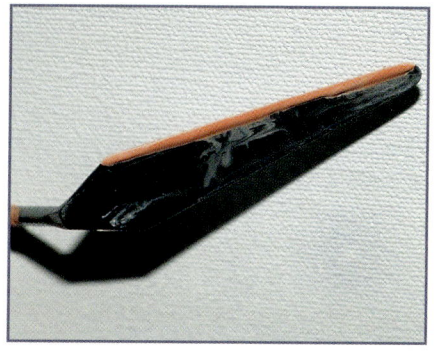

Blending colors: Apply each color quickly and generously, overlapping them at least ½". Use a clean, towel-dried brush and work over the overlapped area with elongated figure-8 strokes, frequently wiping the excess paint off the brush. When the colors are mingled, blend with long strokes, brushing back and forth. Begin blending with firm pressure; use a feather touch for the finishing strokes.

Pat-blending: Load the brush generously with Clearblend, lightly wiping off the excess on a paper towel. Apply the highlight color with a different brush, then pat and tap with the blending brush to gradually soften the edges into the background color. Don't work too hard to blend the colors smoothly—an irregular look is more natural.

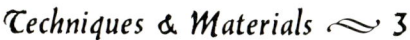

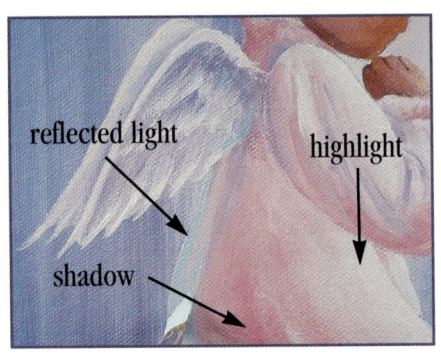

Highlights, shadows, and reflected light: For highlights, blend lighter color into an area that is brighter. For shading, blend darker colors into the shadows. Reflected light appears in shaded areas and actually reflects the paint nearby, whether it is on the background or on the focal object.

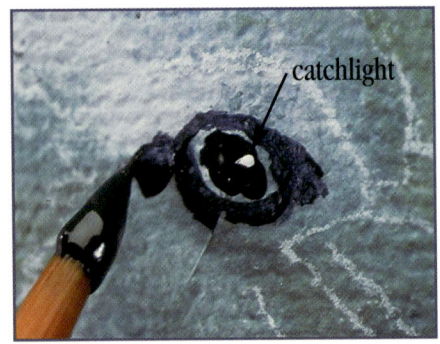

Catchlights: A catchlight is a sharpened highlight on a shiny object such as a bubble or an eye. They may be white or may simply be dots of a brighter color, but usually have sharp edges.

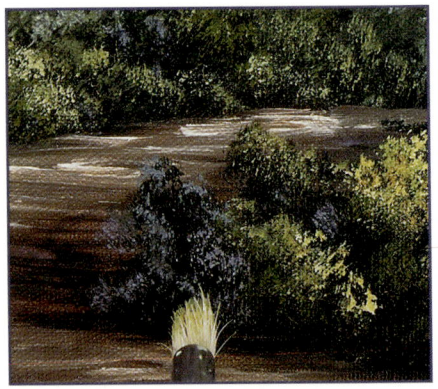

Crunching, stippling and tapping: Occasionally the instructions call for you to "crunch" in a color. Hold the loaded brush perpendicular to the canvas and push straight in, fanning the bristles out a bit. "Stippling" uses the same motion with a little less pressure; "tapping" or "patting" uses even less pressure than stippling. All leave a speckled appearance on the canvas, but the amount of paint varies with the technique.

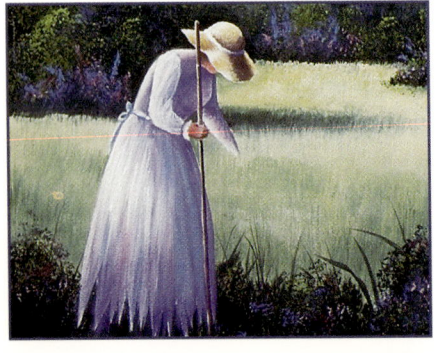

Contrast, perspective and depth: Place dark colors against light and light colors against dark. Darker, more vibrant colors are generally placed in the foreground; lighter, muted colors are applied in the background. Objects of medium value are placed between.

The more distant the object, the smaller it becomes and the closer it appears to the horizon line. Middle ground objects will be farther from the horizon, larger, and more defined. The foreground objects are lowest on the canvas, largest in size and most sharply focused.

Special Techniques

Skies: Work quickly, blocking in the sky colors with a generous amount of paint. Overlap colors ½" or more. Blend immediately with a clean, towel-dried brush until the desired effect is achieved.

Half-dry skies and backgrounds always look streaked; you may have the urge to overwork them, but don't. Allow them to dry completely. After the painting is finished, you will find that a streak or two in the sky or background is realistic. If the appearance is still unacceptable when dry, touch up with a wet-on-dry technique or paint over it completely.

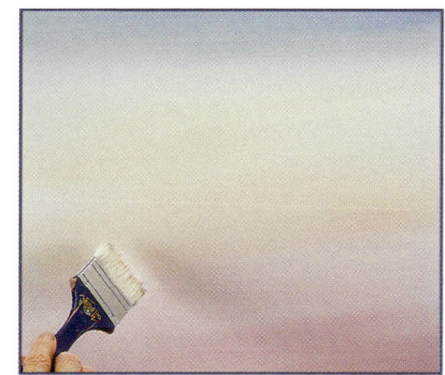

Reflections and water lines: Water works like a mirror, picking up images and colors around it. Visualize your subject matter sitting on a mirror and paint the reflection accordingly. Keep all predominant strokes horizontal.

Add horizontal water lines to make the reflections appear to be underwater. For lines, load the painting knife with Whiteblend and place the edge horizontally against the canvas. Soften the edges with a clean brush moistened with Clearblend. For more coverage, hold the knife at a 45° angle. Reflections can be painted wet-on-wet or added to a dry surface.

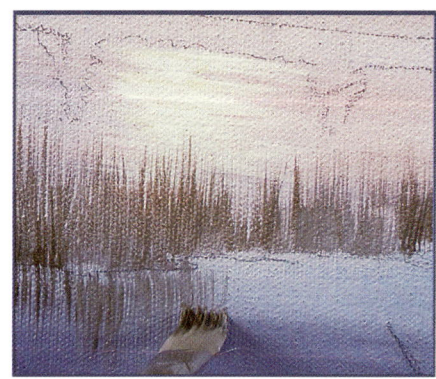

Ocean waves: Oceans and waves can be painted either wet-on-wet or wet-on-dry. Apply the basic colors and blend them using the wet-on-wet technique.

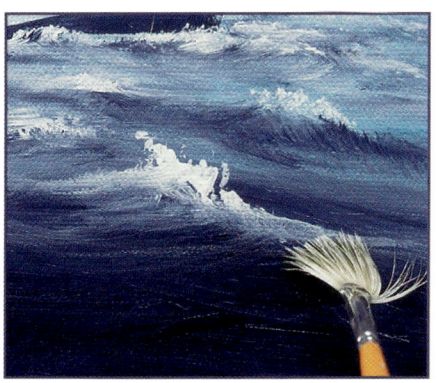
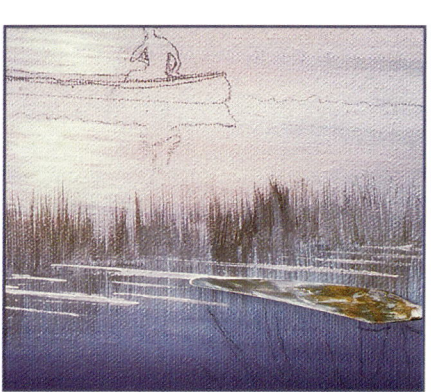

Use a painting knife to paint a tide or reflection line, gradually turning the knife flatter on the canvas as you move it. For distant whitecaps or reflections, add a horizontal highlight below the tide line with either a painting knife or a liner brush. Soften or blend the bottom and side edges with a brush moistened with Clearblend.

Grass: With a variety of tools, strokes and techniques, many different appearances can be achieved. The illusion of grass can be created either wet-on-wet or wet-on-dry.

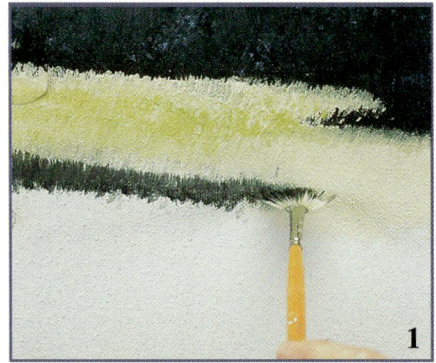

To quickly create a large area or field of grass use two gesso brushes. Alternate one brush loaded with a light color and another loaded with a dark color. For a more controlled appearance or for smaller areas of grass, use the fan or multi-texture brush. To avoid bare spots in marsh or field grass, each additional row should slightly overlap the base of the previous row.

1 Tapping or patting refers to positioning the brush with the handle down, bristles up and almost flat against the canvas. Pat the bristles repeatedly against the canvas. Tap back and forth between the colors on the canvas to create gradual transitions.

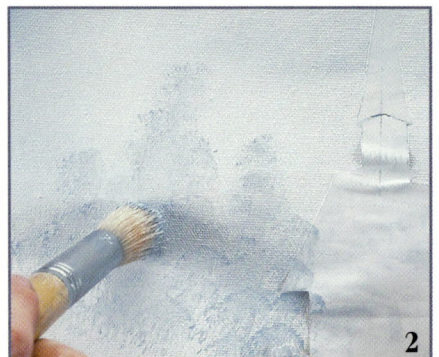

2 When crunching or stippling in the grass, hold the brush perpendicular to the canvas. Press the brush against the canvas with a slightly upward thrust, causing the bristles to arch slightly and the top bristles flare. This will create many irregular grass blades. Be careful to prevent the bristles from sliding upward.

3 To "pull up" or "lift up" grass, stroke the brush upward, using firm pressure at the bottom and applying less and less pressure at the tip until the brush lifts off the canvas. Paint detailed grasses using a liner brush and thinned paint.

Regardless of the brushes or techniques you choose, a general rule for creating depth is to make the grass strokes smaller and closer together and use lighter colors near the horizon. Bolder and larger strokes and darker colors should be used for grass at the bottom of the canvas.

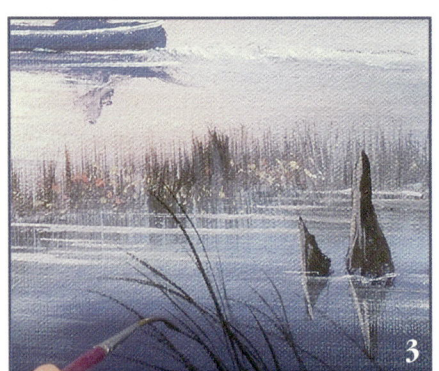

Experiment and you will find that the best results are achieved by using a combination of brushes and strokes and by using both the wet-on-wet and wet-on-dry techniques.

Drying Your Painting

Acrylics dry at an uneven rate. Often the outer edges of an application begin to dry first. This can cause a spotty appearance when drying, but the color will even out when it is completely dry. Acrylics will be darker when dry than while wet.

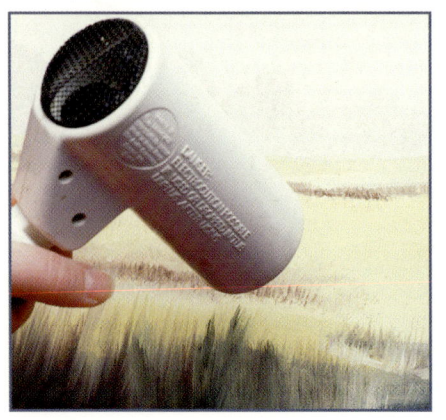

Two techniques that will extend a painting's dry time: Moisten the canvas with water before applying paint, or add a few drops of Slowblend or Grumbacher Acrylic Retarder to each tube color on your palette before mixing. Do not add more than one part medium to two parts paint.

Keep a hair dryer handy when you paint—it can save you a lot of time between steps. Hold the hair dryer a few inches away from the canvas. Use a low temperature and keep moving it around the canvas.

Signing Your Painting

Stand back and look over your painting. Believe it or not, it will be even more beautiful tomorrow! You can sign your painting with watery acrylic paint or a Koh-I-Noor Rapidograph pen.

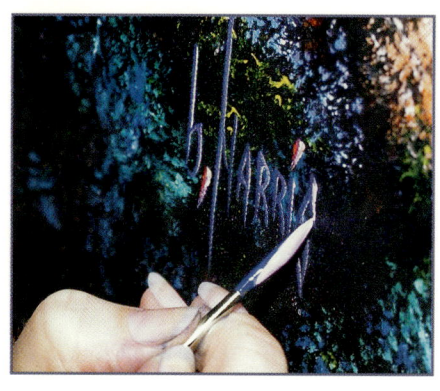

After your painting is completed and signed, let it dry thoroughly, then use a kneaded eraser to remove any remaining pencil or graphite lines. Varnish it with Grumbacher Acrylic Painting Varnish or with Matte Medium.

Cleaning Your Brushes

Wipe excess paint off your brushes with a rag, then wash them with Grumbacher Brush Soap and cool, clean tap water. The soap container has a ridged cleaning surface. Lather the brush and lightly scrub it on the grid. Rinse; towel dry. This will clean and condition the brushes at the same time. Allow them to dry flat to avoid bent bristles.

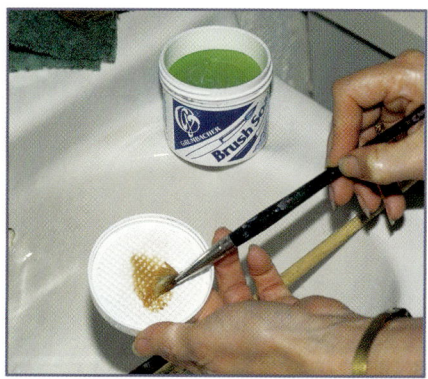

Dry paint can be removed from brushes or other areas with alcohol. Denatured alcohol works best. If a brush is hard with acrylic paint, you may need to soak it for a few minutes before attempting to remove the paint. Be careful with the alcohol—it can remove the finish from some furniture!

Correcting Mistakes

Are you afraid of making a mistake while painting? Don't be! Know up front that you will occasionally make a mistake. We all do. No matter how long you paint or how masterful you become as an artist, you will make a mistake from time to time. The only people not making mistakes are those who are doing nothing at all.

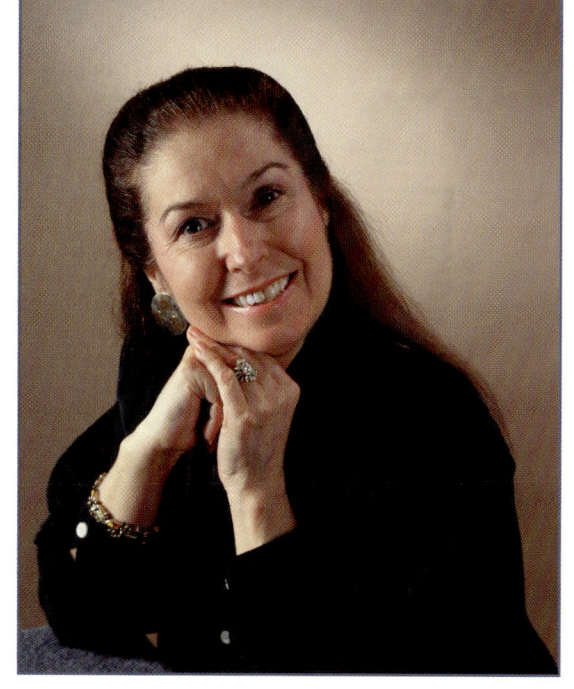

Anything you put on your canvas can be corrected. If it is wet, you simply wipe it off. If dry, you can scrub it off with a toothbrush moistened with Slowblend. For tougher jobs, use a wire brush from the hardware store, or simply paint over it!

Because acrylics dry quickly, it is best to stop and fix obvious errors as they occur. Keep a clean, damp sponge handy to wipe them out. It is also best to dry your painting thoroughly between steps; then errors will simply wipe off, leaving the dry paint undisturbed.

If you have painted a fat limb or a crooked line, you know it right away. Use a clean, moist angle brush to push excess paint back into the line or remove it.

If you have really goofed—and the goofy thing has dried—you can still fix the painting. If it is a mistake covering a large area, just paint over it. Train yourself to think creatively! Could you cover it with foliage or a cloud?

The best source of correcting techniques is to view them as they are demonstrated in my workshops. Hope to see you there! Now, let's paint!

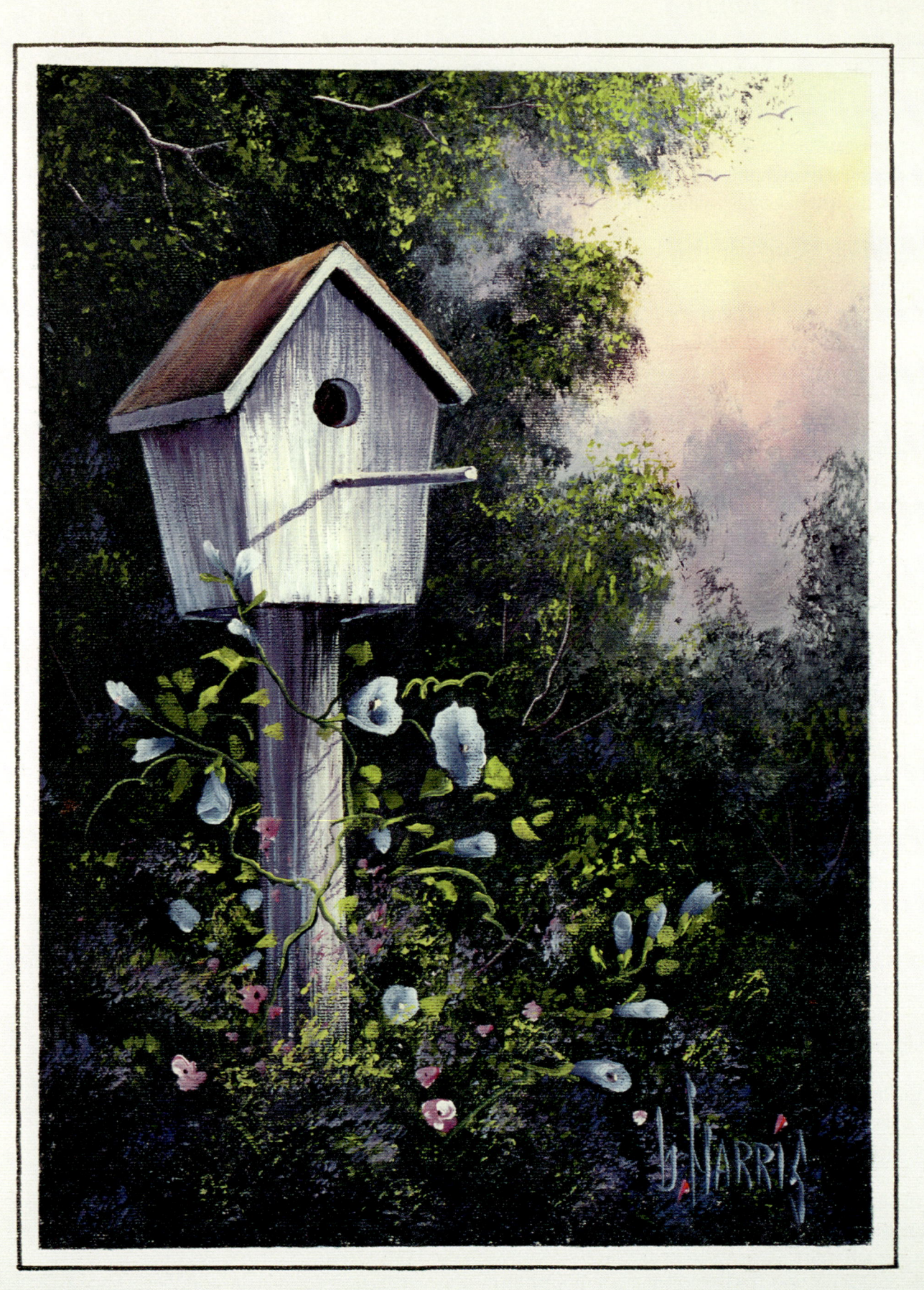

Home Tweet Home

Grumbacher Acrylic Colors
Burnt Sienna
Cerulean Blue
Dioxazine Purple
Hooker's Green
Payne's Gray
Thalo Crimson
Thalo Yellow Green
Yellow Ochre Light

Brushes
#101 Gesso Brush, Size 2"
#1060 White Bristle Fan Brush, Size 1
#4403 Sable Essence® Angular Bright Brush, Size ½"
#4610B Golden Edge® Bright Brush, Size 6
#4623 Golden Edge® Liner Brush, Size 2
#1600 Multi-Texture Brush, Size ½"
#1500 Hake Brush, Size 2"
#582 Eterna Bristle Round Brush, Size 8 and 12

Other Supplies
16"x20" Stretched Canvas
Grumbacher Clearblend
Grumbacher Whiteblend
16"x20" Mat Template (12"x15½" Opening)
Matte Medium
Rapidograph Pen #2.0
Rapidograph Waterproof Ink: Payne's Gray
Masking Tape
Tapered Painting Knife
Natural Sponge, Stylus
White Graphite Paper
Wet Palette
Grumbacher Acrylic Painting Varnish

"Home Tweet Home" is for my friend Linda Loring—owner of The Crafty Lady Arts and Craft store in Yalesville, CT. Her special request for a birdhouse painting inspired me to create this. We hope you like it.

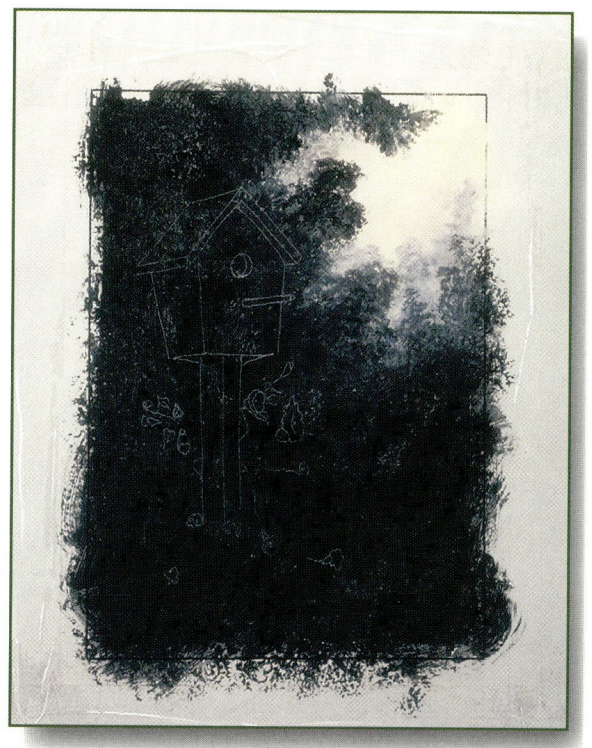

Palette
Before you begin, prepare these color mixtures:

Dark Blue-Green—3 parts Payne's Gray, 2 parts Cerulean Blue, 1 part Hooker's Green

Cream—1 part Whiteblend, a touch of Yellow Ochre Light

Pink-Cream—1 part Cream, a touch of Thalo Crimson

Blue-Gray—1 part Cream, a touch of Dark Blue-Green

Burgundy—2 parts Burnt Sienna, 1 part Dioxazine Purple

Dusty Purple—3 parts Payne's Gray, 1 part Dioxazine Purple, a touch of Whiteblend

Rust—2 parts Cream, 1 part Burnt Sienna

Medium Green—2 parts Cerulean Blue, 1 part Thalo Yellow Green

Bright Green—1 part Thalo Yellow Green, 1 part Whiteblend

Yellow-Green—1 part Thalo Yellow Green, 1 part Cream

Light Cerulean—2 parts Cerulean Blue, 1 part Whiteblend

Canvas Preparation: Refer to page 2 in the techniques section for instructions on French matting to mat this canvas. Use Rapidograph #2.0 pen filled with Rapidograph waterproof ink.

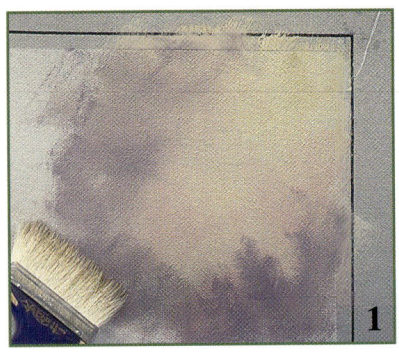

1 **Sky:** Paint the upper right corner of the sky cream with the fan brush. Use the uncleaned brush to apply dashes of pink-cream randomly in the wet paint. Continue with the same brush and blue-gray to paint distant trees along the bottom and left side of the sky area. Blend the edges with the Hake brush.

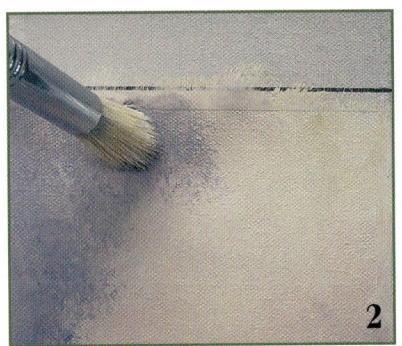

2 **Distant trees:** Stipple slightly darker blue-gray distant tree shapes around the edges of the sky with the large round bristle brush, being careful not to cover all the previous less defined shapes. Occasionally add a touch of light cerulean to the brush.

3 Lightly load a clean, moist sponge with dark blue-green and tap around the wet background to create the middle tree shapes. Occasionally add a touch of blue-gray to the uncleaned sponge.

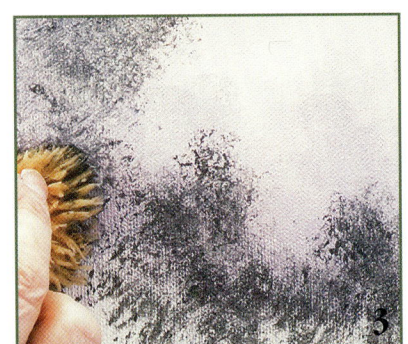

4 **Trees:** Use the palette knife to pile dark blue-green over the canvas, avoiding the areas you've already painted. Spread the paint around with the gesso brush. Tap around in this wet paint with a clean moist sponge to create a foliage-textured look. Dry completely and transfer the birdhouse, with the front roof peak 5" from the canvas top and 6½" in from the left side.

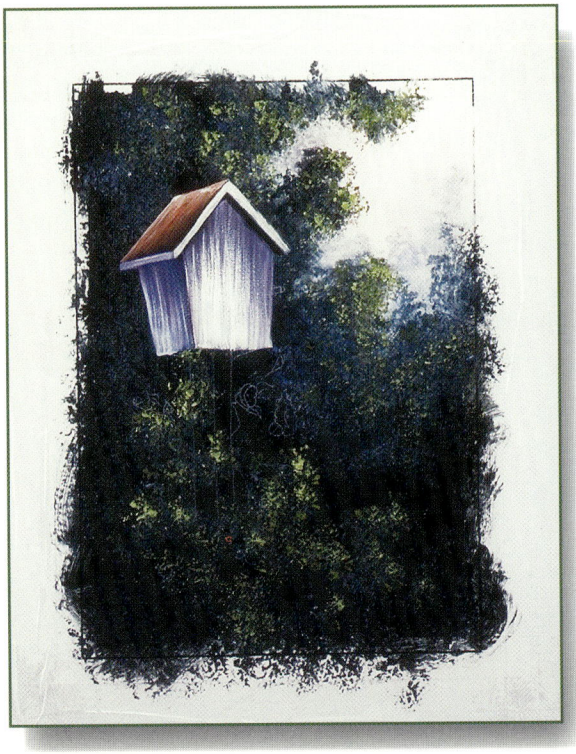

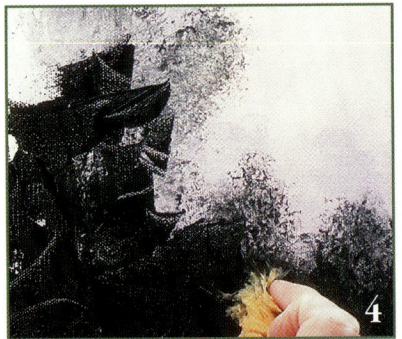

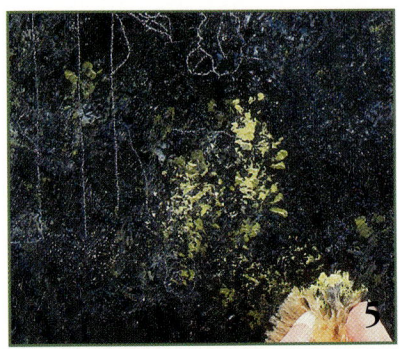

5 **Tree highlights:** Follow the large photograph, left, to place the highlights. Mix blue-gray and light cerulean on the sponge and lightly tap reflected light sparsely throughout the dark foliage. Add medium green to the uncleaned sponge; tap it along the right and top sides of the dark foliage. Add bright green to the uncleaned sponge and tap it along the far right side of each foliage clump.

6 **Roof:** Paint the top half of the roof rust with the angular brush. Add Burnt Sienna to the uncleaned brush to paint the roof center. Add burgundy to the uncleaned brush and paint a shadow along the front and bottom edges of the roof. Blend slightly with a clean angular brush, following the angle of the roof. Use the liner brush to paint burgundy shadows under the eaves.

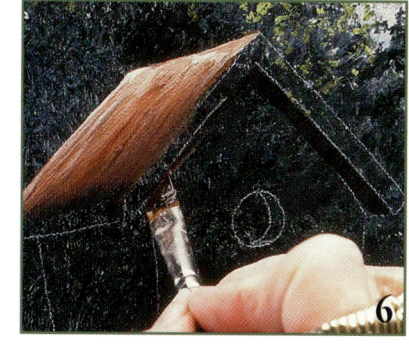

7 **Eaves:** Paint the front edge of the roof with the angular or small round brush using cream and dabs of pink-cream. Clean the brush and paint the side edge of the roof with dusty purple, occasionally adding cream to the brush to lighten the color.

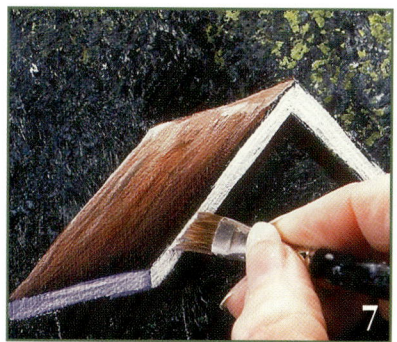

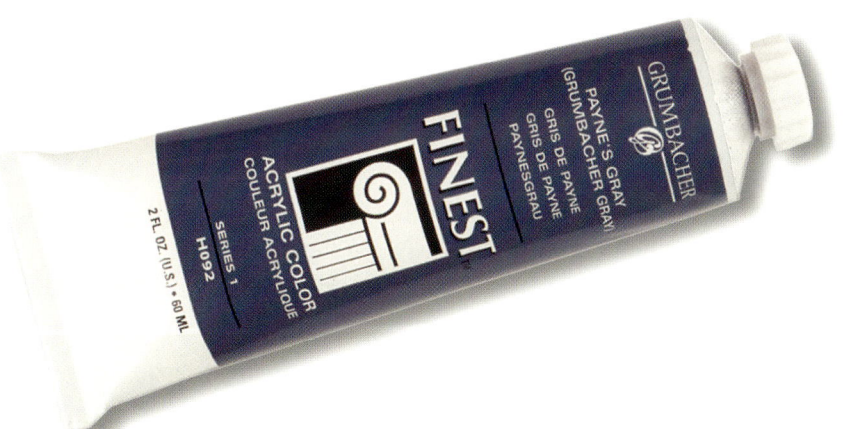

8 **Birdhouse side:** Paint the birdhouse side dusty purple with the angular brush. Using the same brush, stroke light cerulean up from the bottom over the lower portion of the dusty purple, leaving it streaky. Highlight the back edge with light cerulean.

9 **Birdhouse front:** Paint the birdhouse front with the angular brush, starting at the top with dusty purple and alternately adding Whiteblend, pink and light cerulean to the brush as you come down the front. To add wood grain, stroke light cerulean thinned with Clearblend vertically up from the bottom with the multi-texture brush. Clean the brush; add thinned pink then thinned cream to the same area. Dry and repeat if necessary.

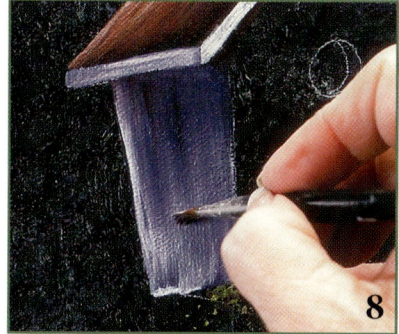

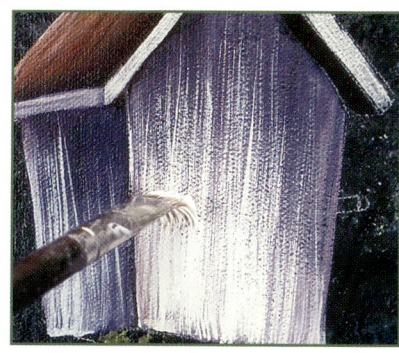

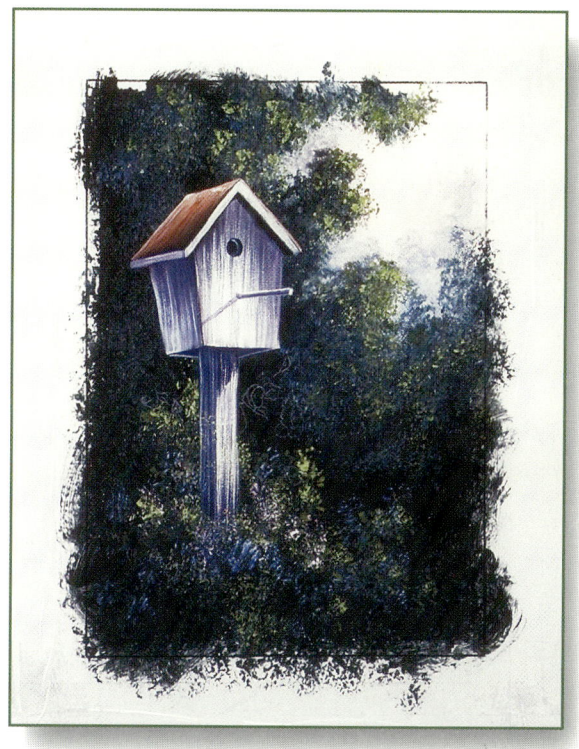

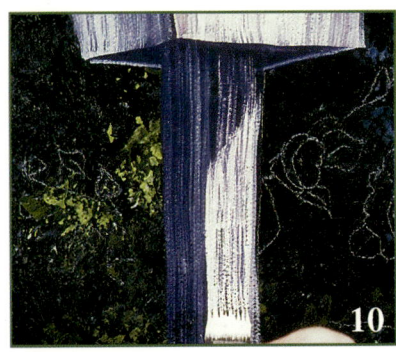

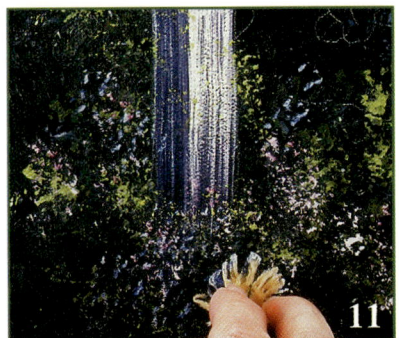

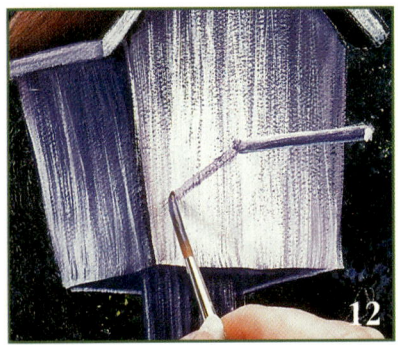

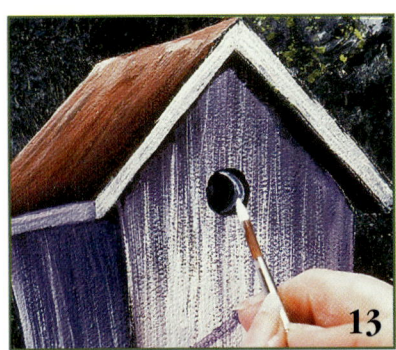

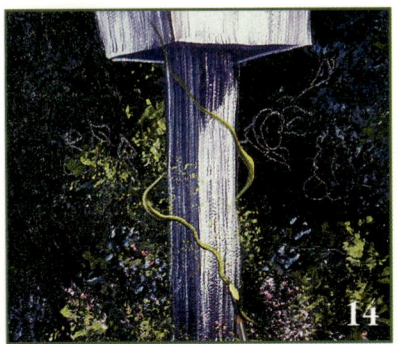

10 **Post:** Paint the bottom of the birdhouse and the pole dusty purple with the angular brush. Blot the bottom of the wet pole to blend it into the bushes. Add cerulean reflected light along the edges of the birdhouse bottom with the liner. Highlight the front of the pole with cream on a clean angular brush. Thin a little pink and cream with Clearblend; apply on the pole front with the multi-texture brush to add wood grain. Apply light cerulean reflected light streaks on the left pole side with the liner. Dry. Add additional streaks on the pole as needed.

11 **Leaf highlights:** Use a lacy area of the sponge to lightly tap light green leaf highlights around the pole in the foreground foliage. Use a clean section of the sponge to add a few dabs of pink for tiny blooms in the foliage. Add light cerulean to the uncleaned sponge and repeat.

12 **Perch:** Use the liner brush to paint the top of the perch cream and the bottom dusty purple. Blend slightly with a clean liner brush. Add a cream circle at the tip of the perch and a thin line of light cerulean reflected light under the perch. Paint the perch shadow and the shadows on the pole with a translucent, watery mixture of dusty purple, water and Clearblend. Make sure all the shadows are at the same angle.

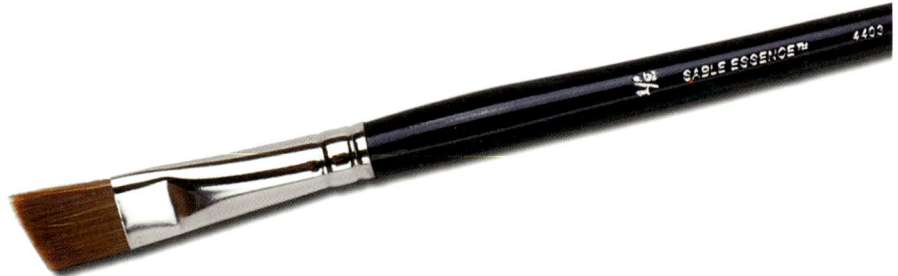

13 **Hole:** Paint the hole with the bright brush and burgundy. Add a half moon on the right side as shown with light cerulean, then add a thin line of Titanium White on the left edge of the half moon. Blend the half moon slightly, then dry. Use the liner brush to add a thin line of rust on the top right edge of the roof. Dry.

14 **Vines & tendrils:** Double-load the liner brush with dark blue-green and yellow-green. Make sure that the paint is thin enough to flow smoothly from the brush. Follow the photo on page 8 to paint the vines and tendrils around the pole.

15 **Morning glories:** Load the angular brush with Cerulean Blue and dip the long tip into Whiteblend. Stroke the brush back and forth on a clean spot on the palette to blend the paint gradually in the brush. Hold the brush with the Whiteblend on the outside edge of a large morning glory. Follow the photo to paint the

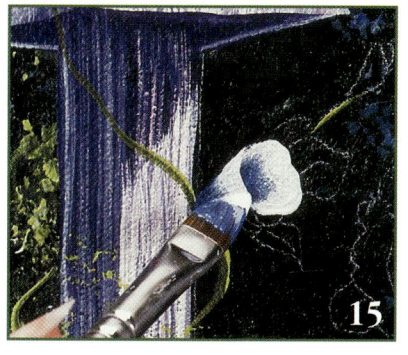
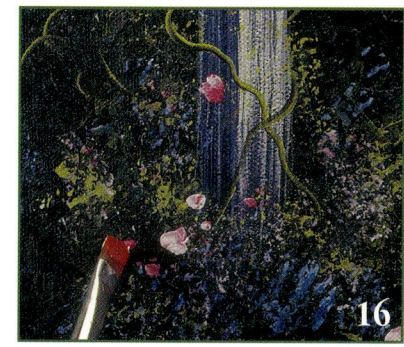

back side of the flower, lift (reload the brush if needed), then repeat to paint the front side. Repeat, making several sizes and shapes of blooms. Add little dabs of blue and white among the vines to suggest small flowers. Apply a Payne's Gray stamen dot in the centers with the liner brush. Brush-mix Yellow Ochre and cream on a clean liner and dot on each stamen to highlight them.

16 **Pink flowers:** Follow step 15 to double-load the angular brush with Thalo Crimson and Whiteblend. Paint little flowers randomly in the foliage by pressing the brush on the canvas. While wet, squiggle the tip of the brush around in the paint to create a rose-like blossom. Add some smaller flowers with little dabs of the double-loaded brush.

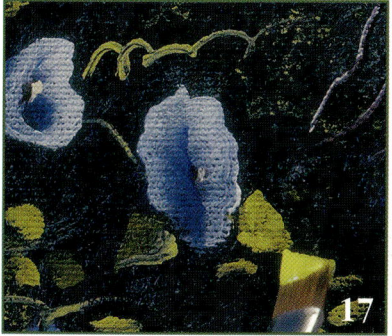

17 **Leaves:** Double-load the bright brush with medium green and yellow-green for the light leaves and dark blue-green and yellow-green for the darker leaves. Press the brush down as you pull it gently, then pull it away from the canvas releasing pressure. Follow the photo on page 8 for placement.

18 **Birds:** Use the liner brush and a blue gray thinned with Clearblend to add a few small birds in the sky. For the suggestion of bluebirds coming to your birdhouse, add a touch of rust to the uncleaned brush and apply it to the birds' breast area.

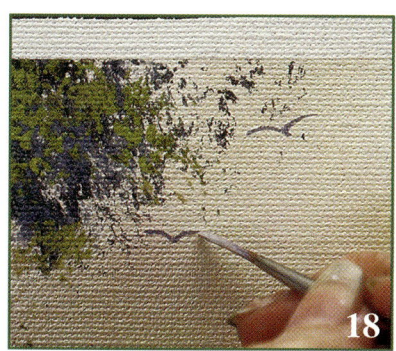

19 Double-load the liner brush with burgundy and cream and add a few twigs in the background foliage, making sure the light side faces the light source in the painting. Dry thoroughly, then remove any excess graphite smudges with a clean moist sponge.

Sign your painting and listen for birds calling to one another on their way home. When your painting is thoroughly dry, spray it with Grumbacher Acrylic Painting Varnish to bring out all the rich texture and colors of the aged wood and bright flowers.

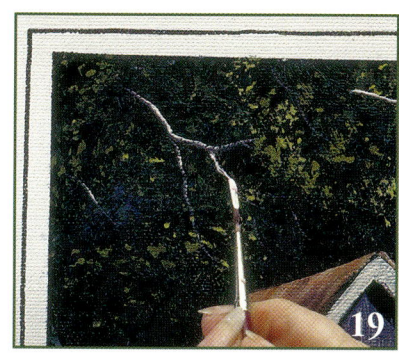

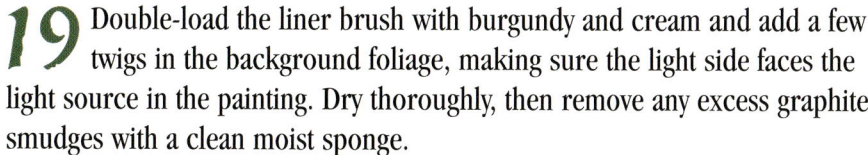

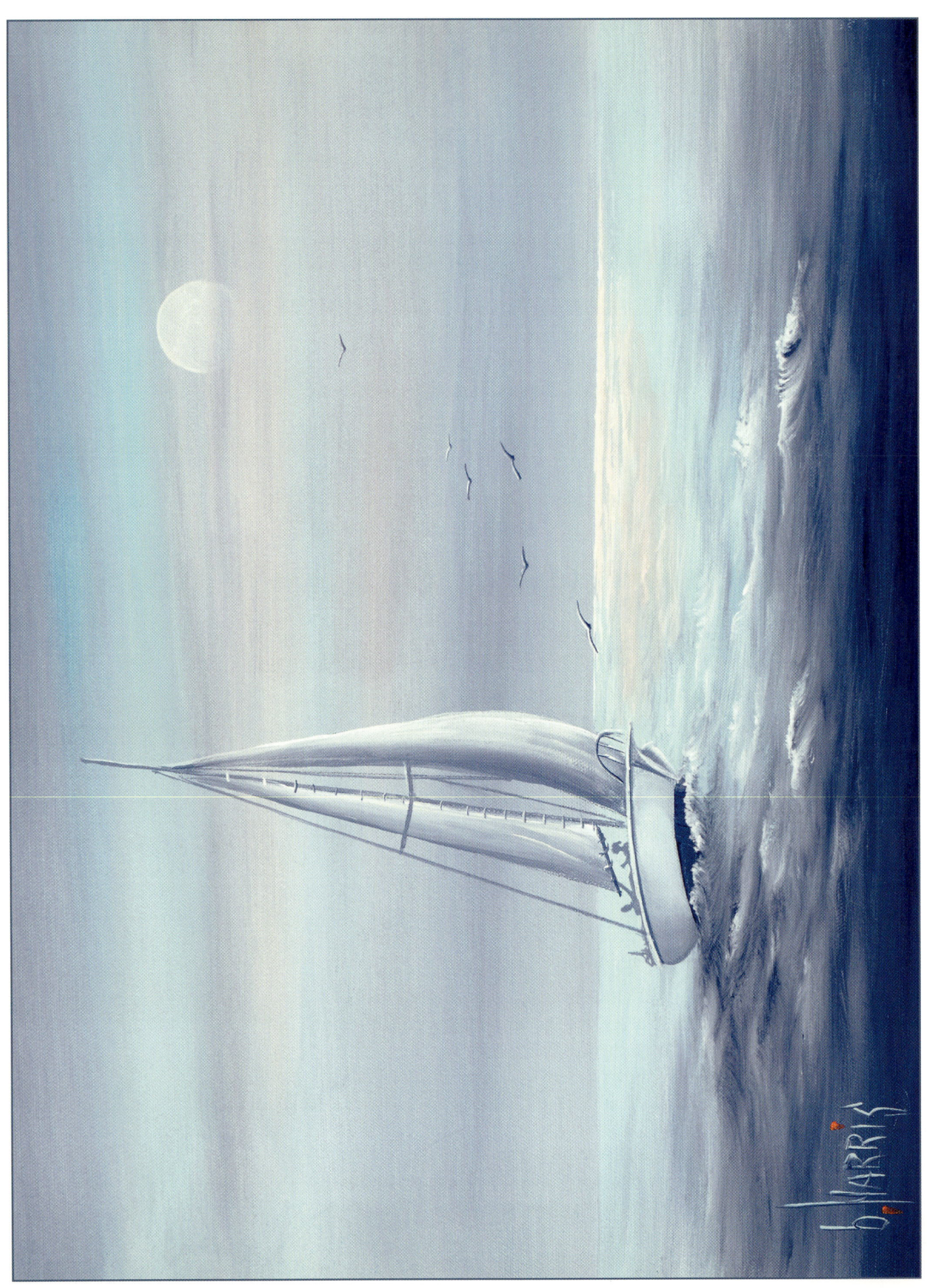

Moonlighting

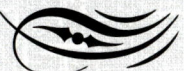

Grumbacher Acrylic Colors
Burnt Umber
Cadmium Yellow Medium
Cobalt Turquoise
Monoazo Orange
Ultramarine Blue

Brushes
Two #101 Gesso Brushes, Size 2"
#1500 Hake Brush, Size 2"
Two #4403 Sable Essence® Angular Bright Brushes, Size ½"
#4623 Golden Edge® Liner Brush, Size 2
#1060 White Bristle Fan Brush, Size 1

Other Supplies
14"x18" Stretched Canvas
Grumbacher Clearblend
Grumbacher Whiteblend
Grumbacher Slowblend
Tapered Painting Knife
Natural Sponge
Black Graphite Paper
Stylus
Wet Palette
Grumbacher Acrylic Painting Varnish

One of my favorite times to go boating is on a moonlit night. The serene, peaceful ambiance is captivating. "Moonlighting" is my impression of those times.

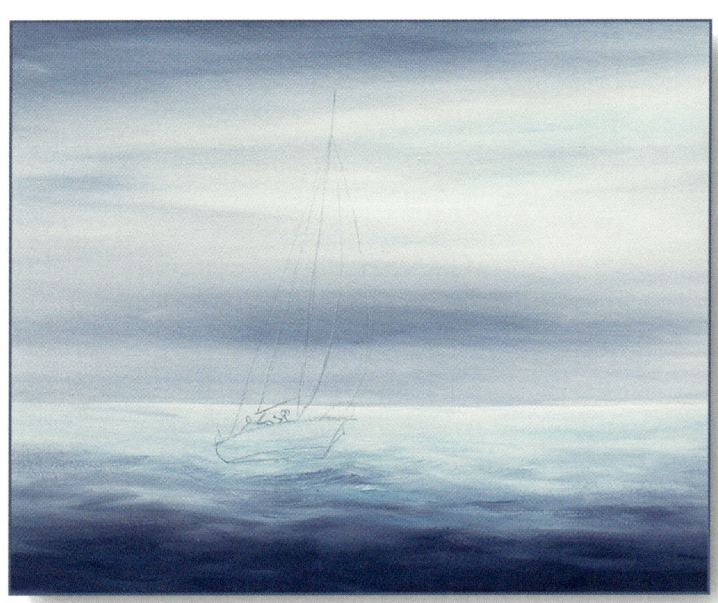

Palette
Before you begin, prepare these color mixtures:

Light Turquoise—3 parts Whiteblend, 1 part Cobalt Turquoise

Navy—8 parts Ultramarine Blue, 1 part Burnt Umber

Medium Blue—3 parts Whiteblend, 1 part Navy

Peach—1 part Whiteblend, a touch of Monoazo Orange

Off-White—1 part Whiteblend, a touch of Cadmium Yellow Medium

Canvas preparation: Draw a horizon line 4¾" above the canvas bottom. Dampen the sky with the gesso brush and clean, cool water. Allow it to soak a few minutes before applying the paint. The canvas should be barely damp, not wet.

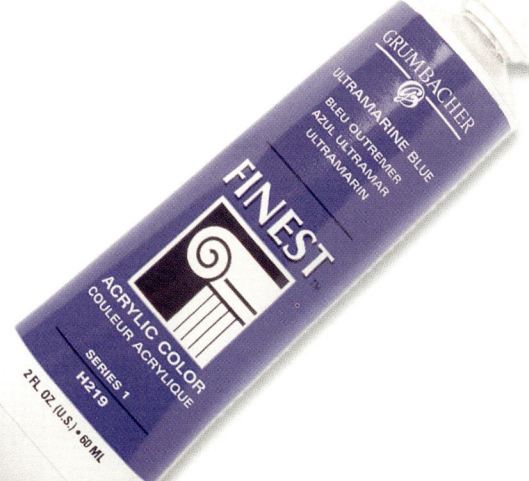

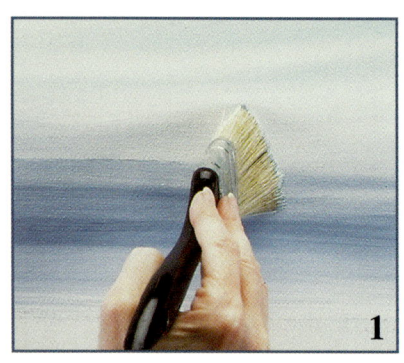

1 Sky: Use the gesso brush to work the sky wet-on-wet. Cover the sky with a generous application of Whiteblend, scrubbing it into the texture of the canvas. Wipe the excess Whiteblend from the brush, then add some light turquoise to the brush. Paint some streaks through the center of the sky. Wipe the excess paint from the brush, add medium blue, then paint streaks in the sky above and below the light turquoise streaks, making the sky darker at the top than at the horizon. Use the fan brush to apply a few small peach streaks in the center of the sky. Blend with a clean, towel-dried gesso brush, using long, horizontal strokes and heavy pressure at first. Gradually lighten the pressure as you finish blending.

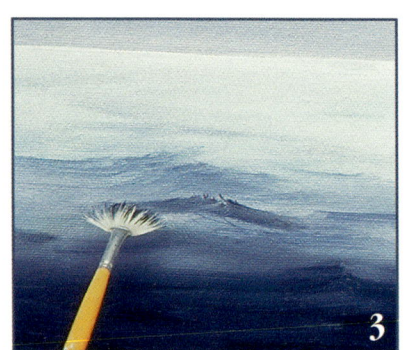

2 Water: Paint and blend the water wet-on-wet. First, paint the water with Whiteblend and the flat bristle brush, starting at the horizon line and ending about an inch from the canvas bottom. Add light turquoise to the brush and streak in the center of the wet Whiteblend. Wipe excess paint from the brush, then use it to apply streaks of medium blue beside and below the light turquoise. Use the gesso brush to apply navy at the canvas bottom, overlapping into the bottom of the medium blue and Whiteblend. Wipe the excess paint from the flat bristle brush and blend the water slightly, creating a gradual transition between the background and foreground water.

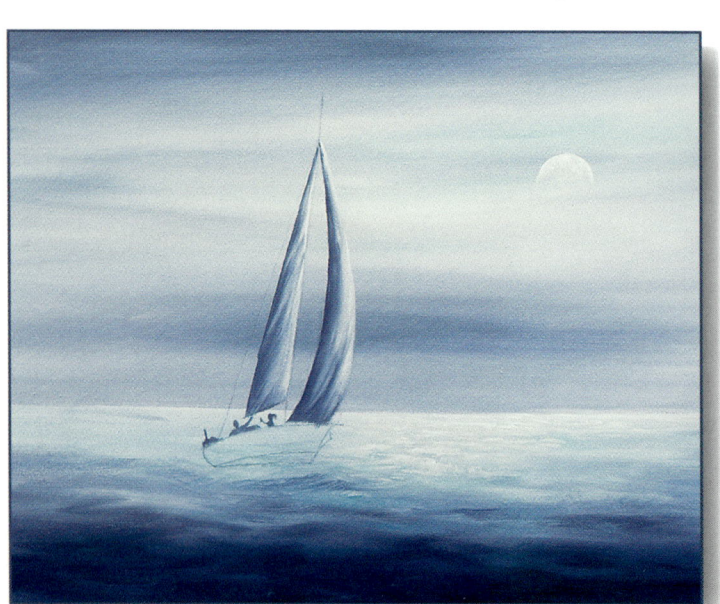

3 Waves: Use a clean fan brush and interconnected, curved strokes swishing back and forth in the wet paint to create waves. Randomly add light turquoise in the dark area and medium blue or navy in the light and turquoise areas with a rocking motion of the fan brush. Make the rocking strokes smaller and flatter near the horizon and gradually larger as you move down. The water movement should be less defined and flatter in the distance than in the foreground. Dry. Transfer the sailboat and moon to the canvas, using black graphite paper. Place the sailboat 7¾" from the left edge of the canvas and 1¾" from the top. Place the moon 5½" to the right of the sailboat and 3" from the upper canvas edge (see picture for placement).

4 **Moon:** Use the angular brush to cover the moon with Clearblend. Load the angular brush with Clearblend, then follow page 3 of the techniques section to side-load the brush with off-white. Hold the angular brush with the off-white on the outer edges of the moon and paint the top two-thirds of the moon. Pat-blend inside the moon, creating splotches in the paint as well as a gradual transition in value. Dry.

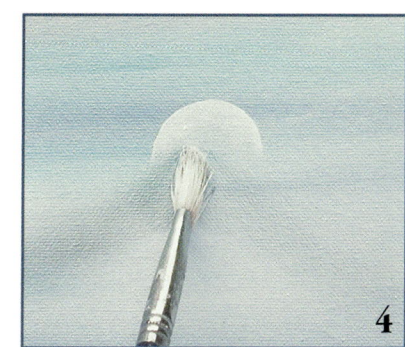

5 **Clouds:** Use the fan brush to cover the moon and the central portion of sky with Clearblend. Brush-mix peach and Whiteblend on the fan brush and apply streaks of drifting clouds over the moon bottom and the sky while the Clearblend is wet. Brush-mix medium blue and Whiteblend on the fan brush and repeat. Blend slightly with a clean, towel-dried fan brush. Dry.

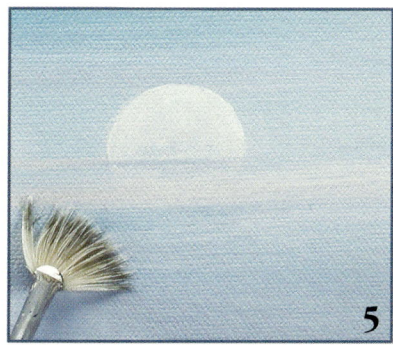

6 **Water reflections:** Use the angular brush to cover the background water area with Clearblend. Using the palette knife, follow page 5 of the techniques section to paint off-white reflections of moonlight in the wet Clearblend. Use a Clearblend-loaded fan brush to soften the edges of these reflections and fade them out on each side. Repeat for a few more lines in the same area, alternating between peach and Whiteblend. Place the majority of these highlights under the moon.

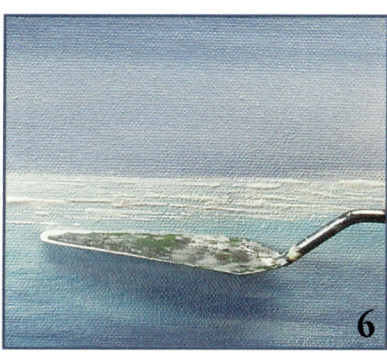

7 Repeat to paint reflections in the middle water area, but apply the paint with the fan brush. Make the reflections farther apart as they come forward. Blend the sides and along the bottom of each highlight with a Clearblend-moistened fan brush. Add and blend additional sky colors underneath the reflections if desired.

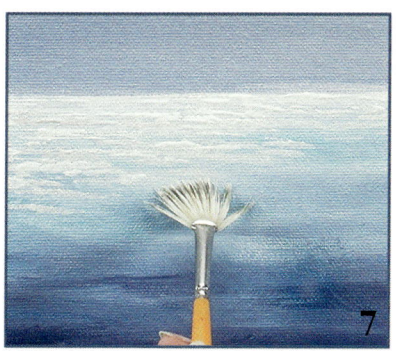

8 **Sails:** Paint and blend one sail at a time with the angular brush, cleaning the brush between colors and before blending. Paint the left side of each sail medium blue and the centers and right sides off-white. Clean and towel-dry the brush before blending. Add a few medium blue streaks angled across the sails to indicate folds in the fabric. If needed, blend slightly with a clean, towel-dried brush.

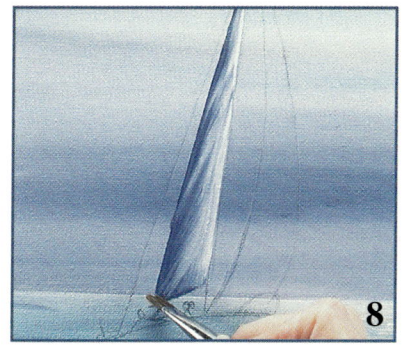

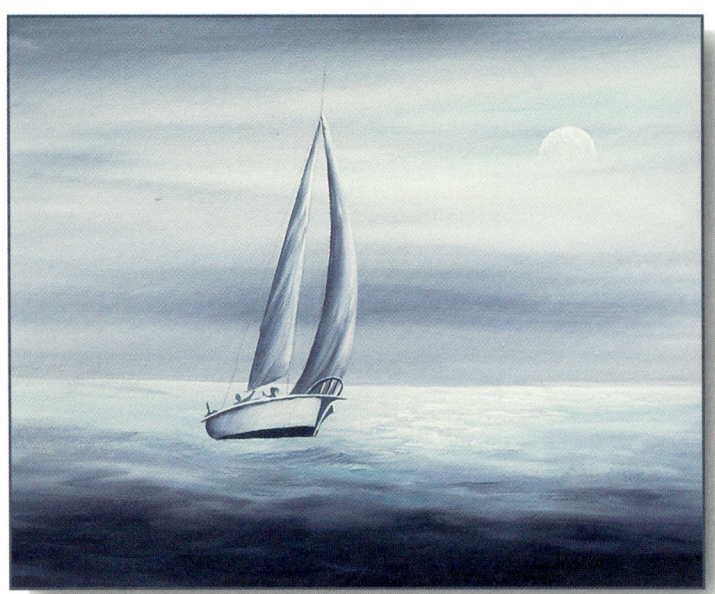

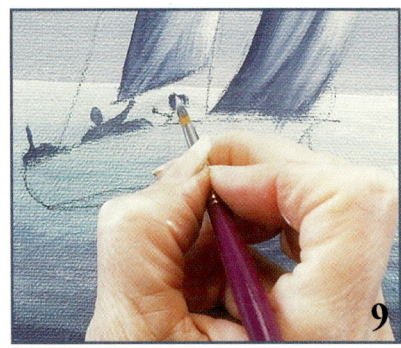

9 **People:** Paint the man, woman and items inside the boat medium blue using the small round or liner brush; dry.

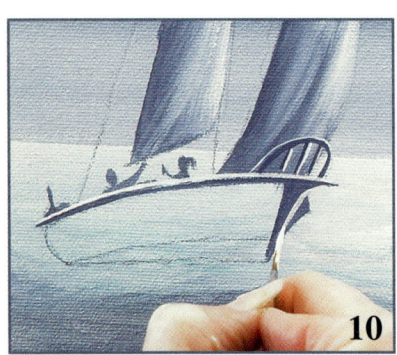

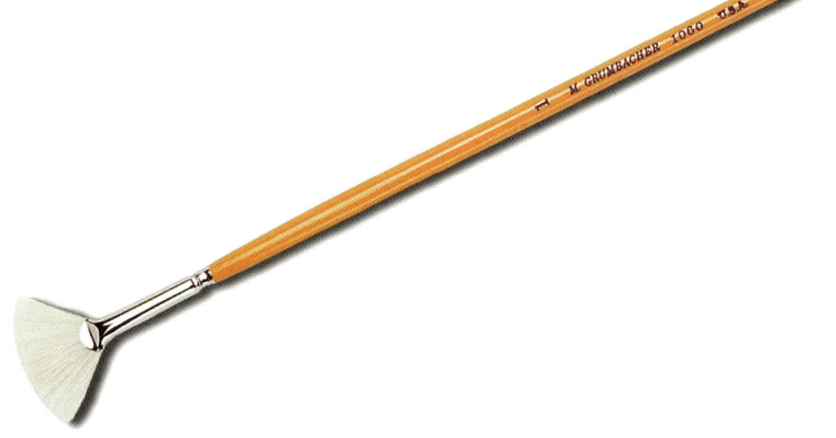

10 **Boat:** Use the liner or small round brush to paint the bow railing, bowsprit and bottom of the gunwale medium blue. Clean the brush, then paint the gunwale and a thin line on the front of the bowsprit off-white. Paint a small section to the right of the bowsprit medium blue, then paint the outer edge off-white. Blend. Highlight the bow railing with off-white.

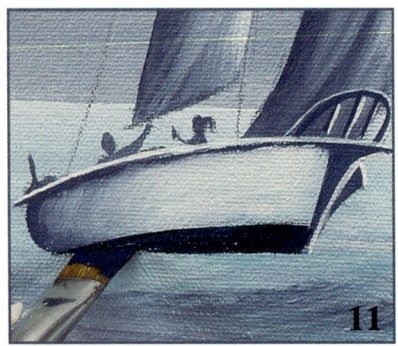

11 Apply medium blue down the back of the boat with the angular brush. Wipe the excess paint from the brush and paint the remaining portion of the side of the boat off-white. Blend as shown with a clean angular brush. Dry. Paint the bottom of the boat navy with the angular brush.

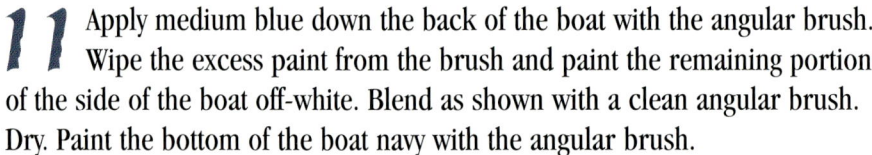

12 **Masts and rigging:** Paint the mast and rigging lines with a watery brush-mix of medium blue and Slowblend. Allow each item to dry before adding the next. Use light pressure on the brush when painting the rigging; dry. Add the cross pieces and rings holding the sails with the same color and brush; dry. Highlight some of this line work with off-white, using the photo on page 14 as a guide.

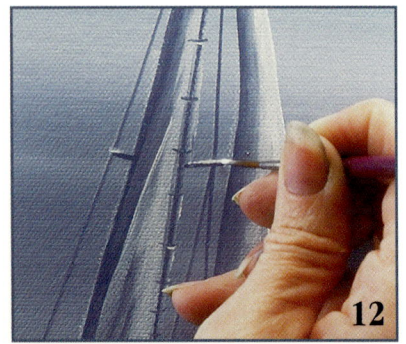

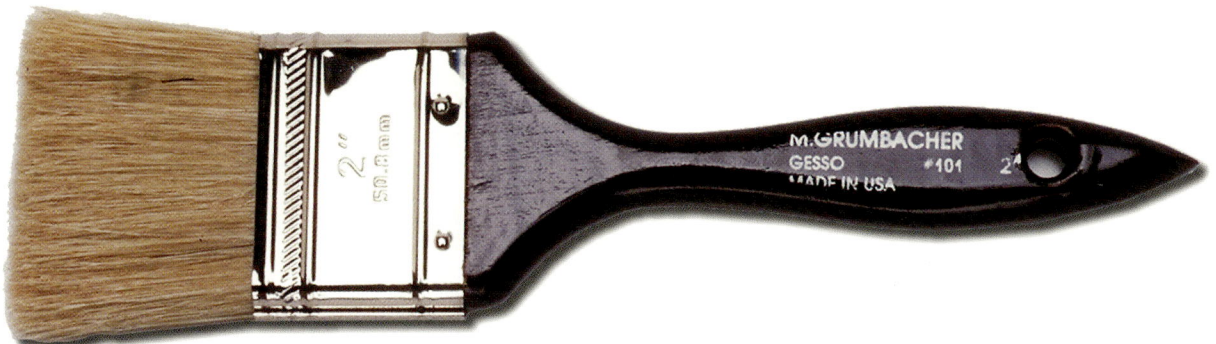

13 **Highlights:** Apply the off-white highlights using the two angular brushes: one for painting and one for blending. Load an angular brush with off-white and the other with Clearblend. Paint the front of the right sail off-white, then immediately blend it back into the shadow area with the Clearblend-loaded brush. Repeat to highlight the back sail, but don't make it as bright. Use the same techniques and brushes to highlight the center of the boat, directly under the woman.

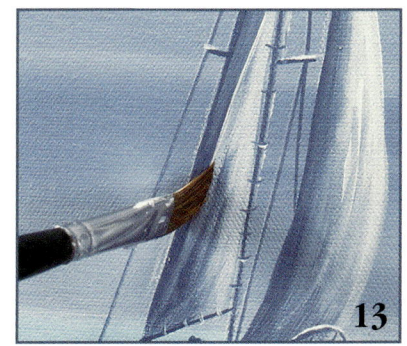

14 **Birds:** Brush-mix medium blue and Slowblend on the liner brush, then double-load it with Whiteblend. Paint as many birds as you like, flying at different angles. Place one or two smaller birds crossing the horizon line to add depth to the painting.

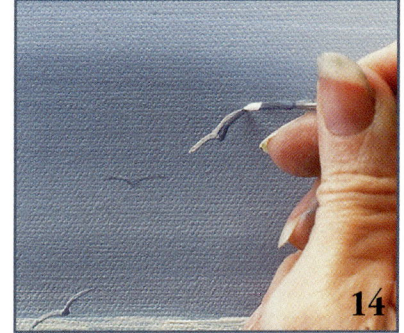

15 **Boat splash:** Cover the area under the boat with Clearblend using the flat bristle brush (add Slowblend for a longer drying time). Stipple off-white waves along the bottom of the boat with the fan brush. Pull the bottom edges of the splashes down into the wet Clearblend with a clean fan brush, using curved strokes to create the wave motion under the boat.

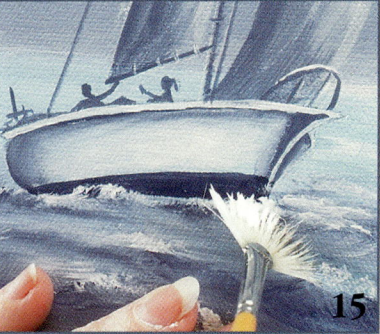

16 **Foreground waves:** Use the flat bristle brush to cover the foreground water area with Clearblend. Stipple a small off-white highlight on top of a wave with the fan brush. Pull the bottom edge of the highlight down with curved strokes to accent the water movement. Repeat for as many splashes as you choose, reapplying the Clearblend if needed. Dry. Stand back and take a look at the painting to see where additional highlights or shadows may need to be placed or strengthened. Apply Clearblend to the area that needs refining, then apply accents or touch up colors over the wet Clearblend and blend. Dry. Repeat until you are satisfied.

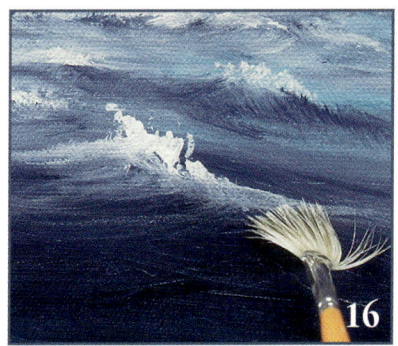

Sign, and set sail for a moonlight adventure! When your painting is completely dry, spray it with Grumbacher Acrylic Painting Varnish to bring out the beauty of the sea!

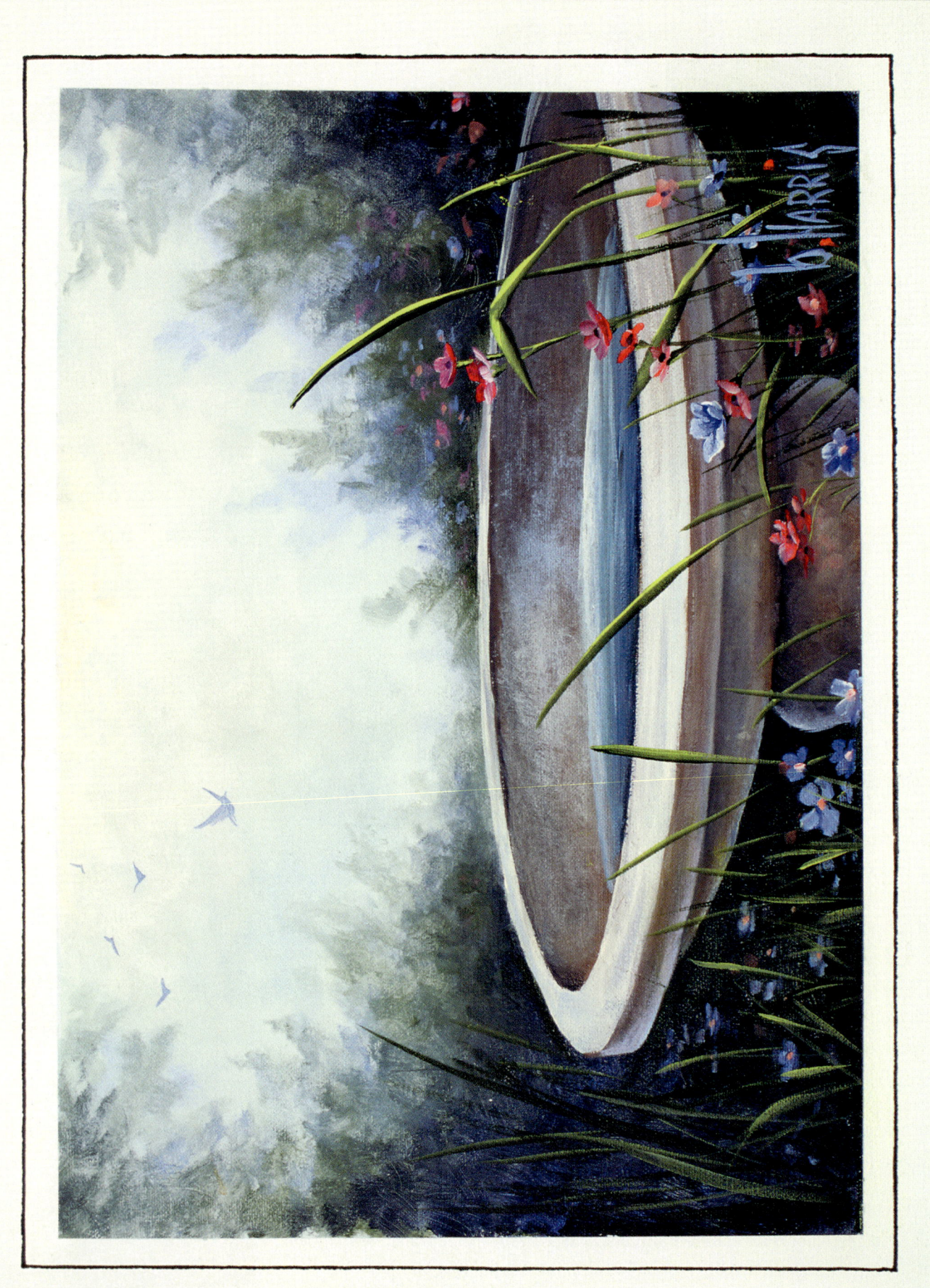

Neighbor's Pool

Grumbacher Acrylic Colors

Burnt Sienna
Cerulean Blue
Monoazo Orange
Payne's Gray
Sap Green
Thalo Yellow Green
Thalo Crimson
Ultramarine Blue

Brushes

#101 Gesso Brush, Size 2"
#1500 Hake Brush, Size 2"
#760F Academy Bristle Flat Brush, Size 6
#1060 White Bristle Fan Brush, Size 1
#4403 Sable Essence® Angular Bright Brush, Size ½"
#4623 Golden Edge® Liner Brush, Size 2
#4610B Golden Edge® Bright Brush, Size 6

Other Supplies

16"x20" Stretched Canvas
Grumbacher Clearblend
Grumbacher Whiteblend
Tapered Painting Knife
16"x20" Mat Template (12"x15½" Opening)
Matte Medium
Rapidograph Pen #2.0
Rapidograph Waterproof Ink: Black
Masking Tape
Natural Sponge
White and Charcoal Graphite Paper
Stylus
Wet Palette
Grumbacher Acrylic Painting Varnish

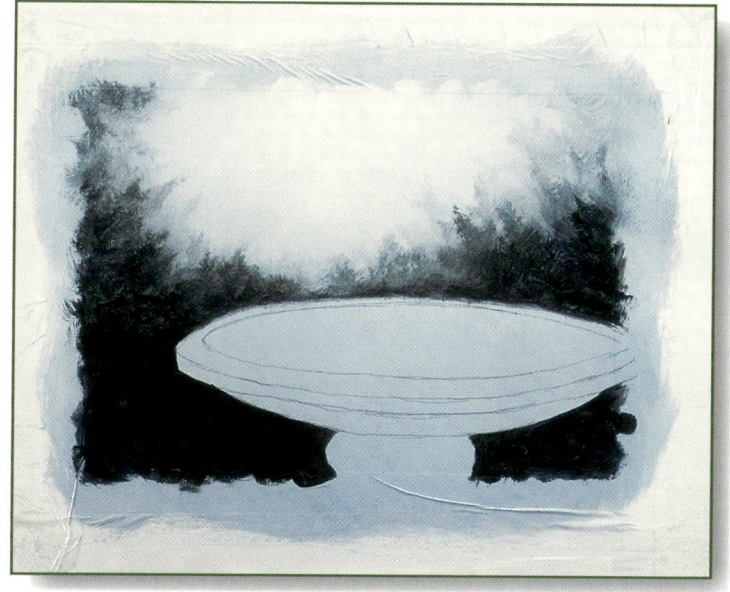

Palette

Before you begin, prepare these color mixtures:

Light Peach—1 part Whiteblend, a touch of Monoazo Orange

Light Gray—1 part Whiteblend, a touch of Payne's Gray

Taupe—3 parts Burnt Sienna, 2 parts Ultramarine Blue, 2 parts Whiteblend, a touch of Thalo Crimson

Navy—1 part Ultramarine Blue, 1 part Payne's Gray

Dark Green—1 part Navy, 1 part Sap Green

Yellow-Green—1 part Thalo Yellow Green, 1 part Whiteblend

Gray-Green—1 part Navy, 1 part Yellow-Green

Light Cerulean—1 part Whiteblend, 1 part Cerulean Blue

Light Ultramarine—1 part Whiteblend, 1 part Ultramarine Blue

Violet—2 parts Ultramarine Blue, 1 part Payne's Gray, ½ part Thalo Crimson, 6 parts Whiteblend

Medium Gray-Blue—4 parts Peach, 1 part Navy

Canvas Preparation: Refer to page 2 in the techniques section for instructions on French matting to mat this canvas. Use the gesso brush to paint the entire area inside the tape light gray. Dry thoroughly, then transfer the design. The left side of the birdbath is 5" from the left canvas edge and the top of the bath is 7¼" above the bottom canvas edge.

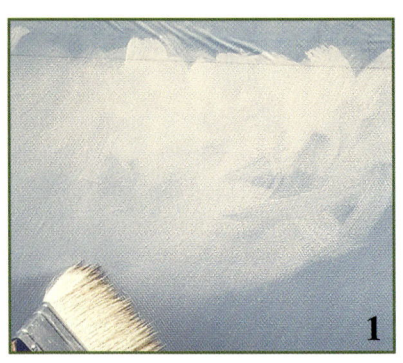

1 **Sky:** Apply the sky and background foliage loosely and quickly. Use a very moist Gesso brush to paint the background area above the birdbath with a generous coat of Clearblend. Apply light peach densely in the top center of the canvas using the flat bristle brush and loose, erratic strokes. Apply less and less light peach as you move away from the top central area so that it gradually disappears into the gray at the bottom of the sky. Blend and fluff with the Hake brush, making the sky blustery.

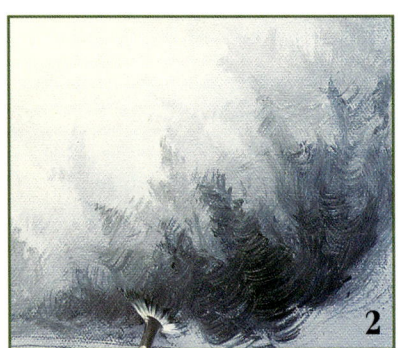

2 **Distant trees:** Apply the distance foliage a small area at a time to make it easy to blend while wet. Apply Clearblend before you start in each area and when the paint becomes too sticky to blend. Hold the fan brush vertically and paint the most distant trees medium gray-blue with erratic swishes. Blend slightly with the hake brush for a soft, out-of-focus appearance. Add gray-green to the uncleaned fan brush and repeat to apply and blend closer foliage.

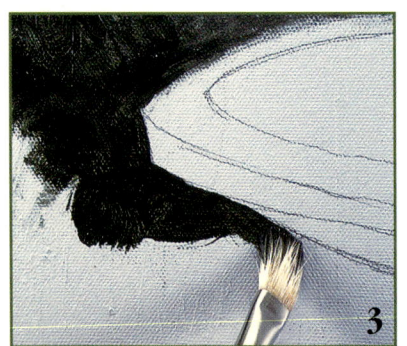

3 Alternate adding navy and dark green to the brush to make even darker, closer foliage. Bring these dark values down around the birdbath. Soften some top edges with the hake brush to create a gradual transition from light to dark foliage.

4 **Birdbath bowl:** Paint the top rim of the birdbath light peach with the angular brush. While it's wet, add medium blue-gray or navy streaks to make the concrete look older. Blend slightly with a clean, towel-dried brush.

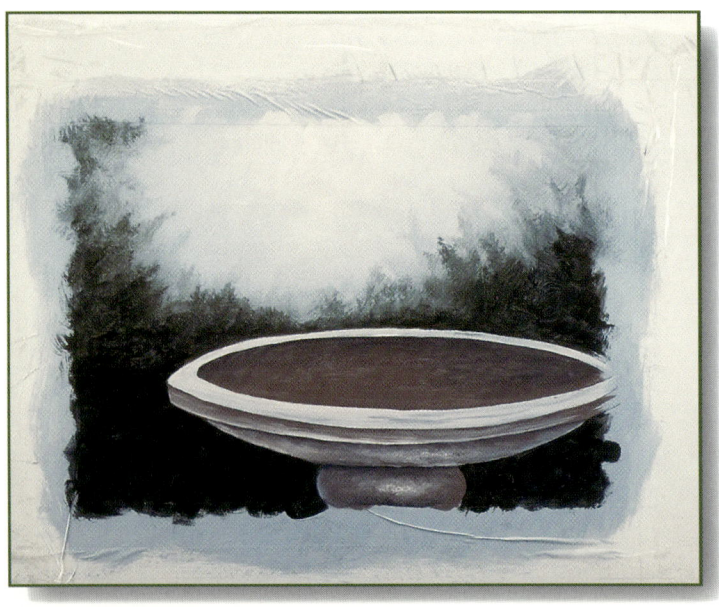

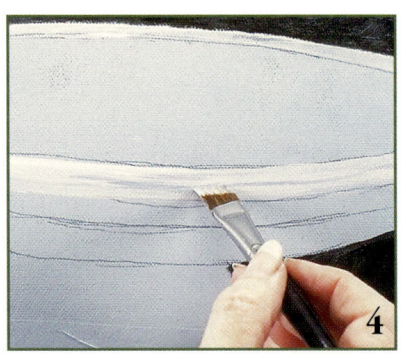

5 Paint the inside of the birdbath taupe with the flat bristle brush. Shadow the right side and under the rim with Payne's Gray. Lightly blend the shadow into the wet taupe.

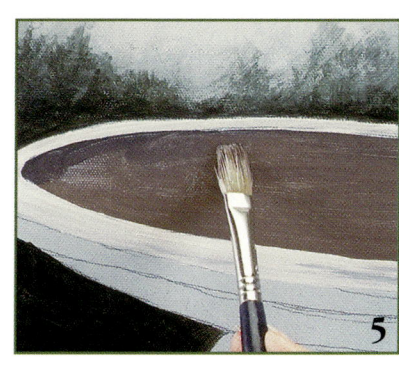

6 **Birdbath rim:** Paint the upper portion of the outside with the angular brush and taupe. While it's wet, brush-mix Payne's Gray and taupe and add a shadow at the top edge. Add streaks of light peach highlight through the center and along the bottom of this area. Blend slightly, leaving a rough appearance.

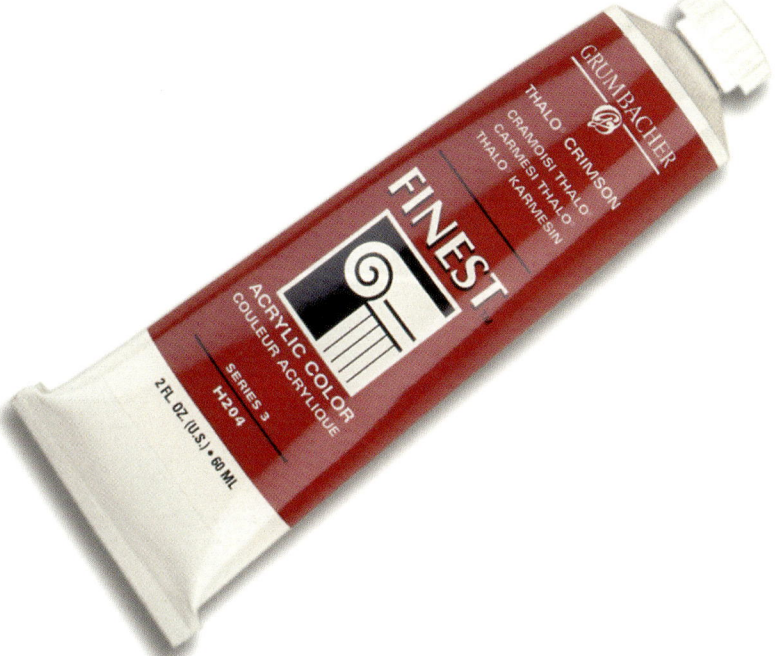

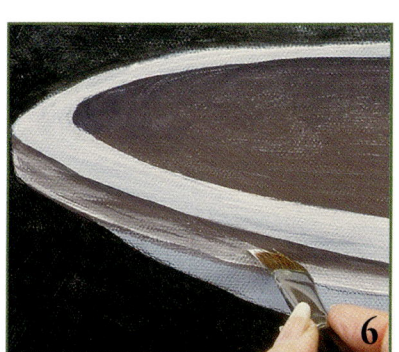

7 Paint the outside of the birdbath bowl taupe with the angular brush. While it's wet apply dark shadows under the rim and at the base with Payne's Gray. Add light peach in the center and on the bottom left edge. Add light ultramarine on the bottom right edge. Tap the wet paint with a clean, towel-dried flat bristle brush to create a gradual transition between colors.

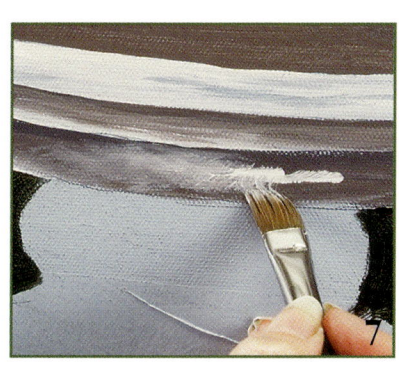

8 **Pedestal:** Use the angular brush to paint the pedestal taupe. Add Payne's Gray shadows at the top and bottom of the pedestal. Apply light peach in the center. Tap the wet paint with the towel-dried flat bristle brush to create a gradual transition, but leave the textured look of rough cement. Dry.

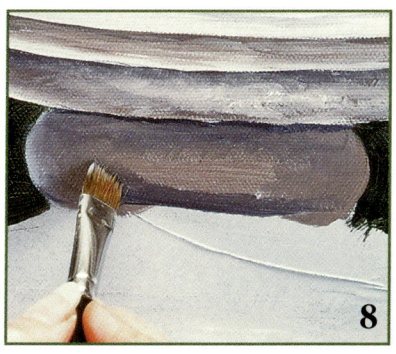

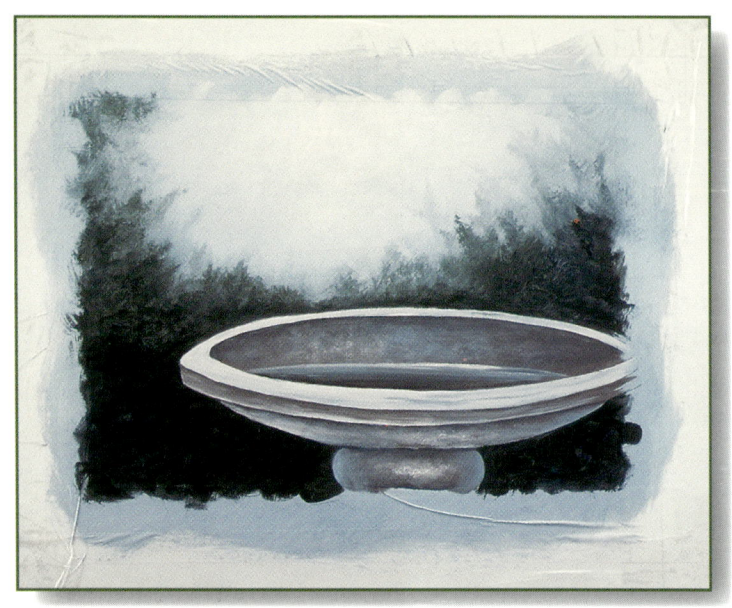

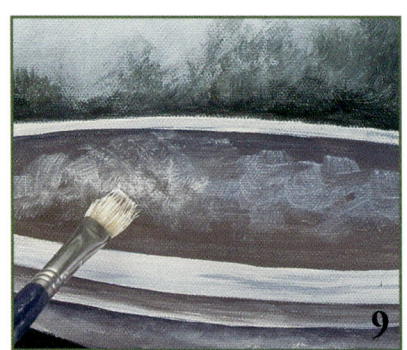

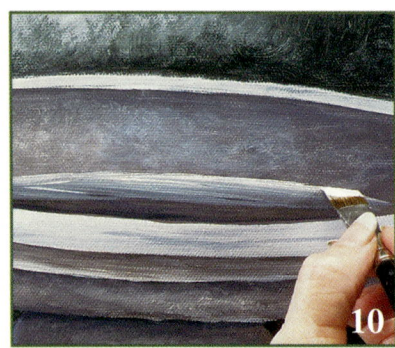

9 Inside the birdbath: Paint the inside of the bowl with the flat bristle brush and Clearblend. While wet, add dabs of light peach just left of the center and dabs of both light gray and light ultramarine just right of the center. Tap a clean flat bristle brush in these colors to blend, leaving no hard edges and allowing the taupe to show through. Dry.

10 Water: Use the flat bristle brush to cover the water area inside of the bowl with Clearblend. While wet, add horizontal streaks of medium gray-blue, navy and dark green across the Clearblend with the angular brush. Apply horizontal streaks of light cerulean and light peach across the top of the water area. Blend slightly with horizontal strokes. Dry.

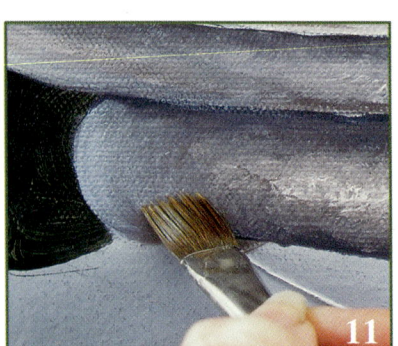

11 Birdbath highlights: Working one area at a time, cover the left side of the bowl, pedestal and side rim of the bowl with Clearblend. Alternate applying light peach, light gray and light cerulean reflected lights in each area with the angular brush. Tap to blend with a clean, towel-dried angular brush. Repeat on the right side of the bowl, pedestal and rim, using light ultramarine and violet reflected light.

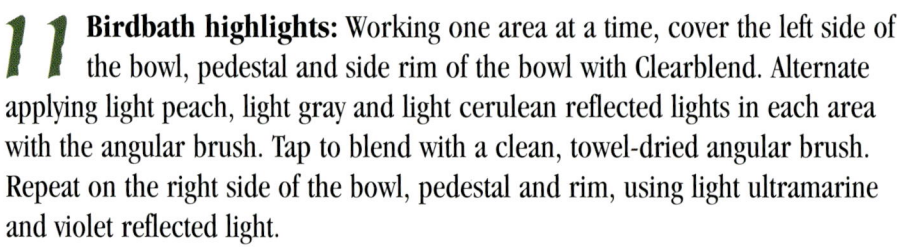

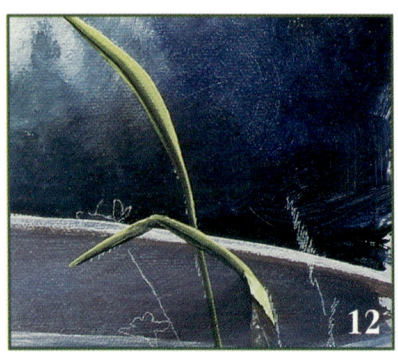

12 Foreground foliage: Transfer the flowers to the canvas, using the white graphite paper. To paint the large grasses on the right and in the center, alternate using either dark green, navy or gray-green for the dark value double-loaded on the angular brush with yellow-green. Load the longer bristles with yellow-green and the shorter ones with the dark color. Hold the brush vertically with the light side on the top and barely touch it to the canvas. As you pull down, increase the pressure of the brush against the canvas gradually to make the leaf wider, then gradually release the pressure to create a thin stem. Apply a variety of sizes and heights of grasses around the birdbath.

Bathing Beauty

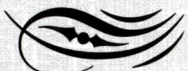

Grumbacher Acrylic Colors
Burnt Sienna
Cerulean Blue
Payne's Gray
Monoazo Orange
Thalo Crimson
Titanium White
Ultramarine Blue

Brushes
#4610B Golden Edge® Bright Brush, Size 6
#4623 Golden Edge® Liner Brush, Size 2
#4403 Sable Essence® Angular Bright Brush, Size ½"
#770 Academy Round Brush, Size 2
#760F Academy Bristle Flat Brush, Size 6

Other Supplies
16"x20" Stretched Canvas with completed painting of "Neighbor's Pool" (pages 20-25)
Grumbacher Clearblend
Grumbacher Whiteblend
Tapered Painting Knife
Natural Sponge
Tracing Paper
White and Charcoal Graphite Paper
Kneaded Eraser
Stylus
Wet Palette
Grumbacher Acrylic Painting Varnish

When Don Agnew, a friend of mine at WJCT in Jacksonville, Florida, was a young boy, he had a pet blue jay named "J.J." This "Bathing Beauty" frolicking in the "Neighborhood Pool" was created with him in mind and to share with you the technique of layering feathers. These techniques are universal and can be used to create any bird you are fond of.

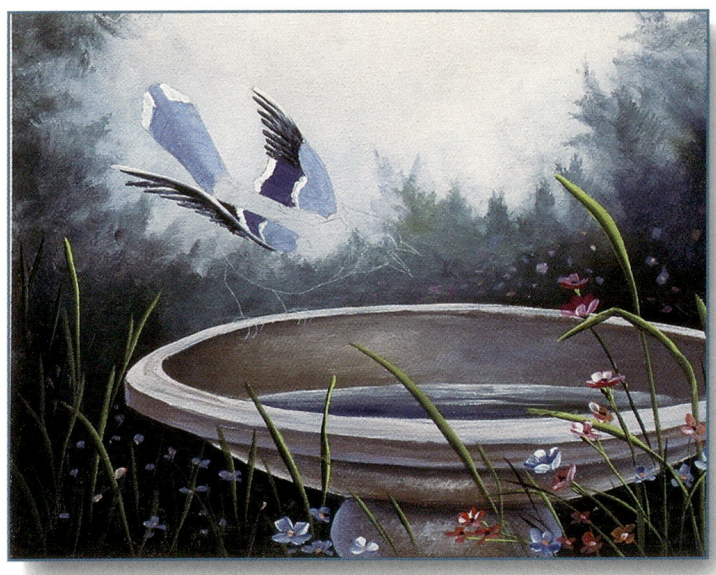

Palette
Before you begin, prepare these color mixtures:

Taupe—3 parts Burnt Sienna, 2 parts Ultramarine Blue, 2 parts Whiteblend, a touch of Thalo Crimson

Light Cerulean—1 part Whiteblend, 1 part Cerulean Blue

Medium Violet—4 parts Ultramarine Blue, 2 parts Payne's Gray, 1 part Thalo Crimson, 4 parts Whiteblend

Light Peach—1 part Whiteblend, a touch of Monoazo Orange

Light Gray—1 part Whiteblend, a touch of Payne's Gray

Canvas preparation: If you painted the small birds in "Neighbors Pool" and now would like to add this "Bathing Beauty," use light peach and the bright brush to paint over the distant birds. Tone the light peach with a touch of light gray if it doesn't match the background (it should be one value lighter than the sky when wet because acrylic paint dries darker). Fade out the edges of this area with a Clearblend-moistened flat bristle brush to blend it into the background. Dry, then transfer the blue jay, positioning the bird's feet on the birdbath rim. Use white graphite paper to transfer the pattern to the dark areas of the painting and charcoal paper to transfer the pattern to the light areas.

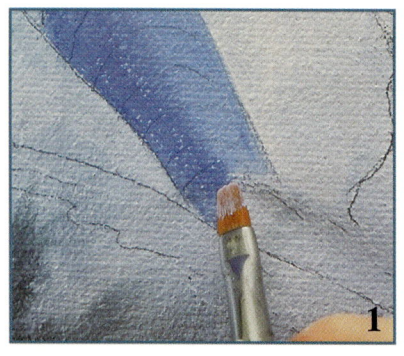

1 **Tail:** Paint the tail light cerulean with the small bright brush. Add Whiteblend to the uncleaned brush and highlight the right side of the tail. Darken the left side by adding a touch more Cerulean Blue to the wet tail. Blend to make a gradual, but visible change in value between the two sides of the tail. While the tail is still wet, add a little medium violet in the center and the left side of the tail and blend.

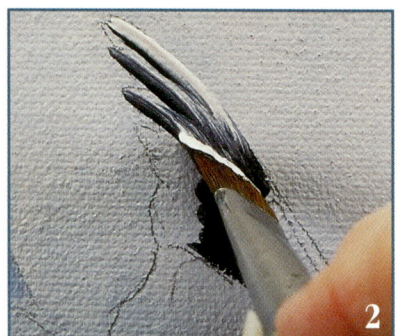

2 **Wings:** Apply the steps to both wings as you go. Use the bright brush and Payne's Gray to paint the center primary feathers. Double-load the angular brush with Payne's Gray and light peach and paint the tips of the primary feathers. With the peach side upward, start at the tip and pull the paint into the wet Payne's Gray. Paint a line defining the forward edge of his right wing.

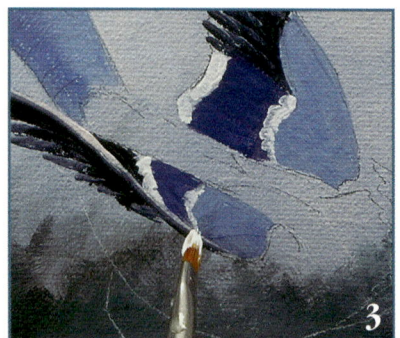

3 **Secondary feathers:** Paint the secondary wing feathers with the flat detail brush and medium violet. Paint the front section of each wing light cerulean. Paint the white markings on the wings and tail as shown with the bright brush and Whiteblend.

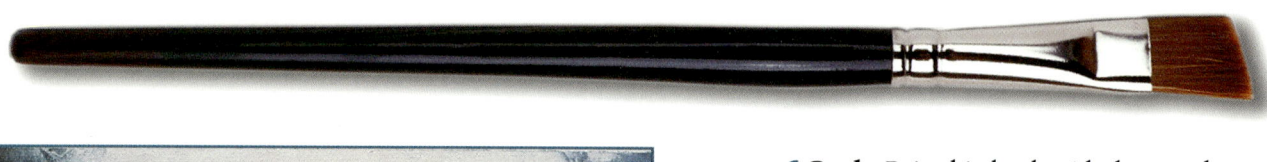

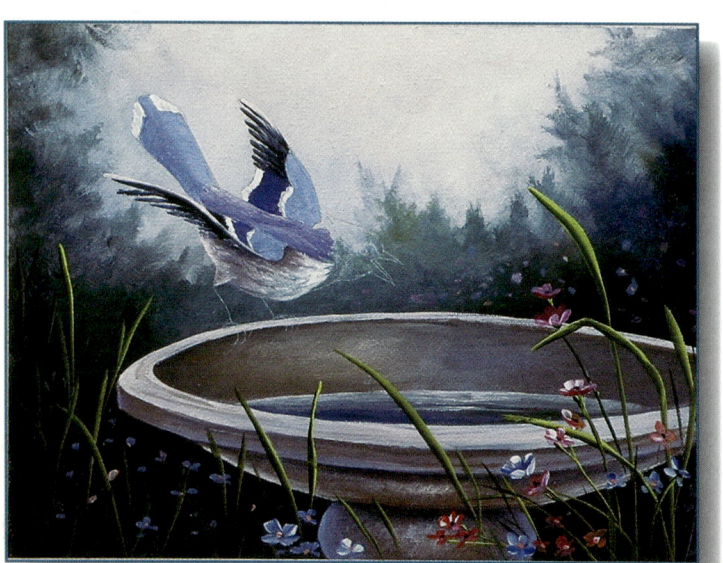

4 **Back:** Paint his back with the angular or bright brush and medium violet. Add a touch of Whiteblend to the uncleaned brush and add short, choppy feather marks on his back. Make all the brush strokes according to the feather growth.

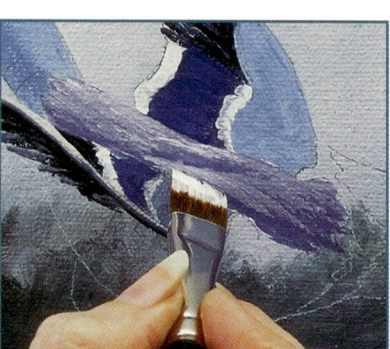

5 **Breast and Rump:** Basecoat his rump and the shadowy section under his wing taupe with the angular brush. Use a clean angular brush and alternate between light peach and medium violet to tap choppy feather marks in the wet taupe.

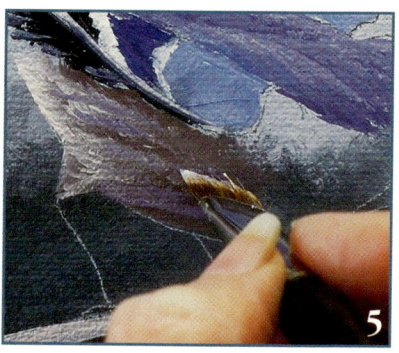
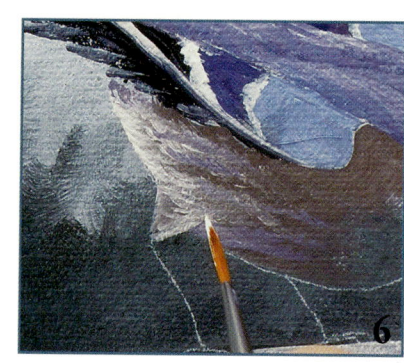

6 **Breast details:** Add a dab of Payne's Gray directly under and around the front of the wing with the bright brush, then tap with the angular brush to create a gradual transition between the body and wing. Use the liner brush and light peach to add reflected light on the outside edge of his rump, stroking horizontally; blend. Use a clean angular brush to paint his breast Whiteblend down to and overlapping into the wet taupe section. Tap to blend, using short, choppy strokes in the direction of feather growth.

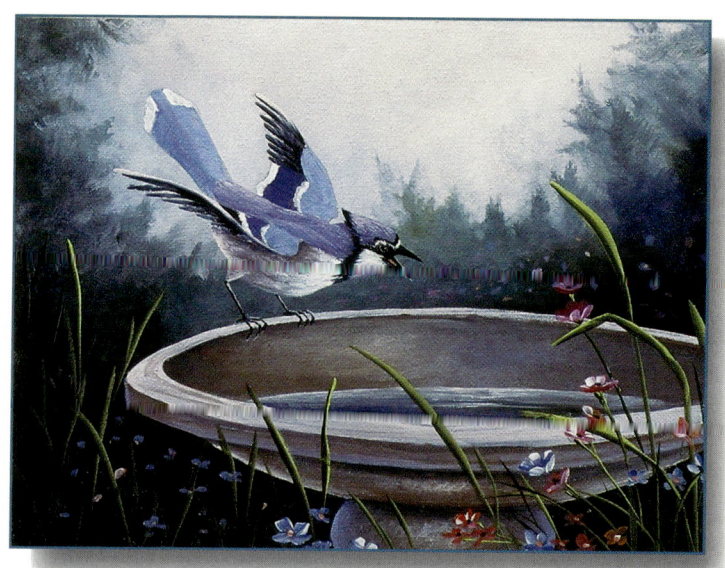

7 **Eye:** Use the liner or small round brush for the detail in the eye area. Paint the pupil Payne's Gray. Dry, then add a Whiteblend catchlight at 2:00. Use Payne's Gray to paint the dark markings around his eye, leaving a tiny space around the pupil for an eye ring.

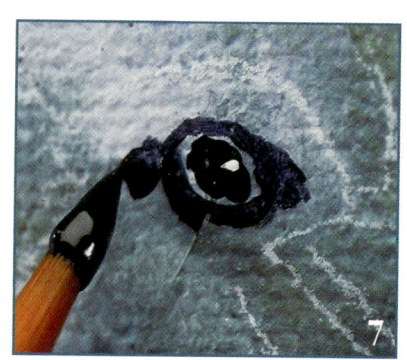

8 **Face:** Stroke the brush in the direction of feather growth as you paint the dark markings on his head and neck with Payne's Gray thinned with Clearblend and the liner or small round brush. Paint his beak with the same brush and Payne's Gray.

9 After the beak is dry, brush-mix Monoazo Orange and light gray on the small round brush and paint his tongue.

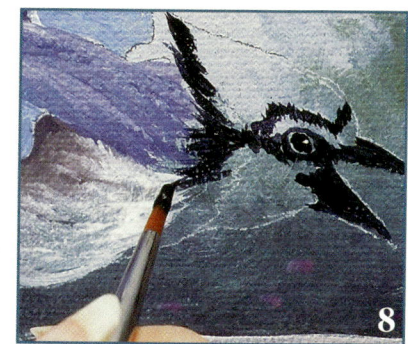
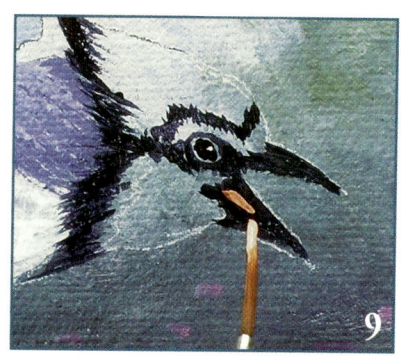

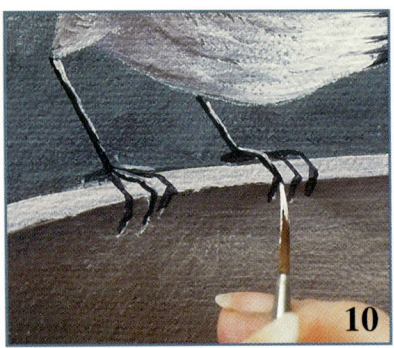

10 **Feet and legs:** Use the liner or small round brush to paint the legs and feet with Payne's Gray thinned with Clearblend. When the feet are dry, add peach and/or light gray highlights to the right side of the legs and the top of his feet.

11 **Face mask:** Use the liner or small round brush and Whiteblend to paint the white markings above his eye and on his chin. Use short strokes going in the direction of the feather growth, and pull the white back over the dark markings. While the chin is wet, alternate adding medium violet and taupe to shade the bottom.

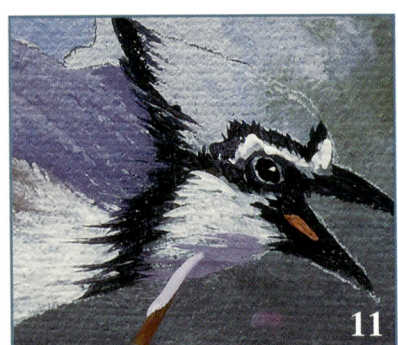

12 **Head details:** Use the angular brush and short choppy strokes to paint the top of his head medium violet. Add a touch of Whiteblend to the uncleaned brush, then add choppy highlight marks in the wet paint along the top of his head. Dry.

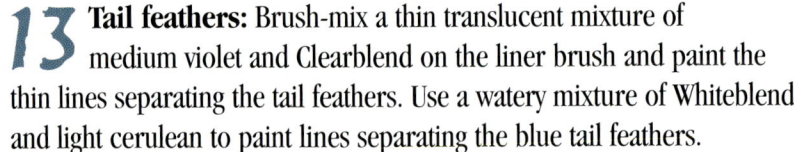

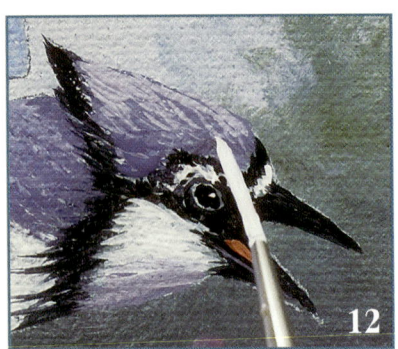

13 **Tail feathers:** Brush-mix a thin translucent mixture of medium violet and Clearblend on the liner brush and paint the thin lines separating the tail feathers. Use a watery mixture of Whiteblend and light cerulean to paint lines separating the blue tail feathers.

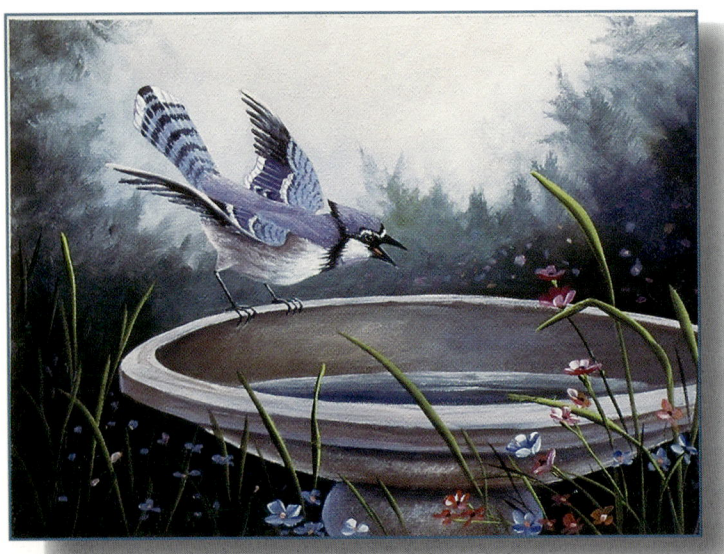

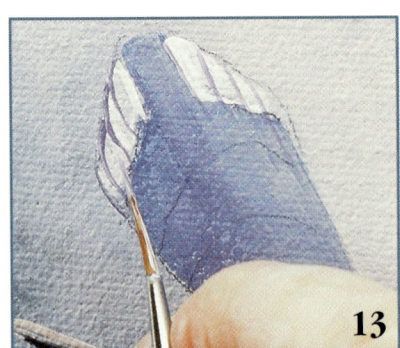

14 **Tail bands:** Use the liner brush and Payne's Gray thinned with Clearblend to add the dark bands across the tail. Apply these bands with very short, choppy strokes in the direction of the feather growth. Paint the bands smaller and closer together as they near the base of the tail.

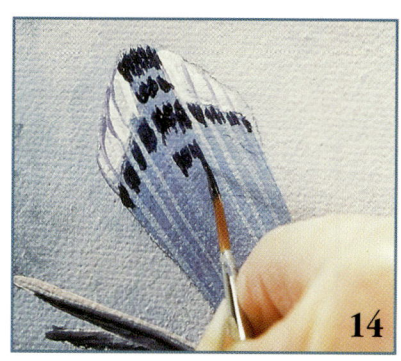

15 **Wing feathers:** Use the liner brush and medium violet thinned with Whiteblend to paint the lines separating the feathers in the medium violet area of each wing.

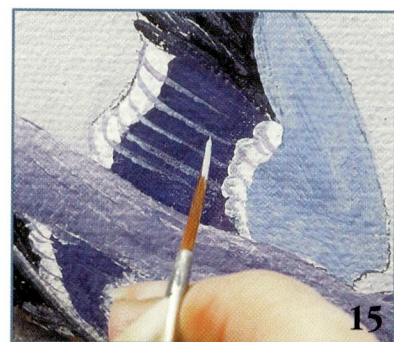

16 **Wing details:** Accent the feather tips where the wing meets the body with Whiteblend, then with Payne's Gray as shown. Brush-mix Clearblend and Payne's Gray on the liner brush and paint the markings on the blue sections of the front section on the wings. Make these markings much lighter and shorter than the ones on the tail.

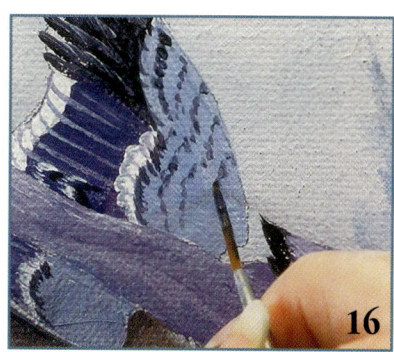

17 **Body details:** Referring to the large phot on page 26, use the liner to paint Titanium White highlights randomly on a few feathers on his face, cheek, breast and the tip of his tail. Repeat with light cerulean thinned with Clearblend and violet thinned with Clearblend. Paint extra strokes where the tail connects to the body, to make it look natural. Add a Whiteblend tip to a few of the gray secondary feathers on his right wing. If needed, strengthen the highlight on the leading edge of the wing with light peach, or light gray. Dry.

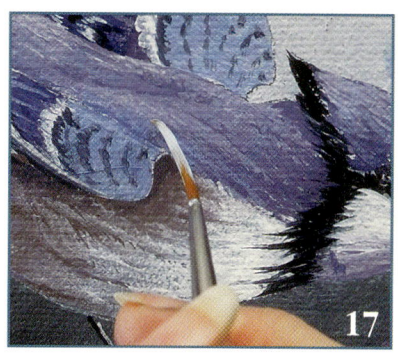

18 Use the angular brush to cover the tail with Clearblend. Add a light peach highlight along the right edge with the angular brush. With a Clearblend-moistened bright brush, fade out the inside edge of the highlight color. Repeat for his back and head, working one area at a time.

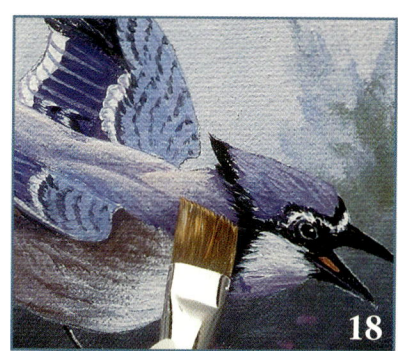

Sign, and put out some peanuts for your blue jays! When your painting is completely dry, erase all excess graphite lines with a kneaded eraser and spray with Grumbacher Acrylic Painting Varnish to bring out every feather of this comical character!

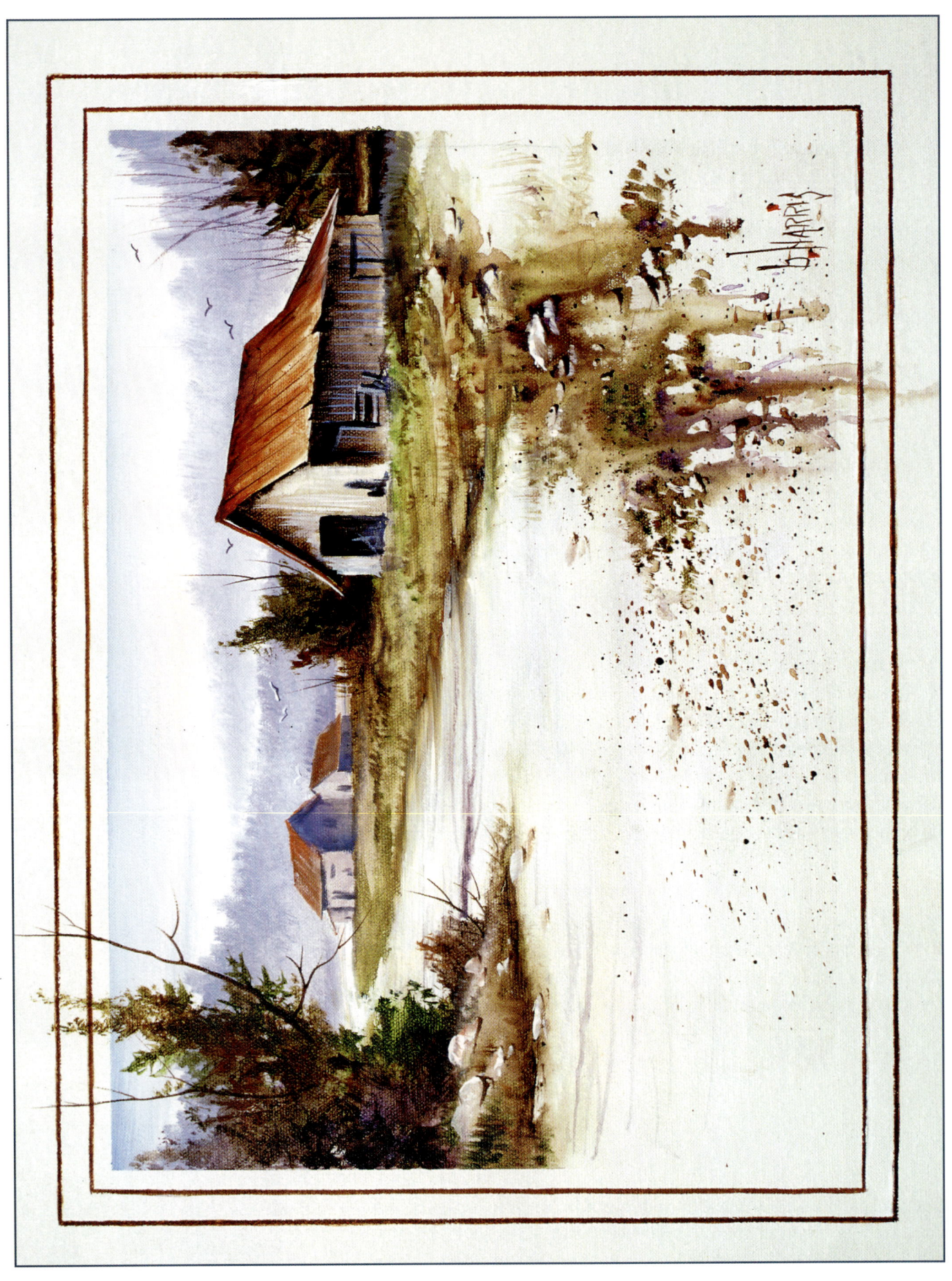

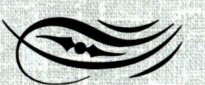

Down the Road

Grumbacher Acrylic Colors
Burnt Sienna
Burnt Umber
Payne's Gray
Dioxazine Purple
Monoazo Orange
Sap Green
Ultramarine Blue

Brushes
Two #101 Gesso Brushes, Size 2"
#1060 White Bristle Fan Brush, Size 1
#4623 Golden Edge® Liner Brush, Size 2
#4403 Sable Essence® Angular Bright Brush, Size ½"
#1600 Multi-Texture Brush, Size ½"

Other Supplies
16"x20" Stretched Canvas
Grumbacher Clearblend
Grumbacher Whiteblend
Tapered Painting Knife
16"x20" Mat Template (12"x15½" Opening)
Matte Medium and Masking Tape
Rapidograph Pen #2.0
Rapidograph Waterproof Ink: Transparent Brown
Natural Sponge
Black Graphite Paper and Ruler
Stylus and Wet Palette
Grumbacher Acrylic Painting Varnish

This lesson is unique because it incorporates two opposite techniques in the same composition—realism and abstraction. The idea of a realistic, rustic barn nestled in an abstract environment was suggested to me by Paulette Jarvey, President of Hot Off The Press. We hope you enjoy it as much as we enjoyed creating it for you.

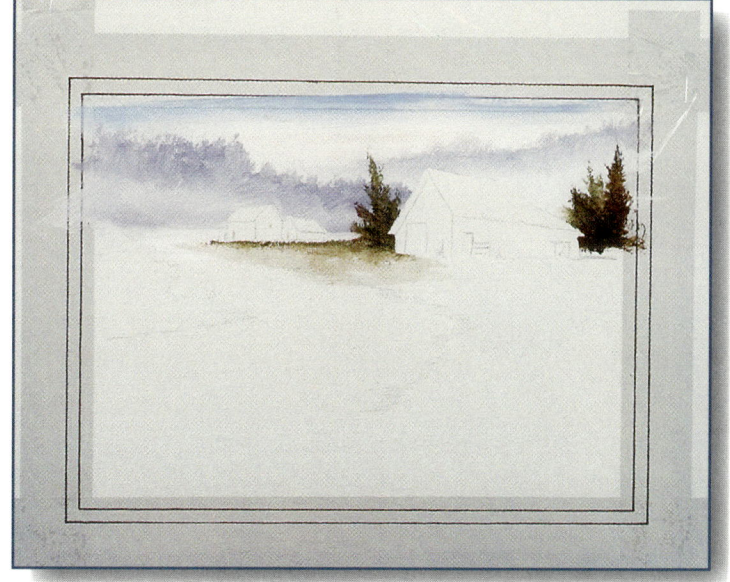

Palette
Before you begin, prepare these color mixtures:

Peach—1 part Whiteblend, a touch Monoazo Orange

Light Blue—6 parts Whiteblend, 1 part Ultramarine Blue

Violet-Gray—4 parts Ultramarine Blue, 1 part Burnt Umber, 15 parts Whiteblend, a touch of Dioxazine Purple

Light Rust—1 part Burnt Sienna, 1 part Monoazo Orange, 1 part Peach, 1 part Violet-Gray

Deep Violet-Gray—1 part Payne's Gray, 1 part Violet-Gray, a touch of Dioxazine Purple

Canvas preparation: Refer to page 2 in the techniques section for instructions on French matting to mat this canvas. After using the mat template to draw the first line, measure ½" in and use a ruler to draw second mat. Cover with masking tape or shipping tape, and seal the edges of the tape to prevent the paint from seeping under it. Transfer the pattern with gray graphite paper, and apply design protectors over the buildings.

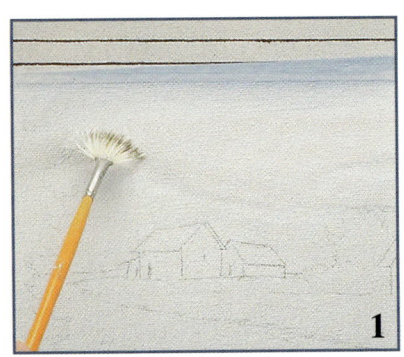

1 **Sky:** Cover the sky area with a generous coat of Whiteblend, applied with the gesso brush. Use the same brush to streak peach through the center of the sky and light blue at the top. Keep these strokes horizontal and use the fan brush to bend any sharp edges.

2 **Distant Hills:** Tap in the farthest hill line with the gesso brush lightly loaded with violet-gray and Whiteblend. Use the fan brush to make the top edges look irregular and uneven, like the tops of trees. Fade out the bottom of this color with Whiteblend.

3 **Middle row of trees and distant road:** Tap in the next row of distant trees in the same manner as in step 4, using the gesso brush loaded with violet-gray. Create an irregular and uneven top with the fan brush, and fade out the bottom with Whiteblend. While wet, streak in the distant curve in the road with peach on the fan brush. Keep your strokes completely horizontal, and the color very pale. Dry.

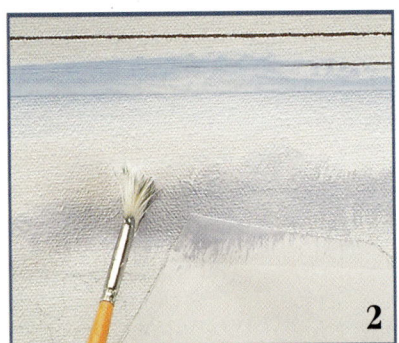

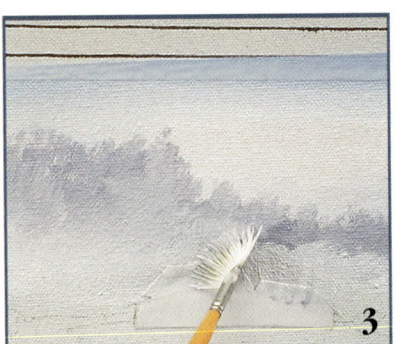

4 **Evergreens behind barn:** Paint these trees in two steps as follows. Apply a little Burnt Umber, a little Burnt Sienna and a little Sap Green directly on the canvas with the fan brush. Tap out the edges of this color with a clean, moist fan brush, creating the feathery outer edges of the trees.

5 Add another clump of these trees just to the left of the barn door, applied in the same manner. Pull a little of this paint down under the trees to begin the ground section. Fade the color into the ground as shown in the photo with a fan brush moistened with Clearblend. Dry, then remove design protectors.

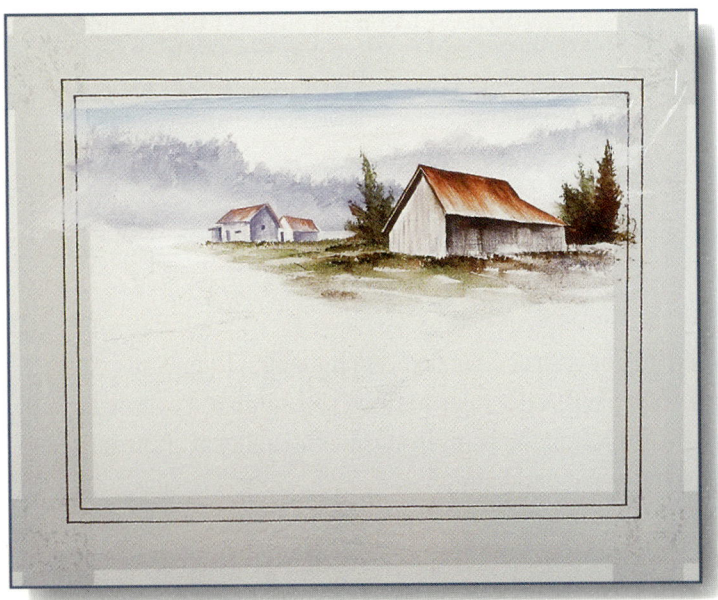

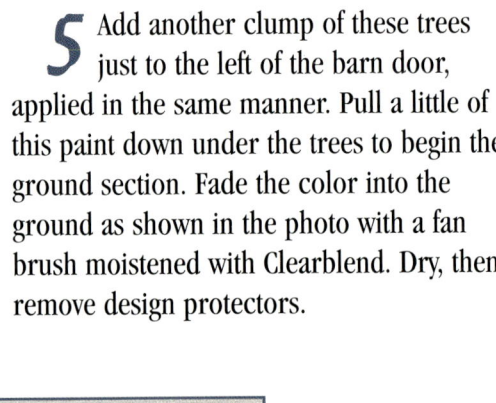

6 **Distant buildings:** Alternate using the bright detail, angular and liner brushes to paint the tiny distant buildings. Paint the top area of each roof (one at a time) with the bright detail brush and rust, and the bottom area with a mixture of rust and Whiteblend. Blend, creating a gradual transition between the values. Alternate using violet gray and peach to paint the fronts and sides of the buildings. Refer to the photo for color placements. Paint the eaves, doors and windows violet-gray.

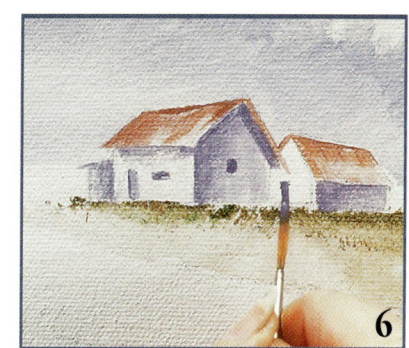

7 **Large barn roof:** Paint the bottom half of the roof with the multi-texture brush and Clearblend. While wet, apply Burnt Sienna to the top of the barn roof with the angular brush. Apply a few dabs of Burnt Umber in the top area of the wet Burnt Sienna. Pull the bottom of the wet Burnt Sienna down over the wet Clearblend with the multi-texture brush, creating a gradual transition in value from top to bottom and directing the strokes according to slope of the roof to create realistic streaks of rust on the tin. Add a thin line of rust color on the edge of eaves on the left side of the roof.

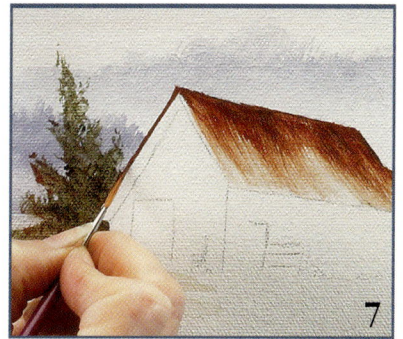

8 **Eaves:** Paint the Burnt Umber eaves under the left side of the roof with the detail bright brush. Use the liner and watery Burnt Umber to paint a thin line under the eaves on the right side of the roof.

9 **Barn side:** Use the angular brush to apply a brush-mixture of Payne's Gray, violet gray and Clearblend under the eaves and along the forward corner of the side of the barn. Use the multi-texture brush loaded with Clearblend to pull this color down to the ground, creating a look of weathered wood. Leave it streaky.

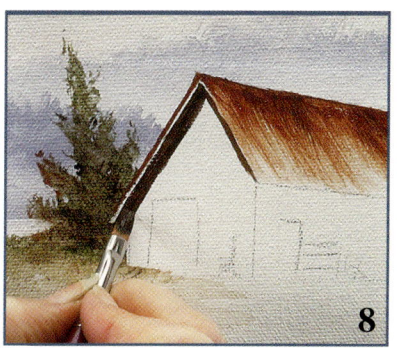

10 **Barn front:** Paint the front of the barn peach with the angular brush, then "dirty" it up a little with some of the color from the side of the barn and some Burnt Umber.

11 **Ground around the barn:** The ground in front of the barn is painted with a watercolor technique. Use the fan brush to dabble some very thin Burnt Umber, Burnt Sienna, Sap Green and light rust in this area. With a clean, wet fan brush, swish these colors vertically, skipping a few spots, to create the ground area out to the road. The ground to the right of the barn is painted in the same manner, only using darker values. When swishing vertically, don't cover all the light areas. They will add interest, and will give you places to put some rocks later on. Add a darker area to the right of the barn.

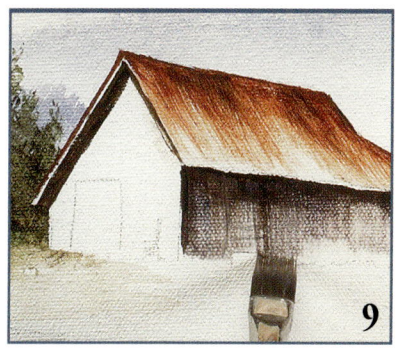

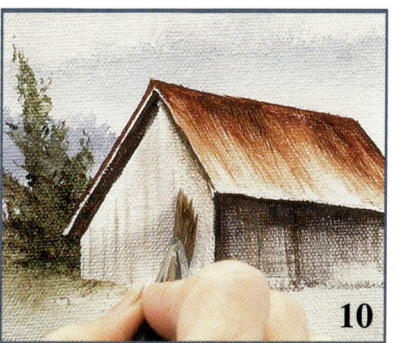

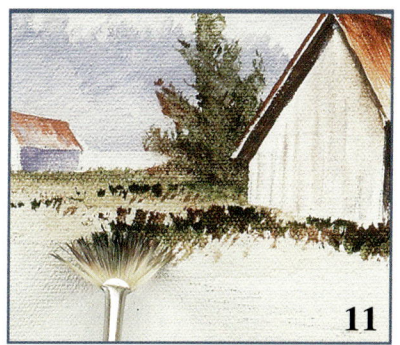

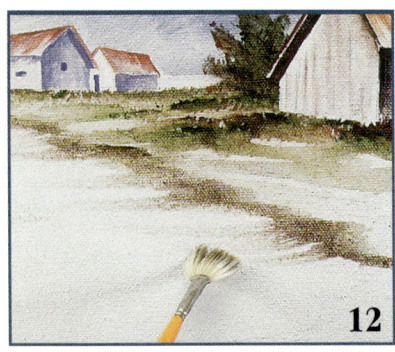

12 **Road:** Add a few more of the grass colors along the edge of the road, and wash them down with a clean brush. Apply horizontal streaks of peach randomly across the road with the fan brush. Let this peach color mix with some of the wet grass color as you stroke the brush back and forth to connect the road and the grass. Add more Whiteblend to the brush as you come forward, painting the road in solid all the way to the edge of the composition.

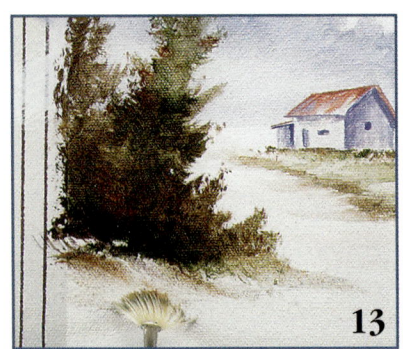

13 **Foreground trees:** These trees are painted in the same manner as the trees behind the barn, first applying several dark, creamy colors, then tapping out the edges with a clean, moist fan brush. While the trees are still wet, use the clean moist fan brush to pull some of the color from the bottom down over the embankment. Add a little extra Burnt Umber at the base of the embankment, and with a clean, moist fan brush, melt this color out over the road and back over the embankment. Tap in a few grasses as well.

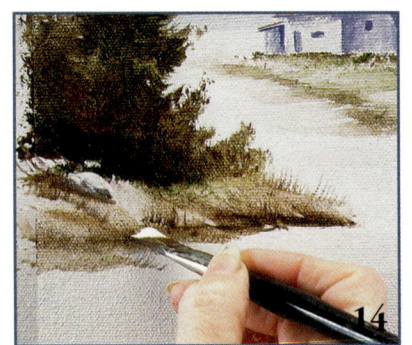

14 **Rocks:** Double-load the angular brush with Burnt Umber and Payne's Gray on the short side, and peach on the long bristles. Holding the brush with the peach side up, press the heel of the brush down on the canvas, creating rocks. Press harder for large rocks, lighter for small ones.

15 **Abstract area:** Paint this section one small area at a time. Use the fan brush to tap in any of the dark colors from the trees and grass. Then, immediately splatter with clean water on the fan brush, and let the watery colors run down as they will.

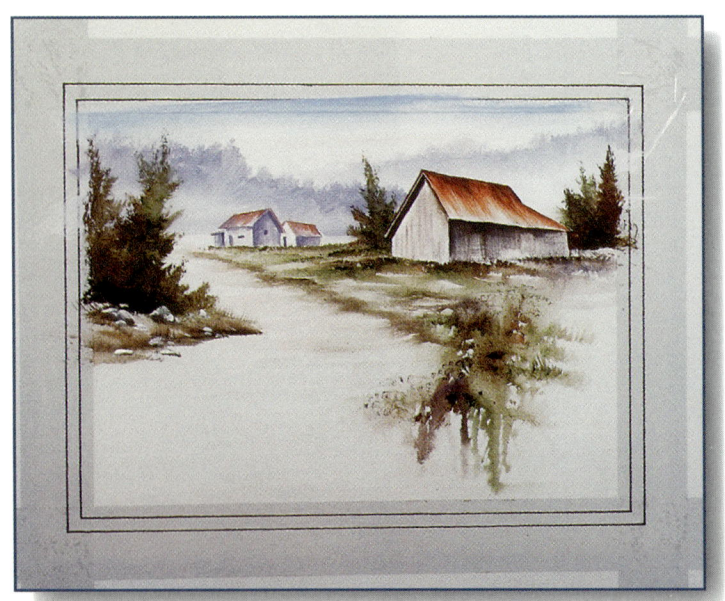

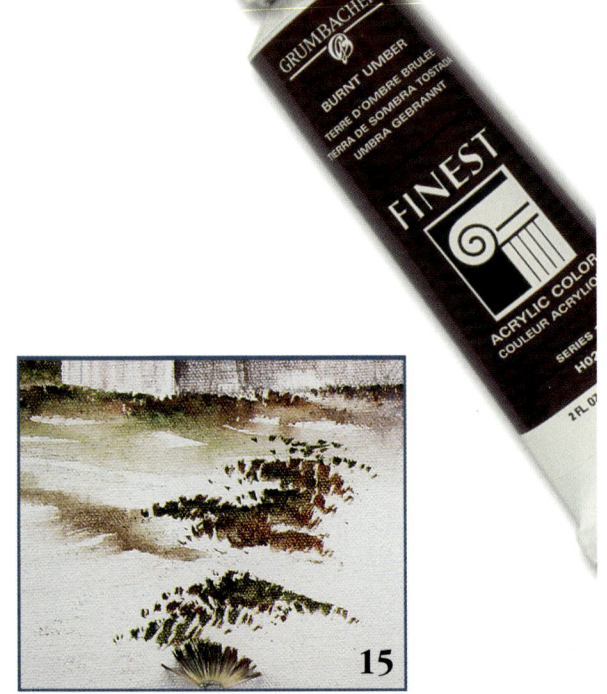

16 If the colors begin to drizzle into an area where you don't want them, remove the paint with a clean, damp sponge. Use a clean, moist fan brush to soften the edges of this area, connecting it to the road, but do not blend away the negative spaces created by the splattering, dripping water. Use a sponge to dry and remove excess paint along the tape.

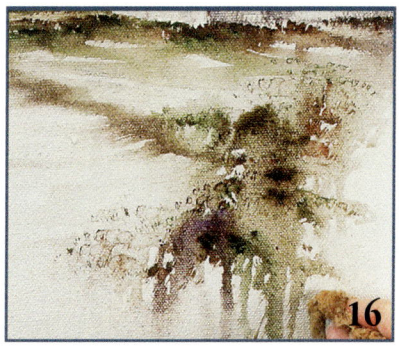

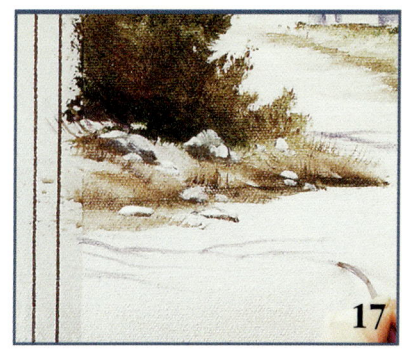

17 **Shadows on road:** Pull some transparent shadows across the road with violet-gray thinned with Clearblend on the liner brush; blot with your finger. Add a few of the double-loaded rocks in this area, too. Splatter with a toothbrush and very watery Burnt Umber, Payne's Gray, light rust, and gray-violet. Remove excess wet splatters with a sponge. Dry completely and remove the tape.

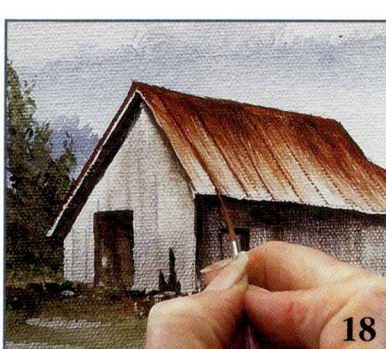

18 **Barn details:** Paint the door with a brush-mixture of Burnt Umber and Payne's Gray on the detail bright brush. Double-load the liner brush with peach and Payne's Gray to add the rest of the detail on the barn, including a fence post or two, and some cracks and broken boards. Be sure to keep the peach side of the brush closest to the light source and the gray side toward the shadows. Apply Burnt Sienna lines on the roof with a liner brush and watery paint.

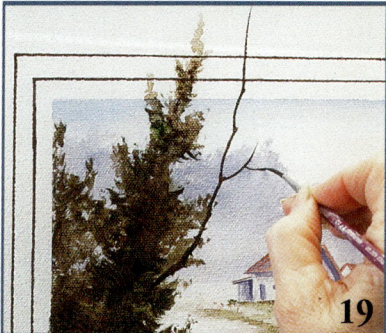

19 **Tree details:** Carry the painting out onto the mat for an interesting look. Add a little more of the wet tree colors onto the evergreens, and with a clean moist fan brush, tap these edges out over the top of the mat. Use the liner brush and watery Burnt Umber to add a few bare trees in this area, carrying some of them over the mat as well. Referring to the large photo on page 32, add a few bare trees behind the barn. Dabble a few more of these colors near the bottom of the abstract area, and splatter with water again, letting some of the drizzles run down on the mat. Remove excess with a clean sponge before it dries.

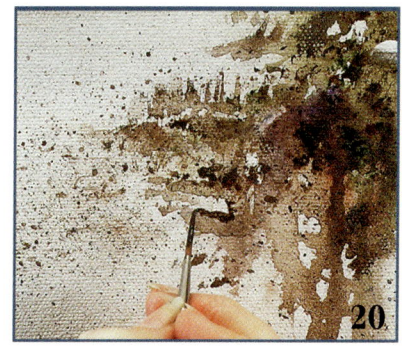

20 **Final details:** Add rocks in the foreground in the lower right with an angular brush double-loaded with Burnt Umber and Whiteblend. Use the liner brush and violet-gray to add a few flying birds. Add watery Burnt Umber shadows around some of the light spots in the abstract area to create additional rocks.

Sign and take a trip "down the road"! When the painting is completely dry, use a kneaded eraser or moist sponge to remove any excess graphite lines. Spray your painting with Grumbacher Acrylic Painting Varnish.

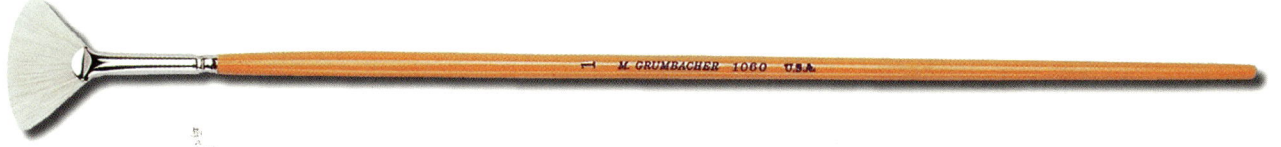

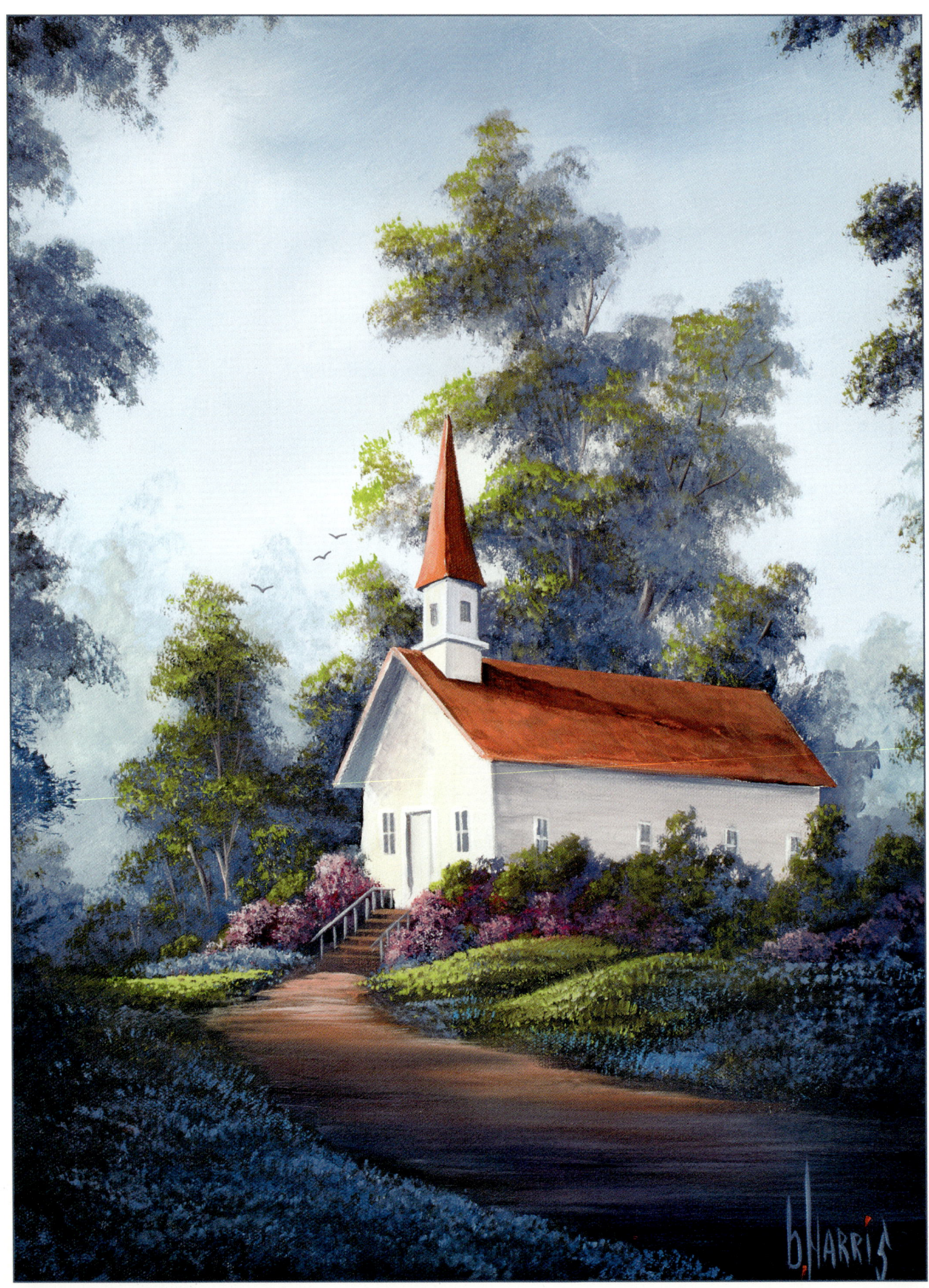

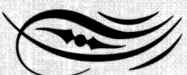

Fellowship

Grumbacher Acrylic Colors
Cadmium Yellow Medium
Cerulean Blue
Monoazo Orange
Payne's Gray
Thalo Crimson
Thalo Yellow Green
Titanium White
Ultramarine Blue

Brushes
Two #101 Gesso Brushes, Size 2"
#1500 Hake Brush, Size 2
#4403 Sable Essence® Angular Bright Brush, Size ⅜"
#4610B Golden Edge® Bright Brush, Size 6
#4623 Golden Edge® Liner Brush, Size 2
#1060 White Bristle Fan Brush, Size 1
#582 Eterna Bristle Round Brush, Size 8 and 12
#760F Academy Bristle Flat Brush, Size 6

Other Supplies
16"x20" Stretched Canvas
Grumbacher Clearblend
Grumbacher Whiteblend
Grumbacher Retarder
Tapered Painting Knife
Adhesive Design Protector
Natural Sponge
Gray Graphite Paper
Stylus
Wet Palette
Grumbacher Acrylic Painting Varnish

Dedicated to Dick and Betty Jo Larsen, two very special people, in memory of their son Rick.

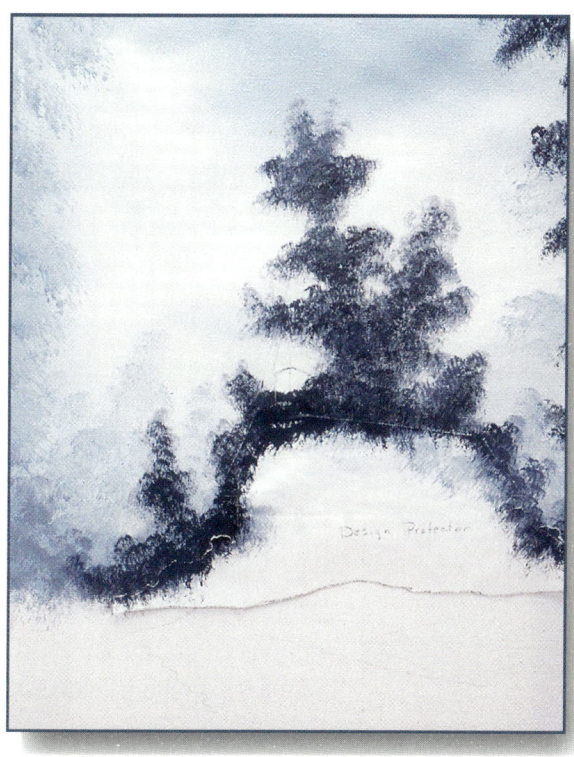

Canvas preparation: Use gray graphite to transfer the church to the canvas. Place the top of the steeple 6" from the top of the canvas and 6½" from the left side of the canvas.

Palette

Before you begin, prepare these color mixtures:

Light Cerulean—1 part Whiteblend, 1 part Cerulean Blue

Medium Blue—1 part Ultramarine Blue, 1 part Payne's Gray, 1 part Whiteblend, a touch of Titanium White

Dark Blue-Green—1 part Ultramarine Blue, 1 part Payne's Gray, a touch of Cadmium Yellow Medium

Dusty Gray-Green—2 parts Dark Blue-Green, 2 parts Light Cerulean, a touch of Thalo Yellow Green

Medium Green—1 part Dusty Gray-Green, 1 part Thalo Yellow Green

Light Green—1 part Medium Green, 1 part Thalo Yellow Green, 1 part Whiteblend

Yellow-Green—1 part Thalo Yellow Green, 1 part Whiteblend

Brown—1 part Monoazo Orange, 1 part Payne's Gray, a touch of Medium Blue

Coral—5 parts Whiteblend, 1 part Monoazo Orange

Peach—1 part Whiteblend, a touch of Monoazo Orange, a touch of Cadmium Yellow Medium

Violet—1 part Medium Blue, 4 parts Whiteblend, a touch of Rose, a touch of Cerulean Blue

Prepare these color mixes as you need them:

Purple—2 parts Ultramarine Blue, 1 part Thalo Crimson, 1 part Whiteblend

Rose—1 part Whiteblend, 1 part Thalo Crimson

Pink—1 part rose, 1 part Titanium White

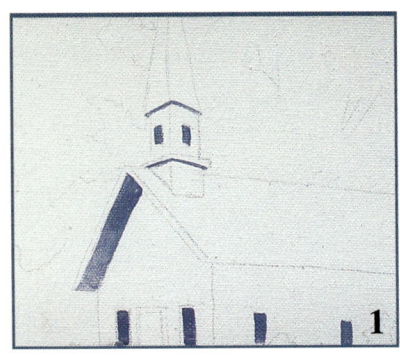

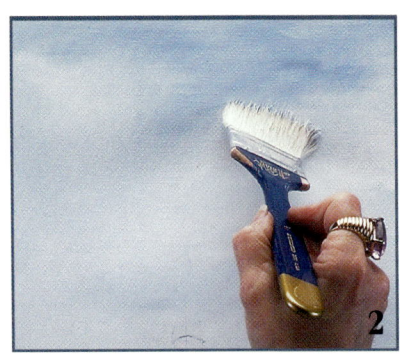

1 **Church preparation:** Paint the windows, door, and the shadows under all the eaves with medium blue and the detail bright brush. Dry thoroughly and place a design protector over the church.

2 **Sky:** Work the sky area wet-on-wet. Moisten the sky with water and Grumbacher Retarder, then use the same brush to scrub a generous amount of Whiteblend into the entire sky area. Immediately pick up light cerulean on the same brush, streak and scrub it into the sky randomly, creating light and dark areas. Keep the cerulean fairly strong towards the top of the sky and lighter at the bottom. Blend slightly with the Hake brush to soften the edges and create a blustery sky.

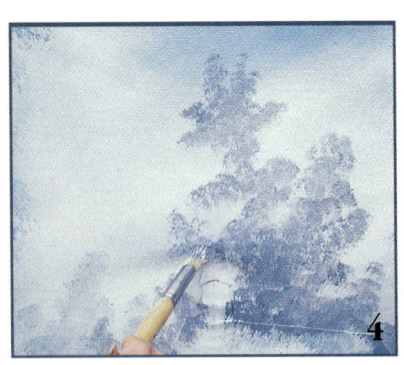

3 **Distant trees:** Create the most distant trees with your large round bristle brush and light cerulean. Stipple these trees directly into the wet sky area, being careful not to get them too dark, too symmetrical, or too perfectly shaped.

4 **Middle trees:** Stipple the mid-ground trees behind the church with the uncleaned small round bristle brush and medium blue. Remember to paint these trees irregularly shaped. Follow the photograph for placement.

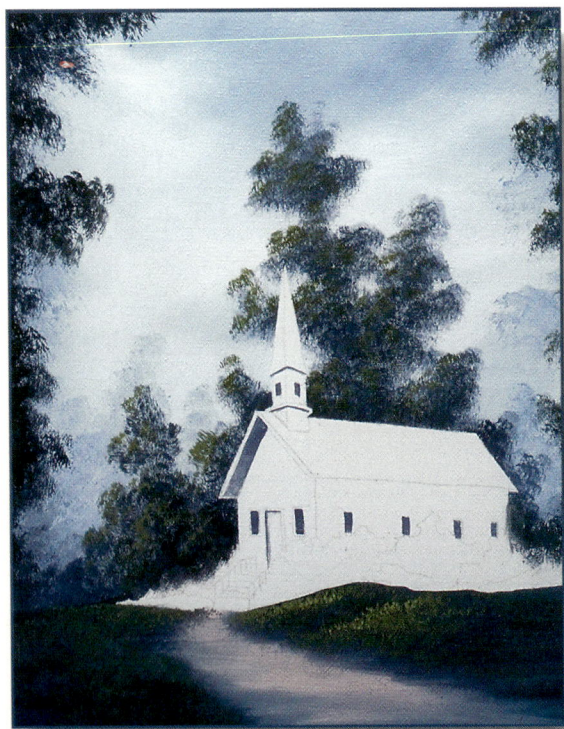

5 With the uncleaned round bristle brush-mix a darker value foliage color using medium blue and dark blue-green. Stipple this color in the centers and right sides of the middle trees and shrubs behind the the church. Do not cover all their previous color nor paint all the way to their right edges. Use the same brush and color to stipple the tall foliage along the right side of the canvas.

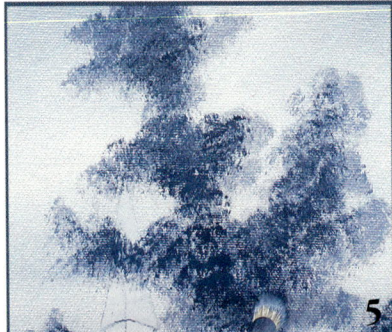

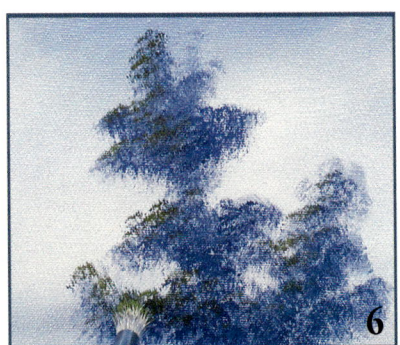

6 **Foreground trees:** With a clean round brush, lightly stipple dusty gray-green in the left two-thirds of the trees and foliage behind the church. Once again, do not cover all the previous color, nor go completely to the left edges of the foliage. With a clean round bristle brush, lightly stipple medium green highlights on the left one-third of these same trees and shrubs behind the church.

7 Grass basecoat: Use the gesso or flat bristle brush and horizontal strokes to basecoat the grassy area with dark blue-green. Details will be added later.

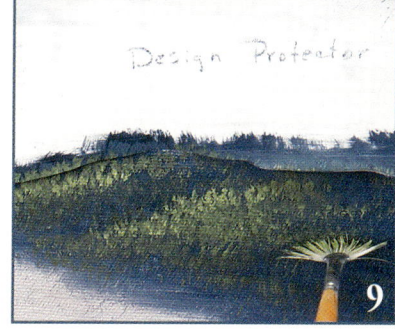

8 Path: Basecoat the path peach with horizontal streaks of the flat bristle brush. Darken the foreground section of the path by alternately streaking dark blue-green, Payne's Gray and dusty gray-green horizontally through the wet paint. Pull a little of the path color into the wet grass area, and pull a little of the grass color into the wet path to connect the two.

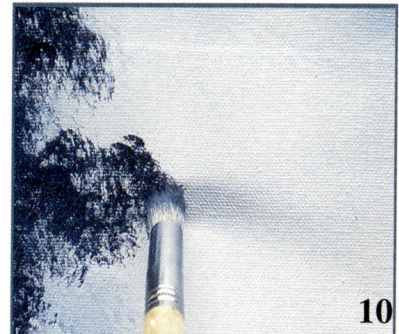

9 Texture in grassy areas: While the grassy areas are still wet, use the gesso brush to tap dusty gray-green reflected light over most of the grass to create texture. With medium green on the same brush, add highlights; to the top two-thirds of the grassy areas. Use the fan brush to stipple light green areas around the front of the church and in the top third of each grassy knoll. Remove the design protector and wipe any paint seepage off the church. Dry thoroughly.

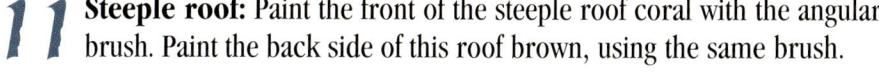
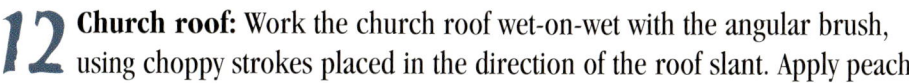

10 Stipple the trees along the left side of the canvas with dark blue-green and the small round brush.

11 Steeple roof: Paint the front of the steeple roof coral with the angular brush. Paint the back side of this roof brown, using the same brush.

12 Church roof: Work the church roof wet-on-wet with the angular brush, using choppy strokes placed in the direction of the roof slant. Apply peach along the top edge. With a clean brush, tap a brown shadow behind the steeple as shown. Paint the remainder of the roof with a brush-mixture of coral and brown. Starting at the top of the roof, use a clean angular brush and a mixture of peach and coral to pat short highlight strokes over the roof (except in the shadow area) to represent shingles. Add coral and a touch of brown to the uncleaned brush to tap shingles in the shadow area. Tap the edge of the steeple shadow to create a gradual transition between colors. Paint the eaves coral with the liner brush.

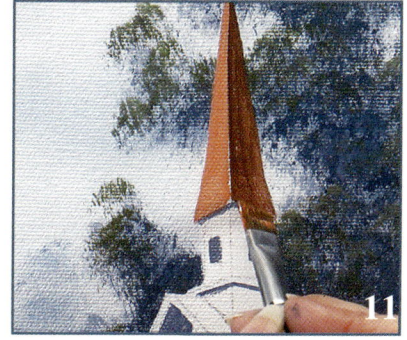

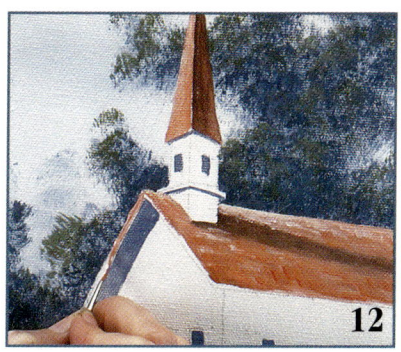

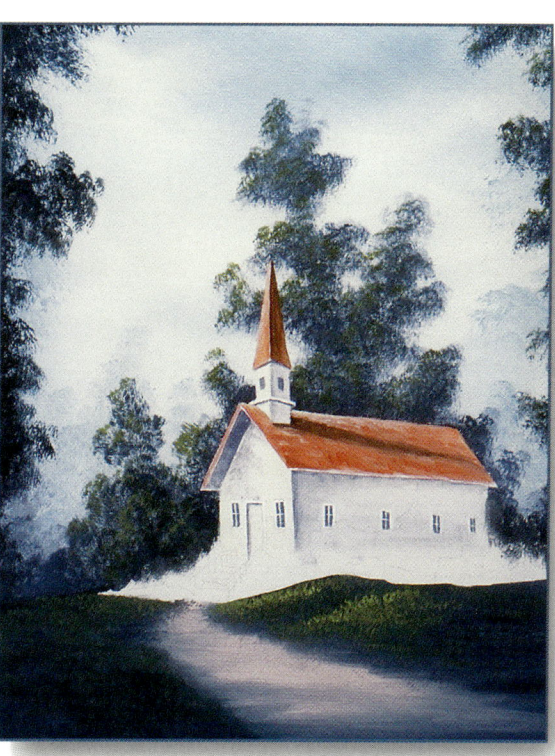

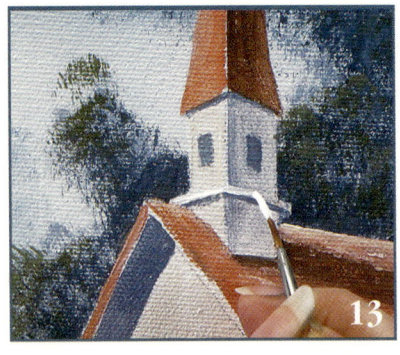

13 Steeple: Paint the front of the steeple with the angular brush and a translucent brush-mixture of Clearblend and peach. With a translucent angular brush-mixture of Clearblend and violet, paint the shadow side of the steeple. Paint directly over the windows and moldings; they will show through these translucent colors. Accent the molding on the steeple with some Whiteblend on your liner brush.

14 Church front: The church itself is worked with the angular brush in the same manner as the steeple. Fill in the front with a mixture of peach and Clearblend, painting right over the windows and the door. While this is wet, pat in an irregular tree foliage shadow on the upper left area with the translucent violet and Clearblend mixture. Use a clean brush to blend this into the peach.

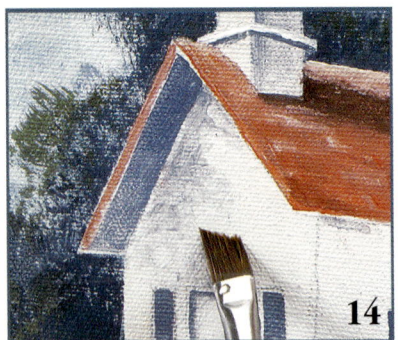

15 Church side: Paint the side of the church with the violet and Clearblend mixture, using the angular brush, and long, horizontal strokes going right over the windows. Add medium blue to the uncleaned brush and darken the shadow directly under the roof and along the front corner. Blend this slightly with a clean angular brush. With the liner brush and Whiteblend, paint the trim around the windows, window panes and door. Stipple the bushes around the steps and along the side of the church with a brush-mixture of dark blue-green and medium blue, slightly darker than the trees around the church.

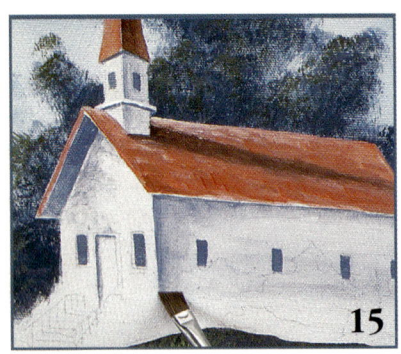

16 Bush highlights: Highlight the bushes around the steps and along the side of the church by lightly stippling with a clean flat bristle brush. Apply medium green to the left two-thirds of each cluster; light green on the left half of each cluster. Apply yellow-green only on the left one-fourth of the foliage around the steps and entrance to the church. Highlight the left third of each cluster in the middle ground trees and shrubs to the left of the church with the light yellow green. While wet, blot to subdue unwanted hard edges. Lightly tap a touch more medium green in the center of these same trees and shrubs if needed, and blot with your finger to correct hard edges. Touch up any area or color that you choose, leaving the trees and foliage behind the church slightly lighter in value and less defined than the shrubs in front of the church.

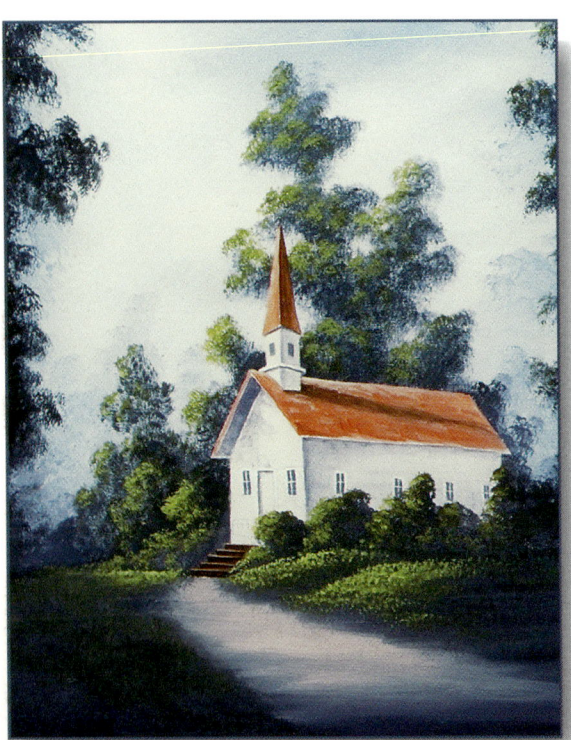

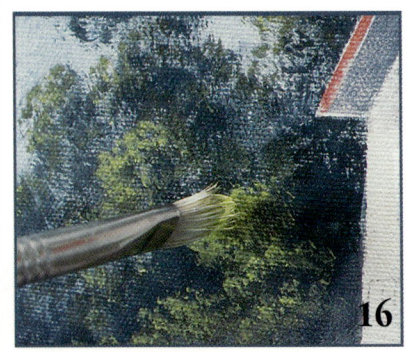

17 **Grass:** With the fan brush, tap dusty gray-green grass up over the bottoms of the shrubs to "plant" them. With a clean fan brush, tap yellow-green grassy area near the church to indicate sun shining down. Stipple dark blue-green bushes in the bottom left corner of the canvas, connecting to the bottom of the tall tree along the left edge of the canvas.

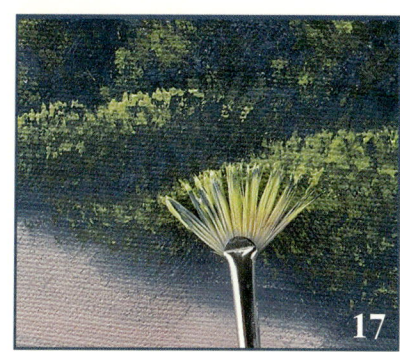

18 **Steps:** Paint the steps brown with an angular brush. Highlight the side edge of each step with coral loaded on the chisel edge of the angular brush. Add dark blue-green for a shadow under each riser with the liner brush.

19 **Flowers:** Randomly stipple clusters of purple azalea blooms in the shrubs in front of the church with a flat bristle brush. Lightly stipple highlights on the top left sides of the purple clusters with a clean bristle brush and rose. Add pink to the uncleaned brush and lightly tap highlights on the left side of the rose azalea highlights in the sunlit areas around the entrance to the church only. Lightly tap the medium blue shadowed blooms around the base of the shrubs with a brush-mixture of Cerulean Blue, Ultramarine Blue and a touch of Whiteblend. Blot the base of the wet flowers to "plant" them. Add a touch of dark blue-green to the blue in the uncleaned brush and stipple a few duller flowers in the shadowy areas of the grass. Highlight the medium blue blossoms with values of light blue, brush-mixed with a clean fan brush using Cerulean Blue and varying amounts of Titanium White.

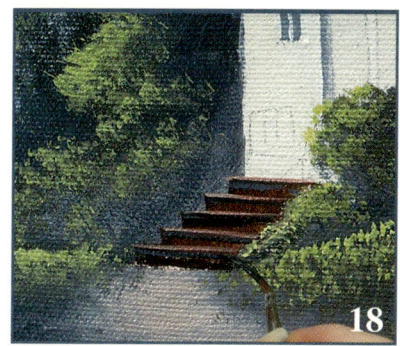

20 **Tree trunks & stair railings:** Double-load the liner brush with Payne's Gray on one side, and peach on the other. Hold the brush with the peach side to the left, and paint the tree trunks. Double-load the same brush with Payne's Gray and Whiteblend, and with the peach side facing the light source, paint the stair railings with an upright post on each step.

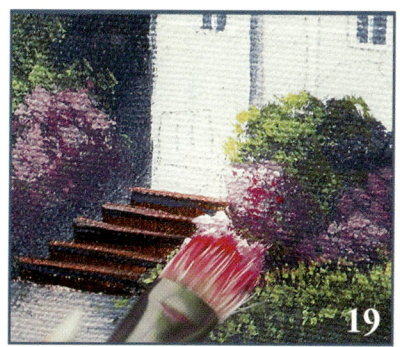

21 **Path Highlights:** Apply Clearblend over the entire path with the fan brush. While wet, apply touch-up colors as needed with the angular brush to include dashes of coral and peach in the sunlit areas, and streaks of medium blue and/or violet reflected light in the shade. Blend into the wet Clearblend with the moistened fan brush. Touch up shadowy areas with dark blue-green or Payne's Gray.

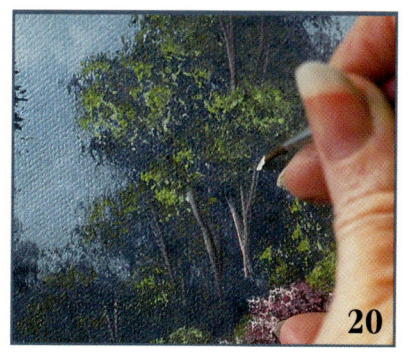

22 **Birds:** With a liner brush and very thin violet, add a few birds in the sky.

Sign, and say your prayers! When your painting is completely dry, use a kneaded eraser or moist sponge to remove any excess graphite lines. Then spray it with Grumbacher Acrylic Painting Varnish to bring out the "amazing grace" of this little chapel.

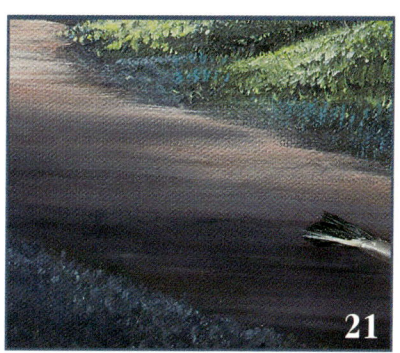

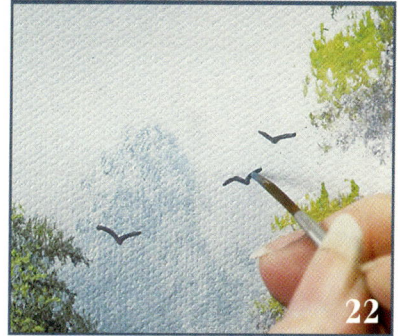

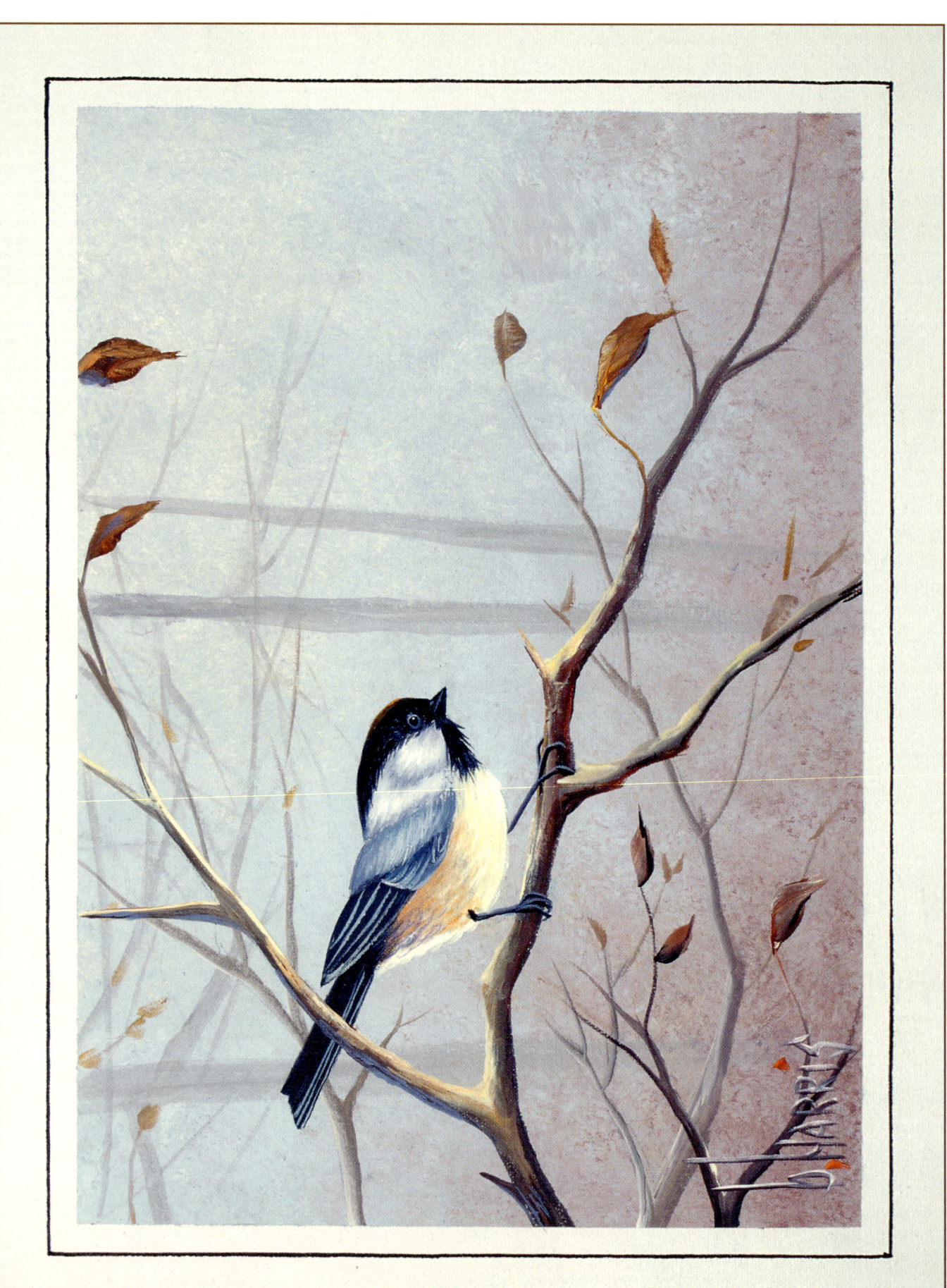

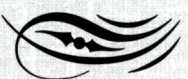

Out on a Limb

Grumbacher Acrylic Colors

Burnt Sienna
Cadmium Yellow Medium
Monoazo Orange
Payne's Gray
Thalo Crimson
Titanium White
Ultramarine Blue
Yellow Ochre

Brushes

#101 Gesso Brush, Size 2"
#4623 Golden Edge® Liner Brush, Size 2
#4403 Sable Essence® Angular Bright Brush, Size ½"
#582 Eterna Bristle Round Brush, Size 8
#1060 White Bristle Fan Brush, Size 1
#4610B Golden Edge® Bright Brush, Size 6

Other Supplies

16"x20" Stretched Canvas
Grumbacher Clearblend
Grumbacher Whiteblend
16"x20" Mat Template (12"x15½" Opening)
Matte Medium
Rapidograph Pen #2.0
Rapidograph Waterproof Ink: Brown
Masking Tape and Wet Palette
Tapered Painting Knife
Natural Sponge and Stylus
Charcoal Graphite Paper
Grumbacher Acrylic Painting Varnish

The black-capped Chickadee is named for its unique song. These friendly little birds are regular visitors to bird feeders in Canada and the northern U.S. They can be heard year-round singing, "Chicka-dee-dee-dee!" The combination of wet-on-wet and wet-on-dry techniques taught in this painting will sharpen your artistic skills and make painting this delightful fellow a snap.

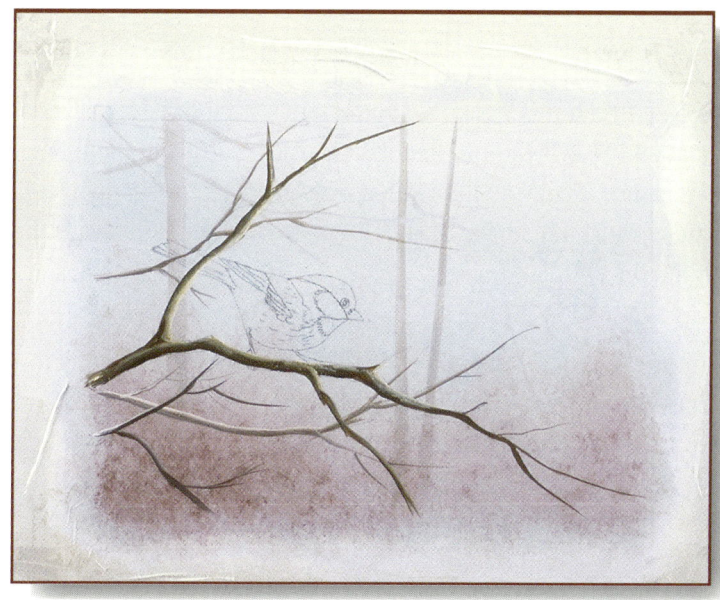

Palette

Before you begin, prepare these color mixtures:

Light Gray—1 part Whiteblend, a touch of Payne's Gray

Peach—1 part Whiteblend, a touch of Monoazo Orange

Light Yellow—1 part Whiteblend, a touch of Yellow Ochre, a touch of Cadmium Yellow Medium

Light Blue—1 part Whiteblend, a touch of Ultramarine Blue

Maroon—1 part Thalo Crimson, 4 parts Burnt Sienna, 3 parts Payne's Gray

Gray-Violet—8 parts Ultramarine Blue, 4 parts Payne's Gray, 1 part Thalo Crimson, 10 parts Whiteblend

Raw Sienna—1 part Burnt Sienna, a touch of Thalo Crimson, 1 part Yellow Ochre, 10 parts Whiteblend

Off-White—1 part Titanium White, a touch of Light Yellow

Canvas preparation: Refer to page 2 in the techniques section for instructions on French matting to mat this canvas. Use Rapidograph Pen #2.0 filled with Rapidograph waterproof ink.

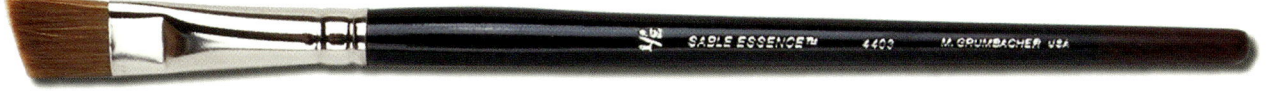

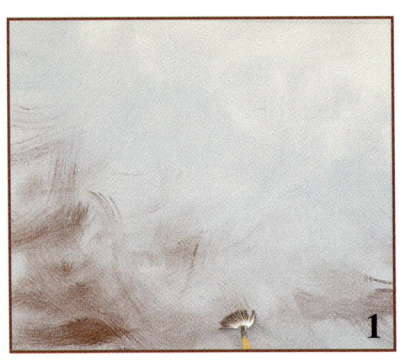

1 **Background:** Paint the canvas light gray with the gesso brush. Dry thoroughly, then use a clean gesso brush to cover the area with Clearblend. Use the fan brush to apply and blend the accent colors into the wet Clearblend at an angle, being careful not to cover the gray background. Begin in the top right corner with peach, getting progressively lighter as you move toward the canvas center. Repeat with yellow in the top right corner and blend. Add light blue, starting at the top left corner. Brush-mix Whiteblend and maroon to make a light maroon and apply it in the bottom left corner, up the left side and along the canvas bottom. Add maroon to the uncleaned brush and darken the area at the bottom left corner.

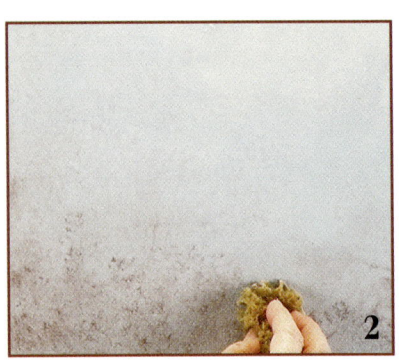

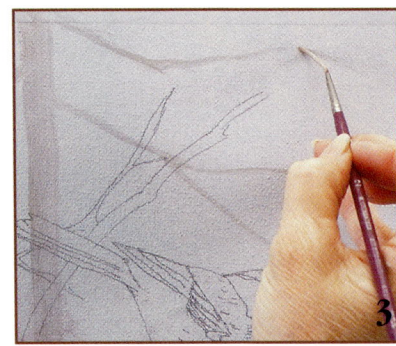

2 Pat-blend the accent colors with a clean, towel-dried sponge to blend and create texture. Tap lightly, moving from light to dark to give the illusion of distant foliage in a misty fog. If you need more color after blending, add it with a clean sponge then pat-blend with a clean area of the sponge. Dry completely, and transfer the design with charcoal graphite paper. The tip of the bird's beak should be 9¾" from the left canvas edge and 7¾" below the top canvas edge.

3 **Distant trees:** Brush-mix light gray and a touch each of Payne's Gray, Burnt Sienna and Slowblend on the angular brush and paint the misty tree shapes in the distance. Set aside the loaded brush for step 4. Lightly blot areas along the trunks with your finger to subdue them. Add the limbs with the same mixture and the liner brush.

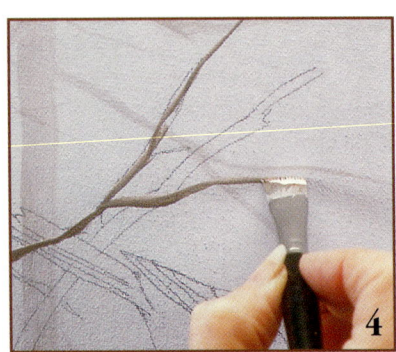

4 **Middle-ground limbs:** Add more Payne's Gray and Burnt Sienna to the angular brush from step 3 and apply a few middle ground limbs crossing over the background trees at the canvas bottom. Add peach to the brush and paint middle ground limbs at the upper left area of the canvas. Use the liner brush and watery mixtures of the same colors to add small branches to those limbs and to paint a middle ground limb at lower left area of the canvas.

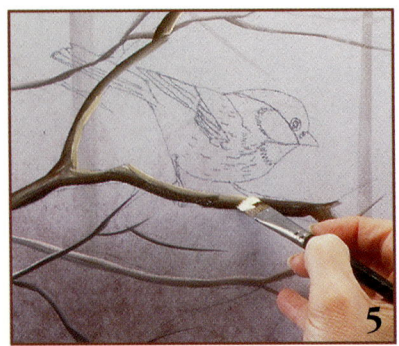

5 **Foreground limb:** Double-load the angular brush with maroon and peach or light yellow; paint the main branches of the foreground limb. Tap around on the limbs with the pointed tip of the angular brush to create texture and variety in value. Add the smaller branches with the liner and a watery mixture of the same colors. Touch up as needed, then dry the canvas completely.

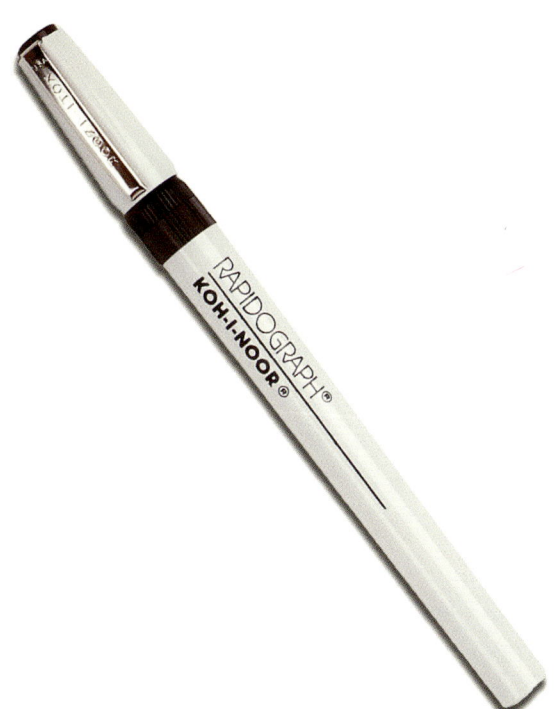

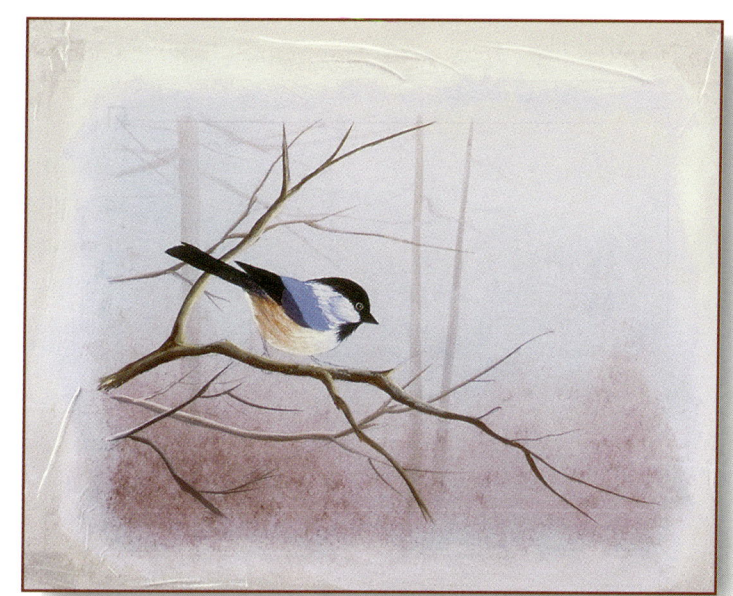

6 **Tail feathers:** Use the angular brush and Payne's Gray to basecoat the tail feathers. Dry and reapply if needed.

7 **Wing feathers:** Use the angular brush to basecoat the top left feathers Payne's Gray. Add Whiteblend to the uncleaned brush and fill in the section below the Payne's Gray section. Add a little Whiteblend and Ultramarine Blue to the uncleaned brush, then paint the wing center as shown.

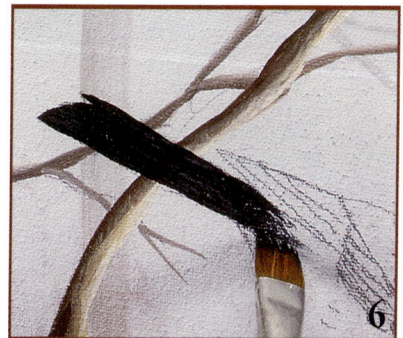

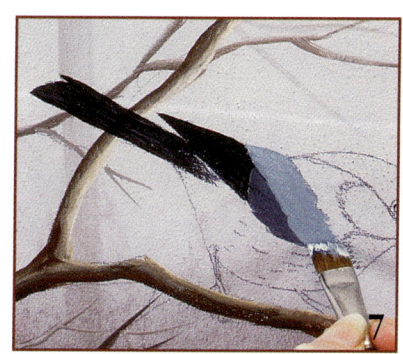

8 **Eye:** Use the liner or the small round brush to paint the pupil Payne's Gray. Dry, then add a Whiteblend catchlight in the pupil at 3:00. Paint the head Payne's Gray, stroking in the direction of the feather growth. Start around the eye, leaving a very thin, unpainted ring around his eye.

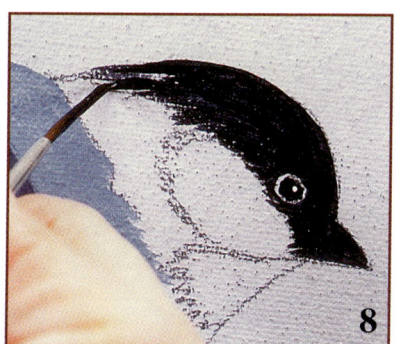

9 **Chin:** Paint choppy Payne's Gray strokes on the chin with the small round brush. Thin the paint with water and pull a few tiny ruffled feathers from this down into the breast area. Apply gray-violet feathery strokes where his head meets the wings and in a "C" around his cheek using a liner or small round brush. Stroke in the direction of the feather growth. Use a clean liner to fill in the remaining cheek and neck areas with Whiteblend. Blend with choppy strokes using a clean, towel-dried small round brush, creating a gradual transition of color but a feathery base. Details will be added later.

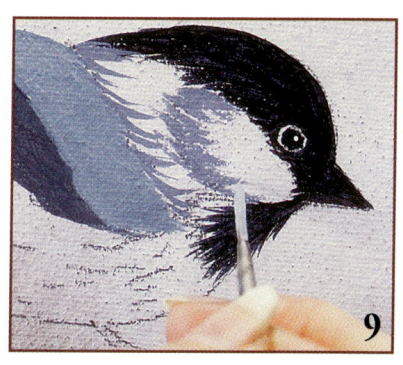

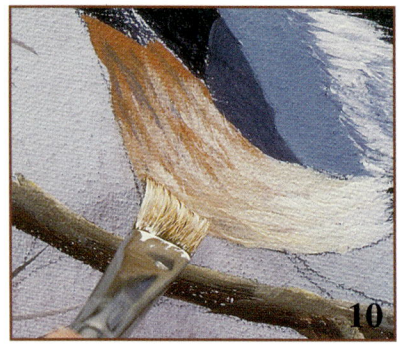

10 **Underbelly and breast:** Use a clean angular brush and short, choppy strokes to paint his underbelly and breast, following the direction of the feather growth. Paint his rump raw sienna, his middle a brush-mix of Whiteblend and raw sienna and his breast pale yellow. Add a few gray-violet shadow strokes with a clean angular brush on his rump, then tap lightly to blend and create texture. Tap and blend with a clean towel-dried angular brush to create a gradual transition of color. Use the liner brush to add a few strokes of Payne's Gray where the tail joins the rump. Repeat with raw sienna and gray-violet. Tap with a clean, dry small round brush to create a gradual color transition.

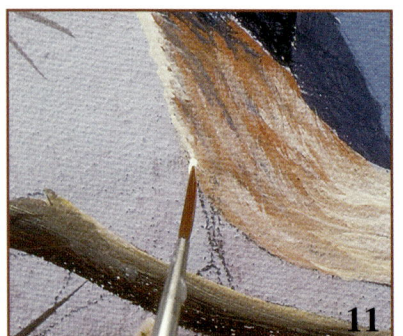

11 **Reflected light:** Use the small round brush to apply tiny off-white strokes on the outside edge of his rump, tucking into the darker rump feathers. Randomly add a few strokes on the rump and body area.

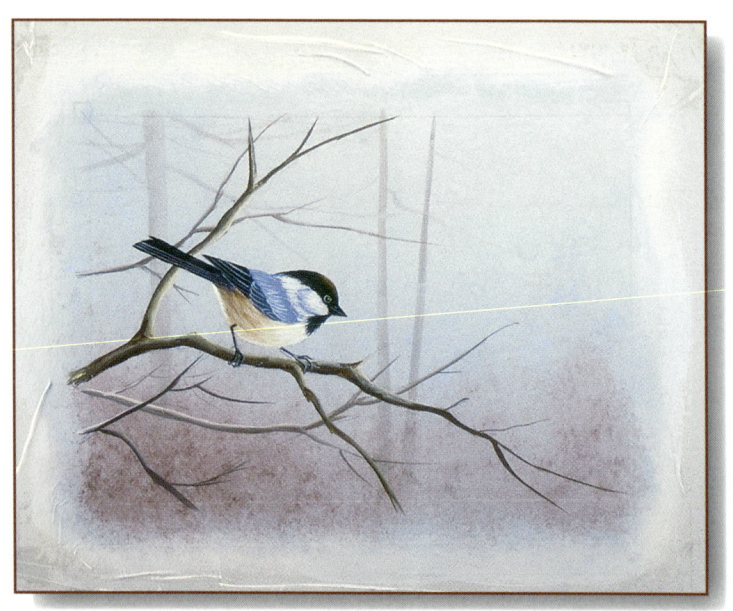

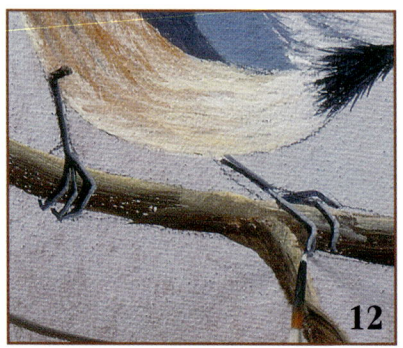

12 **Feet & legs:** Use the liner brush to paint the legs and feet with Payne's Gray thinned with Clearblend. When dry, highlight the tops of his toes and the front of his legs with a little light gray. Dry.

13 **Face details:** Brush-mix raw sienna and Burnt Sienna on the liner brush to make rust. Add tiny, choppy marks of reflected light on top of his head. Fade them back with a Clearblend-moistened liner brush. Thin gray-violet with Clearblend, then use the liner brush to fill in the ring between his eye and face. Add a nostril and a line dividing his beak.

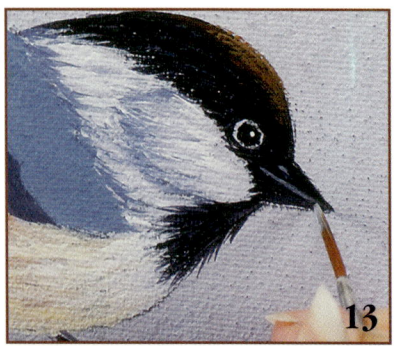

14 **Feather details:** Use gray-violet thinned with Clearblend and the liner brush to apply reflected light on the forward edge of some tail and primary feathers. Brush-mix a touch of Ultramarine Blue and light blue on a clean liner, then add feather markings to the central and front sections of the wing. Add a little Titanium White to the uncleaned brush, then add feather markings in the center of the front wing area.

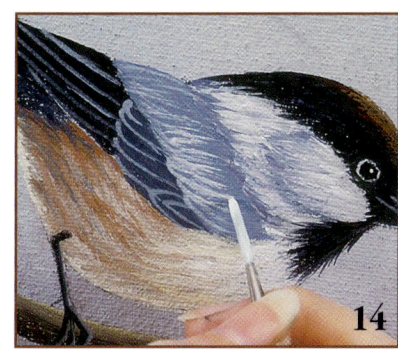

15 **Cheek:** Use the liner brush or small round brush to highlight the centers of the cheek and neck area with short choppy strokes of Titanium White. If necessary, soften them with a Clearblend-moistened brush. Use the liner brush to add a few off-white feather marks on his chest. Dry, then remove any excess graphite lines with a kneaded eraser.

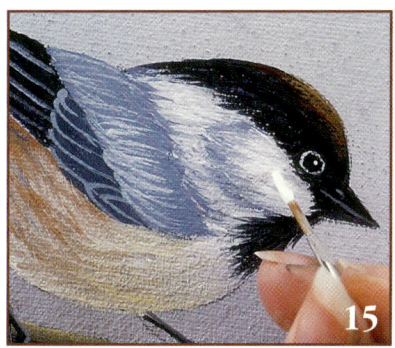

16 Use the liner brush and off-white to add a few choppy reflected light strokes on the foremost limb. Use the angular brush and colors from step 5 to paint the foreground limb over the bird's tail as shown. Tap to blend, then dry the painting.

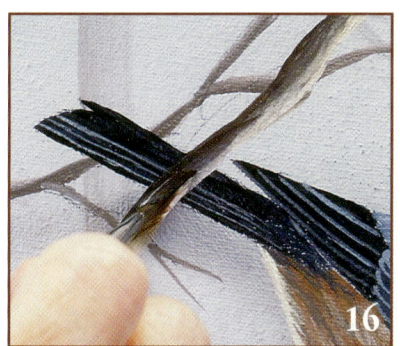

17 **Leaves:** Use the bright brush to paint a few small background leaves in the distance with varying brush-mixes of Payne's Gray Burnt Sienna and Slowblend. Place them randomly and occasionally blot with your finger to keep them very light.

18 **Large leaves:** Load the angular brush with light gray and add a touch of Clearblend and either Burnt Sienna or raw sienna. Paint a few slightly larger, darker and more prominent leaves by pressing the brush down, pulling it gently to form a leaf then lifting it off the canvas. Add maroon, Payne's Gray or any darker color of your choice from the palette to the uncleaned brush and shade the leaves. Create a variety of interesting colors, sizes and shapes of leaves. Add stems to attach the leaves to the branches. Touch up any area that needs embellishing. Remember to be creative— you are an artist.

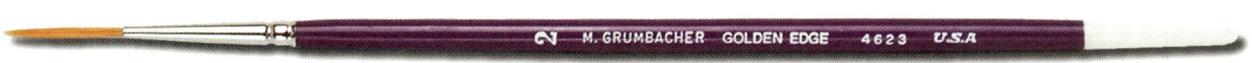

Sign, and go listen to the birds sing. Who knows, you may even see your chickadee! When your painting is completely dry, spray with Grumbacher Acrylic Painting Varnish to make your feathered friend come to life!

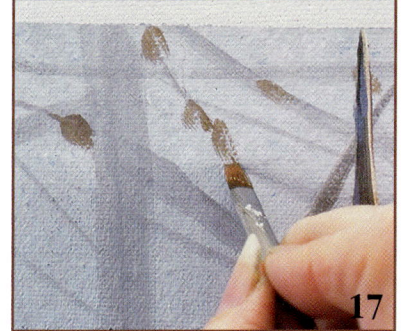

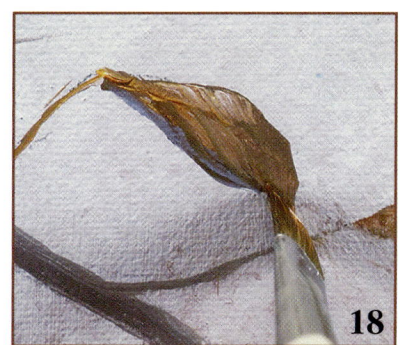

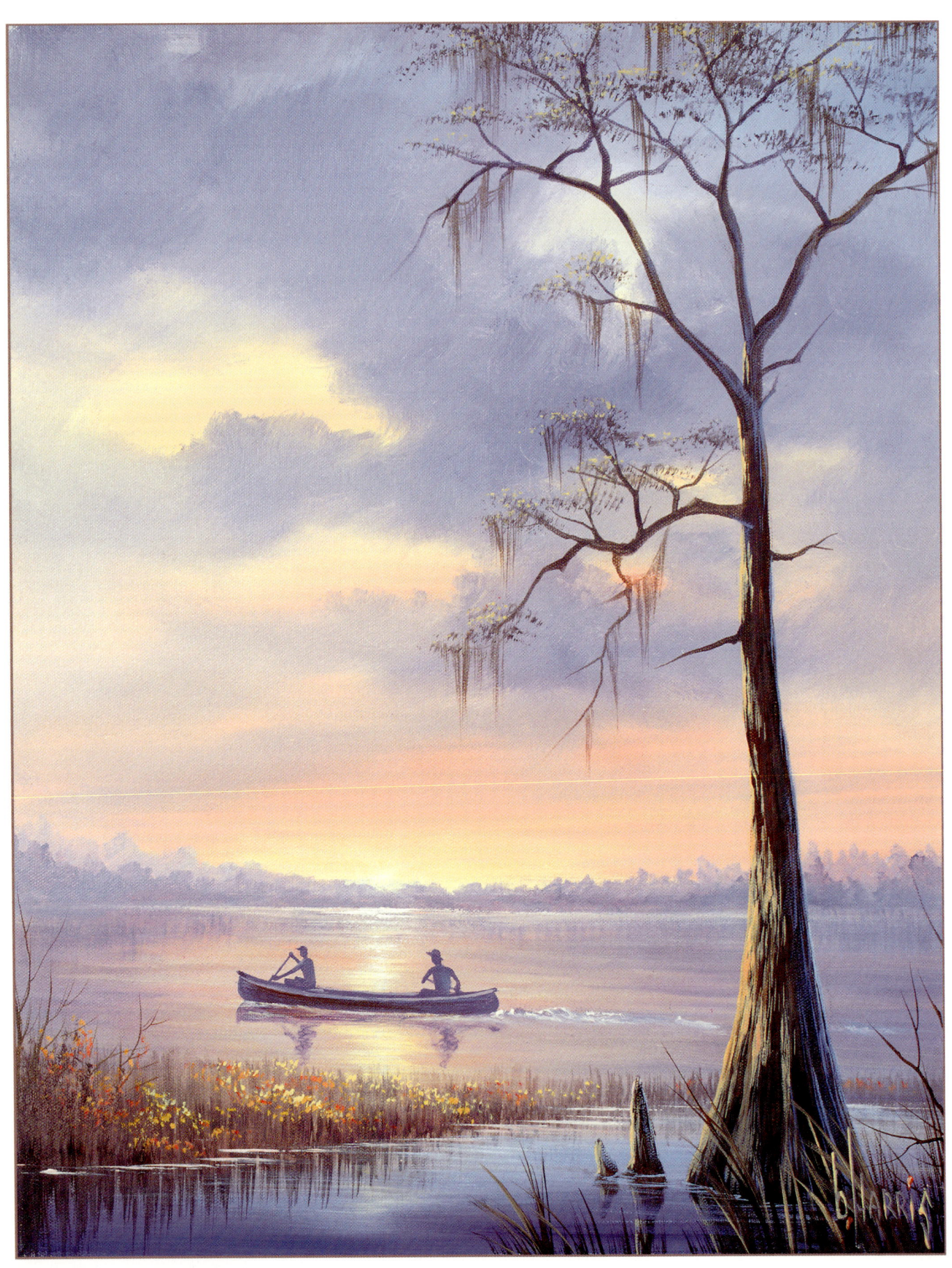

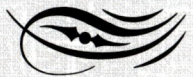

Compass Lake

Grumbacher Acrylic Colors

Burnt Umber
Cadmium Yellow Medium
Cerulean Blue
Grumbacher Red
Payne's Gray
Ultramarine Blue

Brushes

Two #101 Gesso Brushes, Size 2"
#1500 Hake Brush, Size 2"
#1060 White Bristle Fan Brush, Size 1
#4623 Golden Edge® Liner Brush, Size 2
#4403 Sable Essence® Angular Bright Brush, Size ³⁄₈"
#582 Eterna Bristle Round Brush, Size 8
#1600 Multi-Texture Brush, Size ½"
#760F Academy Bristle Flat Brush, Size 6

Other Supplies

16"x20" stretched artist canvas
Grumbacher Acrylic Painting Varnish
Grumbacher Whiteblend
Grumbacher Clearblend
Grumbacher Retarder
Tapered Painting Knife
Natural Sponge
Graphite Paper
Stylus
Wet Palette

Accolades go to Gloria Stegman, one of our most generous T.E.A.M. Artists, for sharing this idea with us. She designed the sketch for this painting on location at a southeast regional T.E.A.M. meeting, held at Compass Lake, Florida. From her description of the beautiful sunset, her sketch and photographs, I created "Compass Lake" for you.

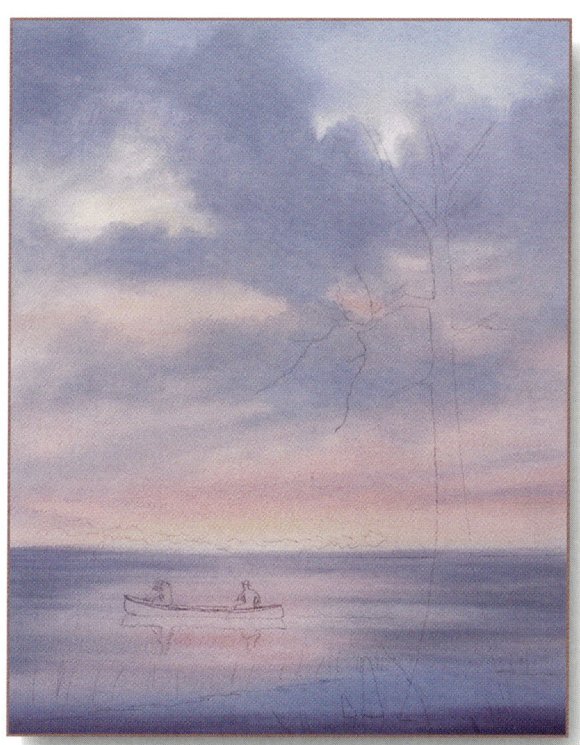

Palette

Before you begin, prepare these color mixtures:

Coral—30 parts Whiteblend, 4 parts Grumbacher Red, 1 part Cadmium Yellow Medium

Peach—30 parts Whiteblend, 2 parts Cadmium Yellow Medium, 1 part Coral

Medium Blue-Gray—6 parts Ultramarine Blue, 6 parts Payne's Gray, 10 parts Whiteblend, ½ part Grumbacher Red

Grape—4 parts Ultramarine Blue, 1 part Grumbacher Red

Violet-Gray—3 parts Medium Blue, 1 part Grape, 3 parts Whiteblend

Cream—1 part Whiteblend, a touch of Peach

Black-Brown—8 parts Grumbacher Gray, 4 parts Burnt Umber, 4 parts Cerulean Blue, ½ part Grumbacher Red

Taupe—1 part Black-Brown, 1 part Whiteblend

Canvas preparation: Sketch the horizon line 6" from the canvas bottom and the grass line 3" from the canvas bottom. Use the gesso brush to dampen the sky area with clean water, Grumbacher Retarder and a touch of Slowblend to extend the blending time when working the sky.

1 **Sky:** Work quickly, applying and blending the sky and clouds wet-on-wet. Scrub Whiteblend into the sky area with the gesso brush. While wet, use the uncleaned brush to apply peach and coral streaks through the sky. Wipe the excess paint from the brush, then apply Cerulean Blue along the canvas top. Blend the colors slightly with the hake brush.

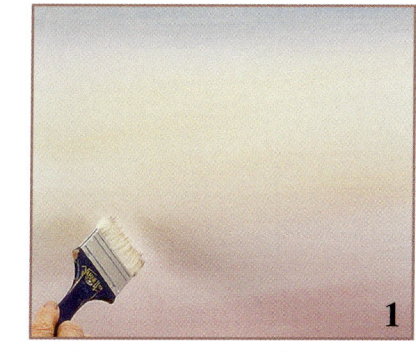

1

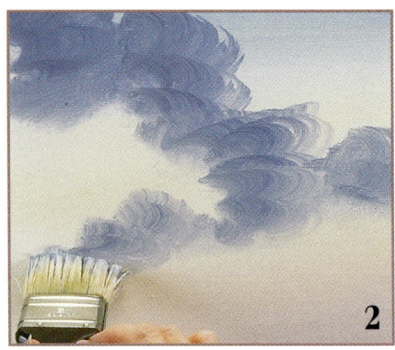

2 Clouds: Working while the sky is still wet, wipe the excess paint from the gesso brush, then scumble irregular medium blue-gray clouds in the sky. Make the clouds larger in the top section of the sky and smaller closer to the horizon.

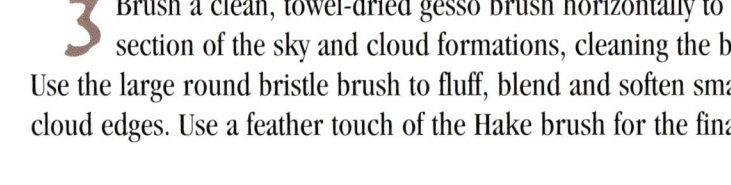

3 Brush a clean, towel-dried gesso brush horizontally to blend the bottom section of the sky and cloud formations, cleaning the brush frequently. Use the large round bristle brush to fluff, blend and soften smaller clouds and cloud edges. Use a feather touch of the Hake brush for the final blending.

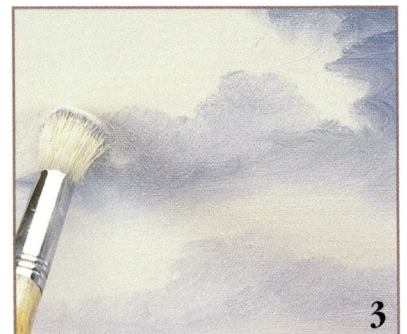

4 Water: Apply and blend the base colors wet-on-wet. Use a clean gesso brush to scrub Whiteblend into the top two-thirds of the water area above the grass line. Hold the gesso brush horizontally and apply streaks of coral in the center of the water as shown in the large picture on page 51. Apply horizontal streaks of medium blue-gray and Cerulean Blue along each side and along the bottom of the canvas, making the water darker in the foreground. Blend rough edges with horizontal strokes of a clean flat bristle brush.

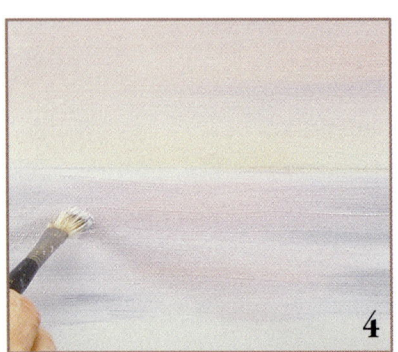

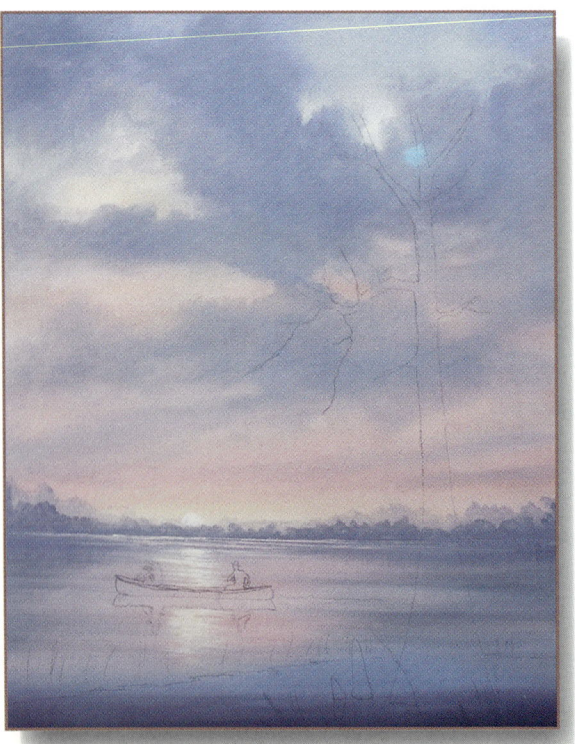

5 Apply Cerulean Blue and Whiteblend below the grass line and grape along the bottom of the canvas. Blend with a clean, towel-dried gesso or flat bristle brush with long, horizontal strokes. Dry completely, then transfer the pattern to the canvas.

6 Sunset: Use a clean gesso brush to cover the lower section of the sky with Clearblend. While it's wet, brush-mix Whiteblend and a touch of Cadmium Yellow Medium on a flat bristle brush to make pale yellow and paint the center bottom of the sky. Add a little coral above it. Blend by stroking horizontally with a clean flat bristle brush. Blend the top portion of the coral into the Clearblend so there is no distinguishable edge.

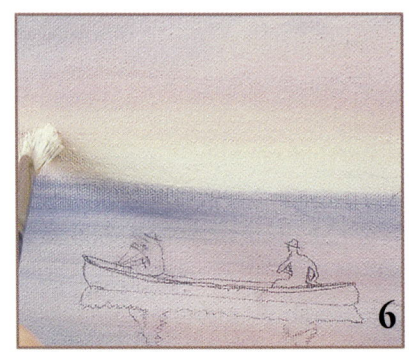

7 Distant trees: Brush-mix violet-gray with Clearblend and a touch of Whiteblend on the flat bristle brush and stipple a translucent distant tree line along the horizon line with the brush corner. Wipe the brush, and stipple another row of slightly darker violet-gray distant trees in front of the first row.

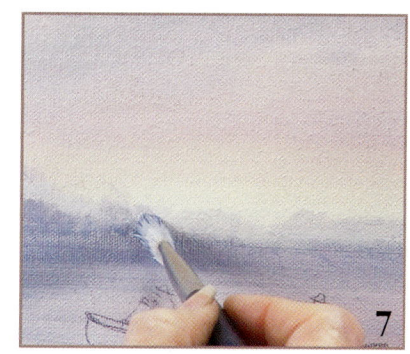

8 Tree reflections: Apply Clearblend over the water with a clean flat bristle brush. Load the multi-texture brush with violet-gray and stroke downward from the tree line to create reflections in the water. Clean and dry the brush, then lightly stroke horizontally over the reflections to soften.

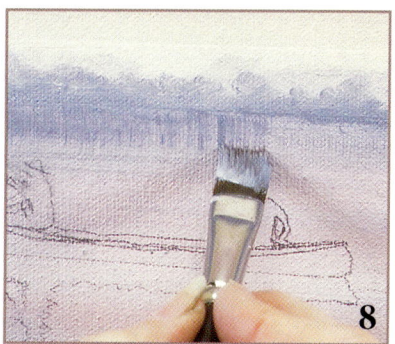

9 Water highlights: Follow the techniques section, page 5, to add a tide line with the painting knife. Use a variety of off-white values, made by mixing Whiteblend and peach. Apply these directly under the brightest part of the sky. Brush-mix off-white on the multi-texture brush and zig-zag horizontally to apply shimmers on the water above and below the canoe center. Blend the edges with a clean, Clearblend-moistened multi-texture brush.

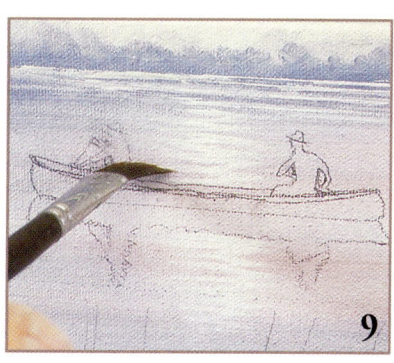

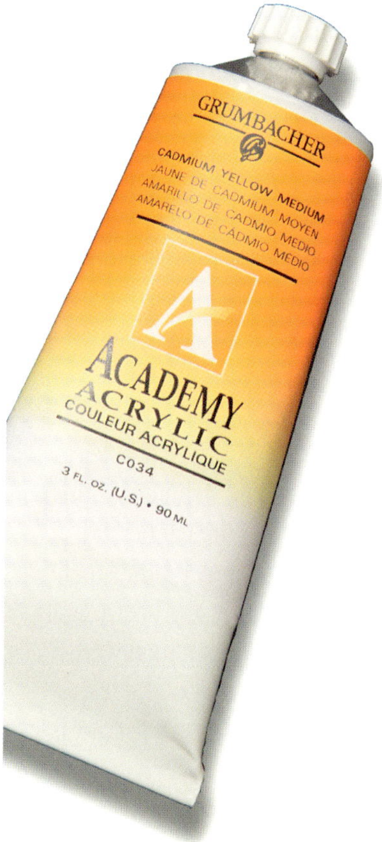

10 Sun: Use the liner brush to apply a Whiteblend half-circle between the two men on the distant tree line. Blot with your finger to subdue; dry.

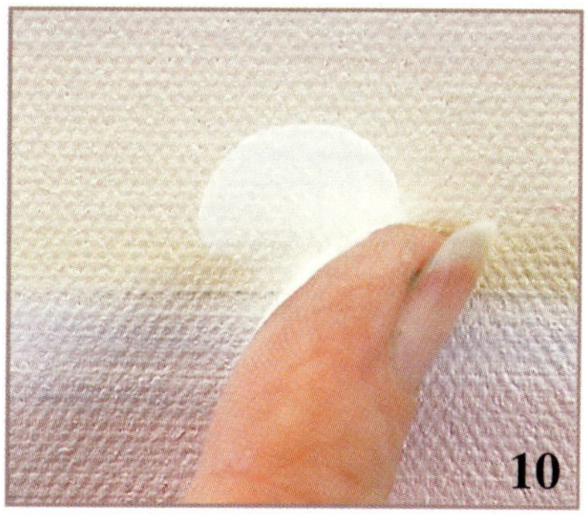

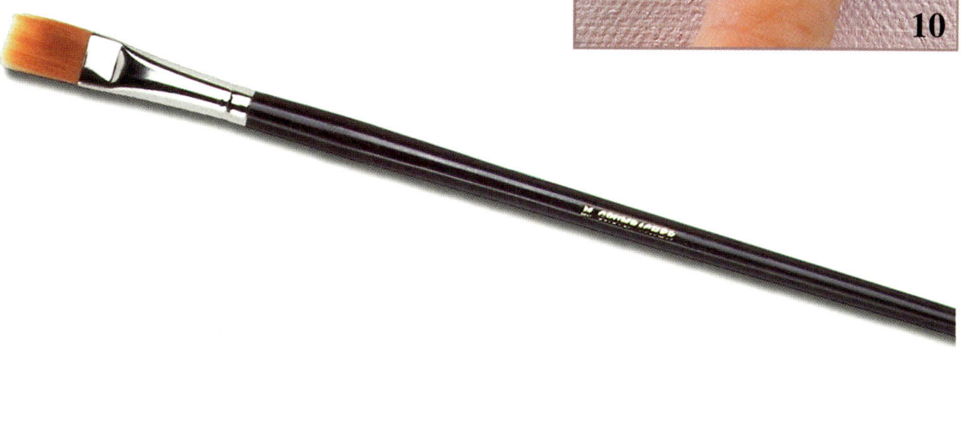

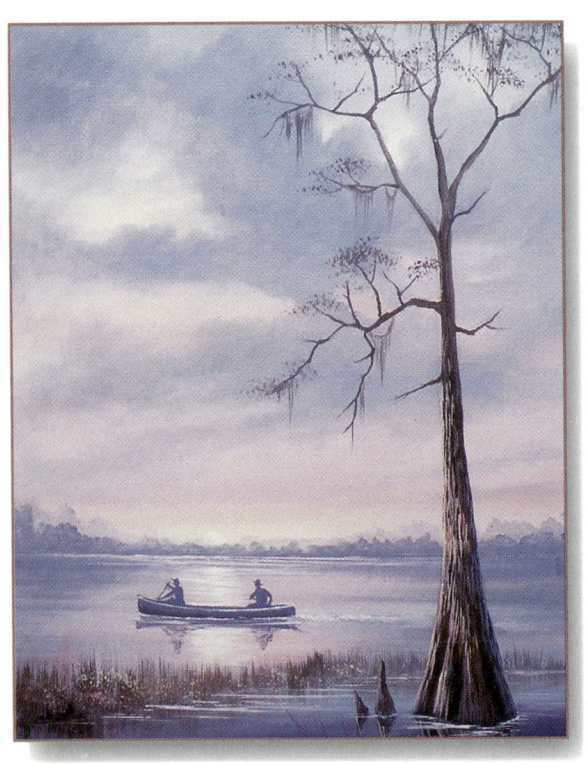

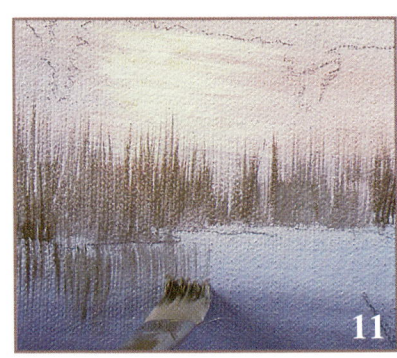

11 **Grasses:** Thin taupe with Slowblend and water on the multi-texture brush. Pull grass up along the grass line, keeping it very short on the right and getting progressively taller to the left. Wet the area beneath the grass line with water and Clearblend. Use the multi-texture brush to pull grass reflections down into the water below the grass. Add black-brown to the brush to darken the taupe and shadow the root areas of the grasses and reflections on the left side of the canvas.

12 **Water lines:** Load the painting knife with Whiteblend mixed with a little peach and follow step 9 to add water lines along the base of the grassy area. Soften the bottom and side edges occasionally with a Clearblend-moistened multi-texture brush.

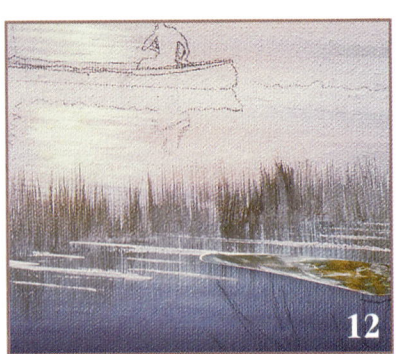

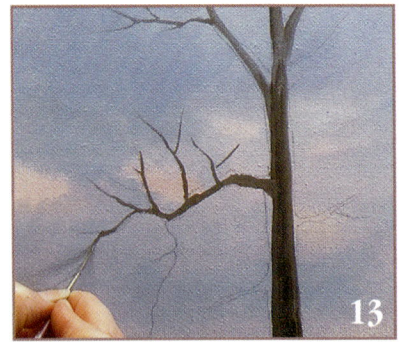

13 **Cypress tree:** Paint the top of the tree taupe with the angular brush. Add black-brown to the brush making the tree gradually darker as you move down. Paint the cypress roots and their reflections black-brown. Thin taupe with Slowblend and water, then use the liner brush to add the branches and smaller twigs. Dry completely.

14 **People and canoe:** Use the small round brush and/or the liner brush and medium blue-gray to paint the people and canoe. Add a Whiteblend edge along the top of the canoe, letting it mix slightly with the medium blue-gray. Add a little black-brown along the very bottom of the canoe and blend.

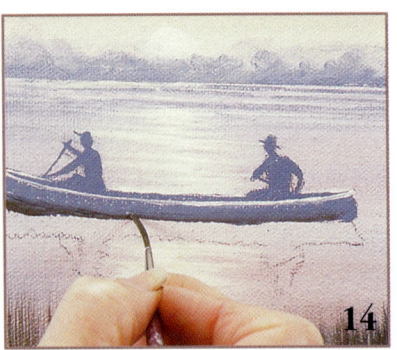

15 **Canoe reflection:** Cover the area under the canoe and behind it with Clearblend. While wet, paint a translucent reflection of the canoe and people and the ripples behind the canoe with a medium blue-gray on the small round brush. Use a Clearblend-moistened fan brush to lightly zig-zag horizontally across these reflections. Use the fan brush and Whiteblend to dab a foamy crest along the canoe bottom and the top of the ripples. Pull the bottom of the wet Whiteblend foam down into the wet Clearblend with a clean fan brush for a wake.

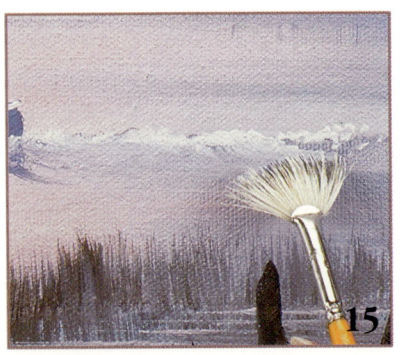

16 Flowers: Use the fan brush and coral, peach, cream, cerulean or any of the colors that you like to stipple weed flowers in the grassy area. Turn the brush horizontally to paint some flowers and vertically to paint others.

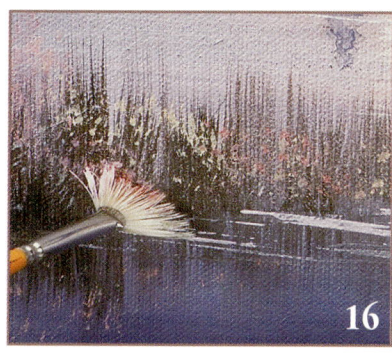

17 Tree details: Hold the angular brush vertically and make short choppy strokes to highlight the cypress tree, the roots and their reflections. Alternate between peach and coral along the left sides. Add taupe to the brush to highlight the central portions. Add black-brown to the brush to highlight the right sides. Add reflected light on the right sides using the liner brush with violet-gray and light cerulean. Brush-mix medium blue-gray and Whiteblend on the liner brush and add water lines in the foreground water, separating the tree and the roots from their reflections.

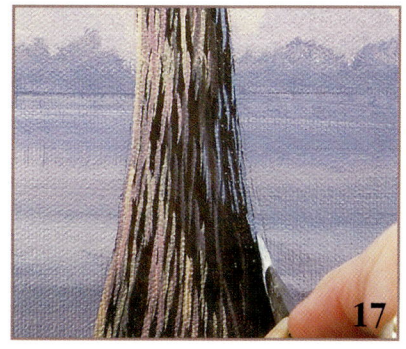

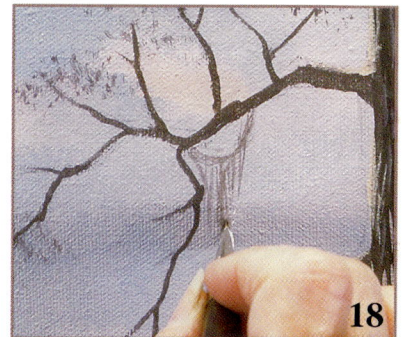

18 Foliage: Tap sparse foliage on some of the limbs with the fan brush and taupe. Use very watery taupe on the multi-texture brush to paint the moss. Occasionally paint a loop of moss, then pull straight down from it with a corner of the brush.

19 Water details: Thin a little Whiteblend with Clearblend on the multi-texture brush, then paint a translucent wash over the reflections of the cypress roots for a watery look. Add Whiteblend to the uncleaned brush, then paint a pale reflection of the setting sun in the foreground water while the wash is wet. Blend the edges with a clean brush.

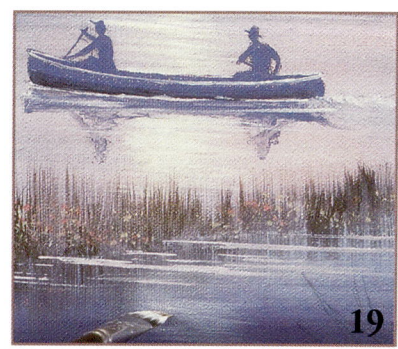

20 Foreground grasses: Thin black-brown with Clearblend on the multi-texture brush. Hold the brush vertically and apply the shorter grasses. Use the liner and thinned black-brown to paint the taller, thinner grasses. Highlight a few of these grasses with taupe or a light color of your choice from the painting with the liner.

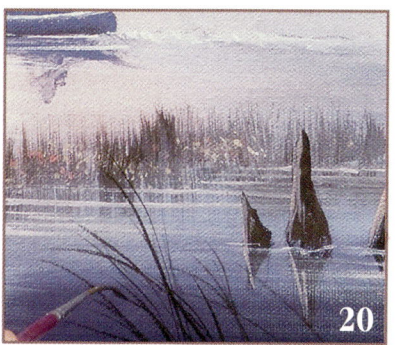

21 Twigs: Double-load the liner brush with black-brown and peach to paint the foreground twigs on the bottom right. Repeat, using taupe and peach for the twigs on the grassy point.

Sign and go canoeing with your favorite friend! When your painting is completely dry, spray with Grumbacher Acrylic Painting Varnish to accent all the lovely colors of a summer sunset!

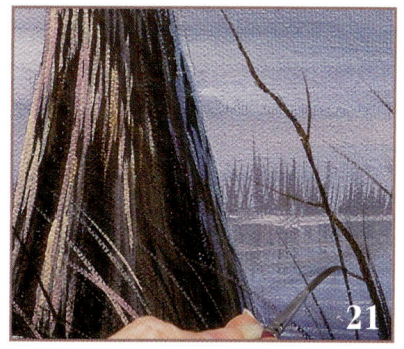

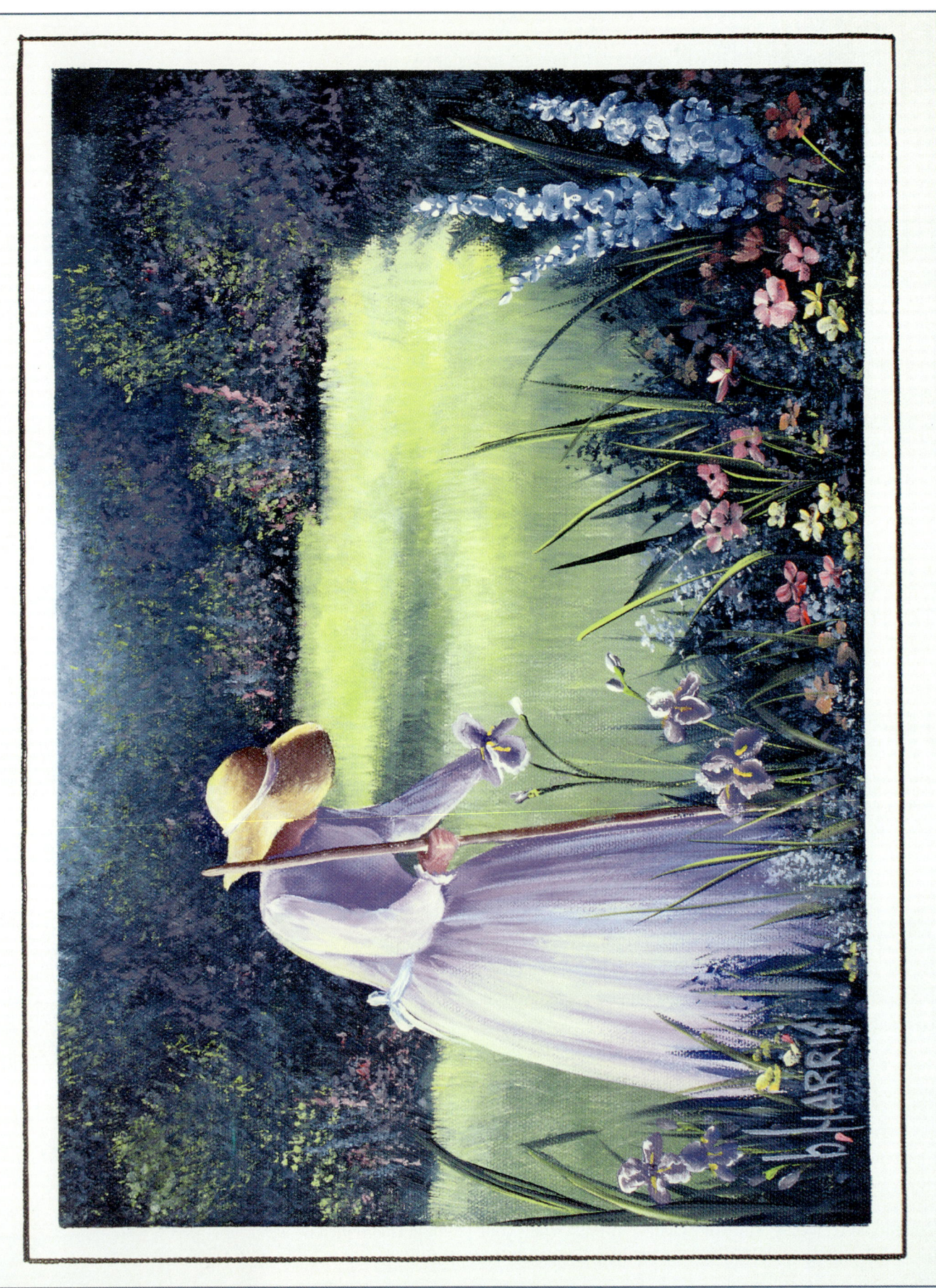

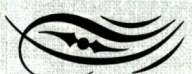

Tending the Garden

Grumbacher Acrylic Colors

Cadmium Yellow Medium
Cerulean Blue
Dioxazine Purple
Grumbacher Red
Hooker's Green
Payne's Gray
Portrayt
Thalo Yellow Green
Titanium White
Ultramarine Blue

Brushes

Two #101 Gesso Brushes, Size 2"
#4403 Sable Essence® Angular Bright Brush, Size ½"
#4610R Golden Edge® Round Brush, Size 6
#4610B Golden Edge® Bright Brush, Size 6
#4623 Golden Edge® Liner Brush, Size 2
#1060 White Bristle Fan Brush, Size 1
#1600 Multi-Texture Brush, Size ½"

Other Supplies

16"x20" Stretched Canvas
Grumbacher Clearblend
Grumbacher Whiteblend
16"x20" Mat Template (12"x15½" Opening)
Matte Medium
Grumbacher Artists' Pen
Masking Tape
Tapered Painting Knife
Natural Sponge
Charcoal Graphite Paper
Stylus
Wet Palette
Grumbacher Acrylic Painting Varnish

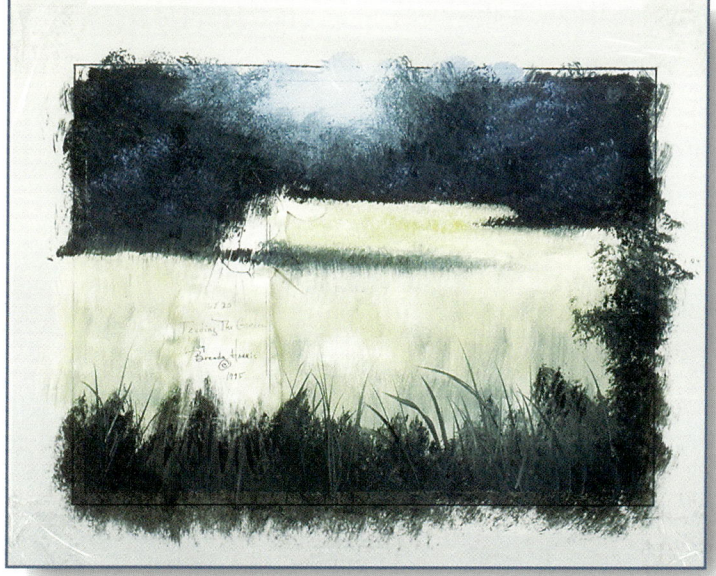

Palette

Before you begin, prepare these color mixtures:

Light Ultramarine—10 parts Whiteblend, 1 part Ultramarine Blue

Pink—1 part Whiteblend, a touch of Grumbacher Red (create a light and a medium value)

Dark Blue-Green—3 parts Ultramarine Blue, 1 part Hooker's Green, 1 part Payne's Gray

Violet-Gray—2 parts Payne's Gray, 1 part Dioxazine Purple, 2 parts Titanium White

Light Violet-Gray—1 part Violet-Gray, a touch of Titanium White

Flesh—1 part Portrayt, 1 part Whiteblend

Flesh Shadow—1 part Portrayt, 1 part Dioxazine Purple, 1 part Titanium White

Pale Yellow—1 part Titanium White, a touch of Cadmium Yellow Medium

Medium Green—1 part Dark Blue-Green, 1 part Thalo Yellow Green, 1 part Titanium White

Bright Green—1 part Whiteblend, 1 part Thalo Yellow Green

Dark Brown—2 parts Dioxazine Purple, 1 part Cadmium Yellow Medium

Off-White—1 part Whiteblend, a touch of Pale Yellow

Canvas preparation: Refer to page 2 in the techniques section for instructions on French matting to mat this canvas. Transfer the pattern from the book with charcoal graphite paper. The top of her hat is 5" from the upper canvas edge and 8" from the left side. Cover the woman with a design protector.

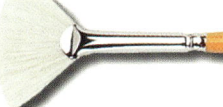

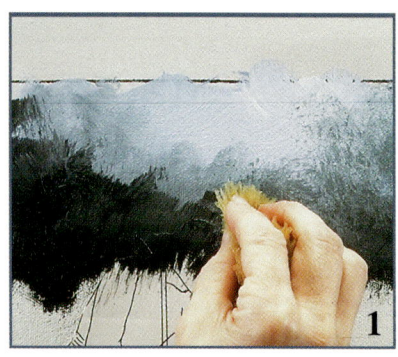

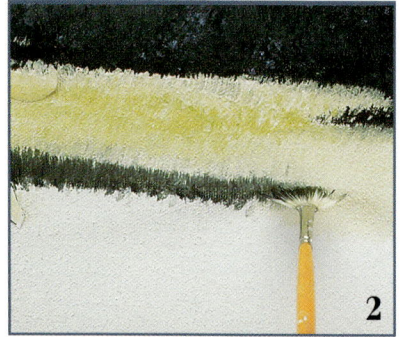

1 **Sky, background trees and bushes:** Paint a small light ultramarine sky area in the top center of the canvas, using a fan brush. Create background trees in a two-step process while the sky is still wet. First, apply dark blue-green distant foliage with the gesso brush, connecting it to the light ultramarine sky. With a towel-dried, damp sponge, pat the edges of these bushes, working into the wet sky area. Sponge-mix and tap a medium value of blue-green (dark blue green and light ultramarine) through the foliage. Add a little more light ultramarine to the sponge and use to tap in texture and some reflected light.

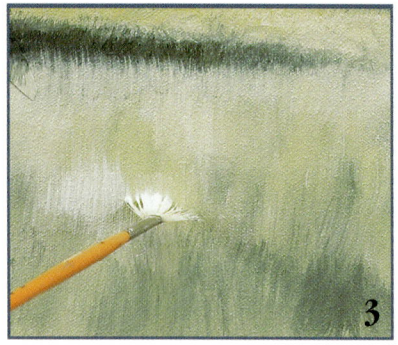

2 **Distant grass:** Continue while the foliage is still wet. Follow the photograph to help in placement of lights and darks. Hold the fan brush with the handle pointing down and tap distant pale yellow grass along the bottom edge of the distant bushes to "plant" them. Continue painting the distant grass by alternating between the pale yellow and bright green. While the grass is wet, tap in a dark blue-green shadow at the base of the bushes on the left behind the woman. Tap the edges of the shadow with a clean, towel-dried brush to soften them.

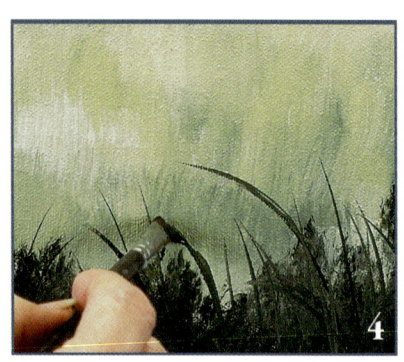

3 **Middle grasses:** Tap in the middle grass area quickly with the gesso or fan brush, using pale yellow, bright green and medium green. Vary the color of the grass by occasionally adding some Whiteblend and dark blue green with the fan brush, keeping it generally lighter in the distance and gradually getting darker as it moves forward. Use your fan brush to lift up and create contrasting grass colors where needed. Refer to the large photo on page 57 for color placements.

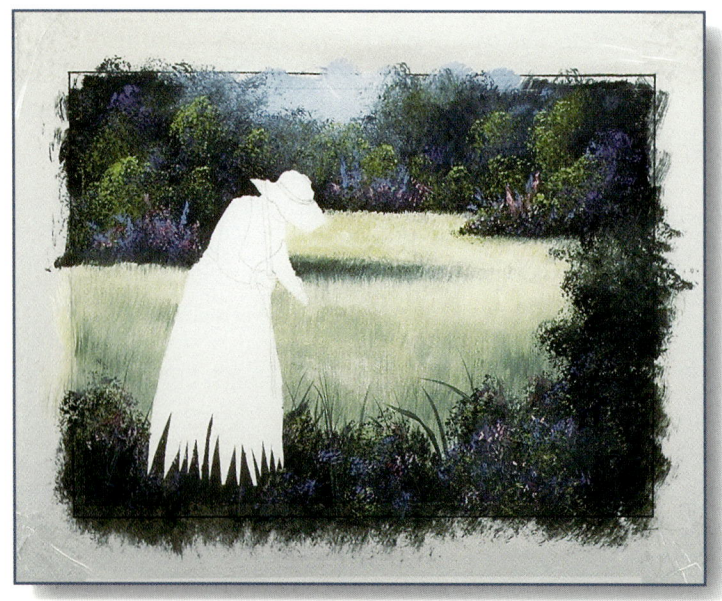

4 **Foreground foliage and grass:** Tap in the foreground bush on the right and the grass along the bottom of the canvas with the gesso brush and dark blue-green. Immediately pull up some of the tall grass stems with the chisel edge of the angular brush turned vertically. Dry. Touch up as needed, working a small area at a time and blending the edges of the "touch-up" with Clearblend.

5 **Foliage highlights:** Add sparse medium green highlights to the foliage by tapping with the damp sponge. Keep these subtle. Add bright green to the uncleaned sponge to create stronger highlights on the top left sides of a few bushes.

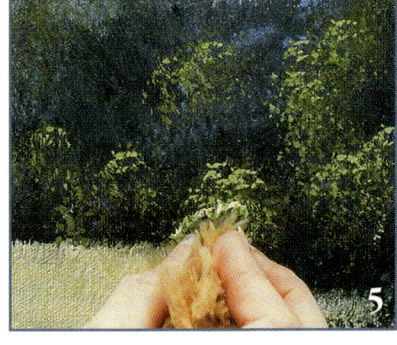

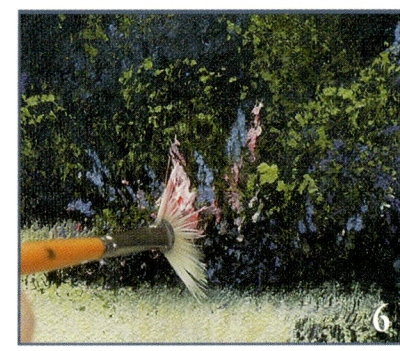

6 **Distant flowers and foreground:** Use a clean sponge to sprinkle flowers and filler in the dark foliage. Paint a few medium pink, light ultramarine, and light violet-gray blossom clusters. Add more tube color to your mixtures for variety in the flower values. With the bright detail brush, randomly add a few dabs of colors to indicate small undefined flowers. Use the fan brush to stipple some taller stalks for a few hollyhocks in the background. Dry completely and remove the design protector. Fill in the space between her right hand and left elbow with the liner brush and a continuation of the grass color behind her.

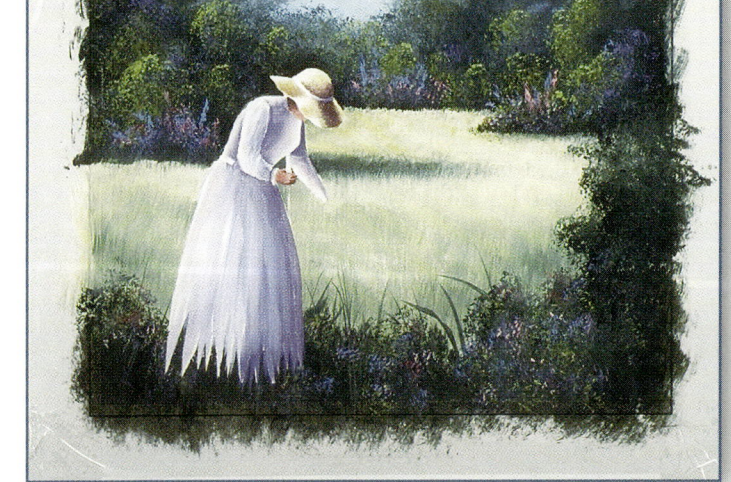

7 **Hat:** Paint the top of the hat pale yellow with the angular brush. Add the shadow on the front of this section with dark brown. Blend the two colors together by tapping with the multi-texture brush to create a look of straw. Brighten the rear crown of the hat with a dab of Whiteblend, and tap it in with the multi-texture brush. Paint the brim of the hat the same way, adding shadows in the areas where the hat dips, and along the front. Use the photograph for a guide. Dry and touch up as needed, softening the "touch-ups" over the hat with a multi-texture brush moistened with Clearblend. Paint the hatband with Whiteblend and a liner brush, then shadow the front with light violet-gray.

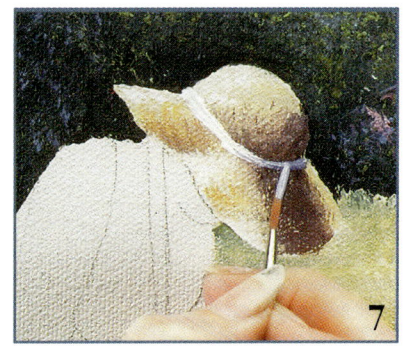

8 **Face:** Paint and blend her face and hand with the small round and liner brushes. Paint the shadow area of the face with the small round brush and flesh shadow. Fill in the rest of the face with flesh. Blend the face colors together.

9 **Left hand:** Paint her right hand flesh with the small round brush. Add some of the flesh shadow mixture to the uncleaned brush and shade the back of her hand and to separate her fingers. Add a dot of Whiteblend for each knuckle and pat slightly to blend.

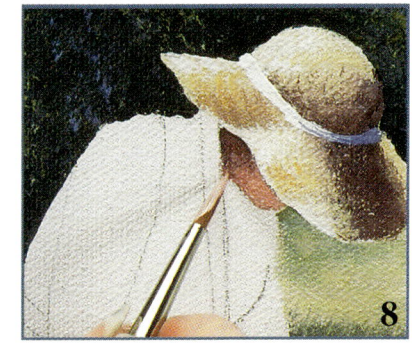

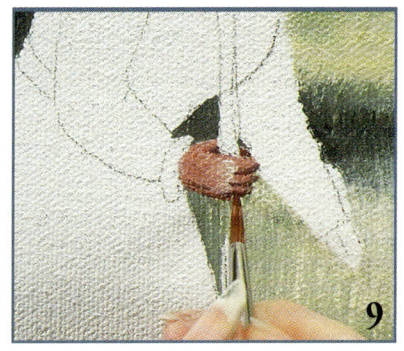

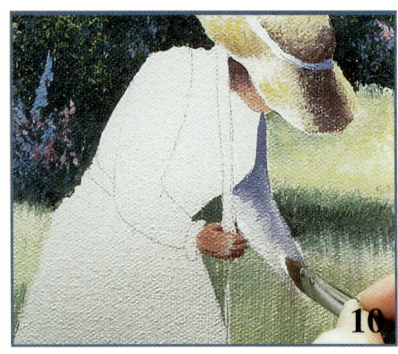

10 Dress: Alternate using the angular, round and detail bright brushes to paint and blend the dress, referring to the photo to see placements of colors. Occasionally brush-mix Titanium White in with the dress colors to create a variety of values and subtle changes in the fabric; final highlights are added later. Beginning with her left sleeve, paint the shadow with varying values of violet-gray using the angular brush. Add Titanium White to the uncleaned brush as you come down the sleeve making the shadow lighter toward the hand.

11 Bodice: Paint the shadows on the bodice with the angular brush and violet-gray. Add Titanium White to the uncleaned brush for the lighter

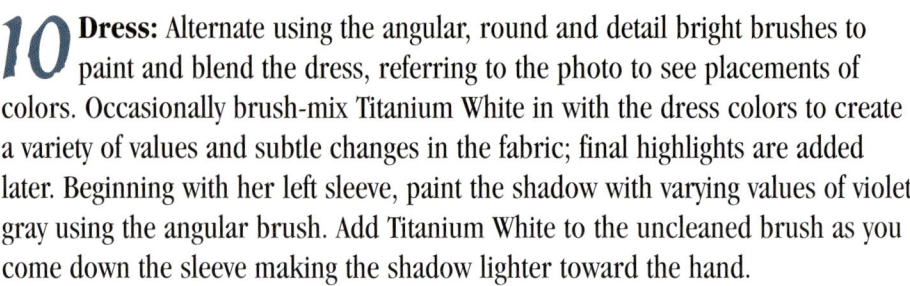

area, and blend between the two colors. Highlight her back and her shoulder with pale yellow. Accent the front of her bodice with pink and light ultramarine. Blend.

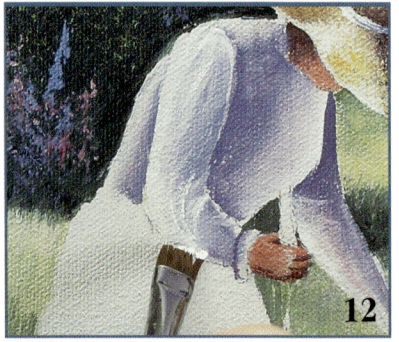

12 Right sleeve: Apply Titanium White to the back of her arm and light violet gray to the front with the angular brush. Add pink and light ultramarine reflected light accents near the shadows on the wet sleeve and blend. Add a violet-gray band behind the lace on the sleeve.

13 Skirt: Paint the skirt from front to back with the angular brush, working wet-on-wet. Paint the front of the skirt values of violet-gray, adding Whiteblend to lighten as you work toward the back. Streak varying values of pink, light ultramarine and Whiteblend accents vertically through the skirt, leaving the violet-gray shadow strong in the area directly under her arm. Dry.

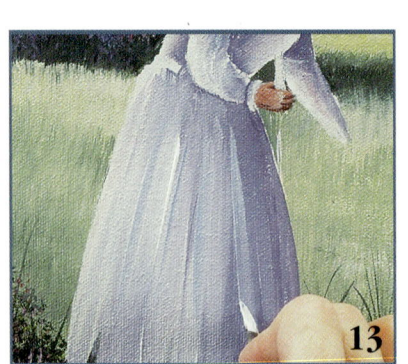

14 Bodice and sleeve highlights: Moisten the sleeves and bodice with Clearblend and add touch-ups and highlights while wet. Apply and blend a few strokes at a time using the detail bright brush to apply color and a

Clearblend-moistened angular brush to blend. Refer to the finished photo for color placements. Use off-white for the brightest highlights along the top of her shoulder, back, right sleeve and ruffle. Brush-mix Cerulean Blue and Whiteblend to make light teal blue on the detail bright brush. Use this to add a

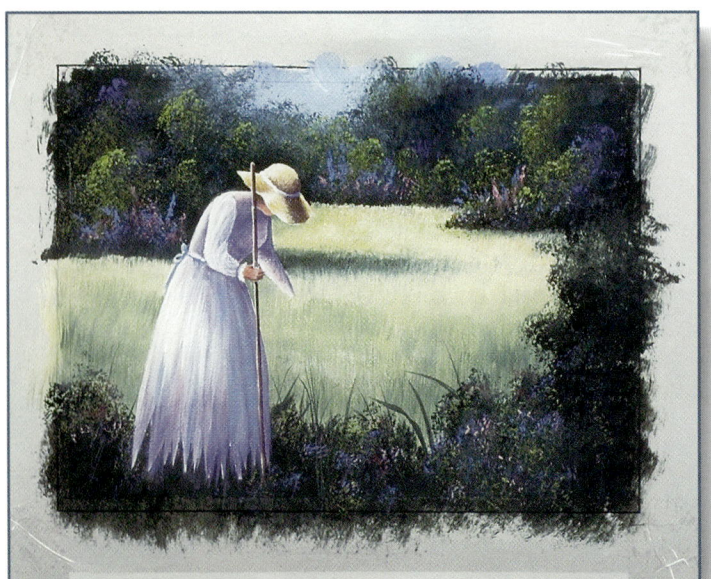

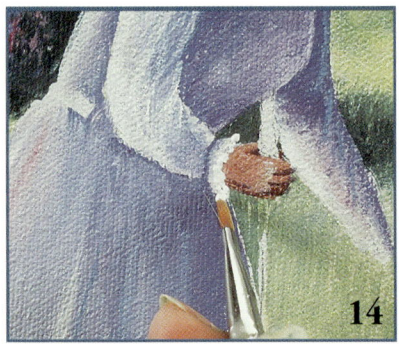

dash of reflected light in some shadowy areas. Use the liner brush to paint her sash light ultramarine, and highlight it with Whiteblend.

15 **Skirt highlights:** Cover the skirt area with Clearblend. Working with two brushes again, add touch-ups as needed. Apply streaks of off-white on the skirt back. Apply reflected lights in the shadow areas with the light teal blue mixture from step 14. Blend them with the Clearblend-moistened brush as before. Dry.

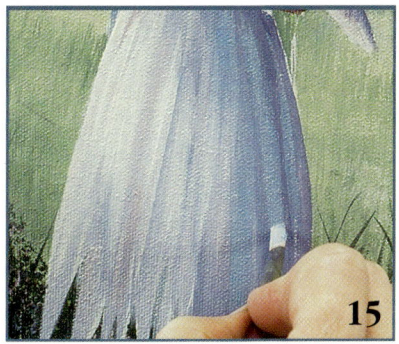

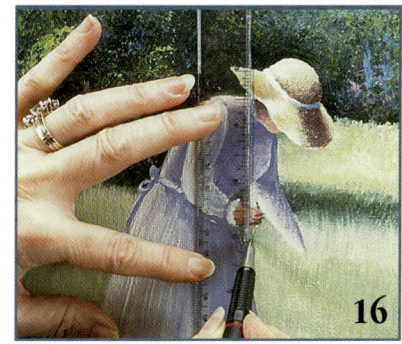

16 **Hoe:** Use a pencil and T-square ruler to draw the hoe handle. Double-load the liner brush with dark brown and pink and paint the hoe handle with the pink on the left. Use the chisel edge of a clean moist angular brush to straighten any uneven edges along the wet hoe handle.

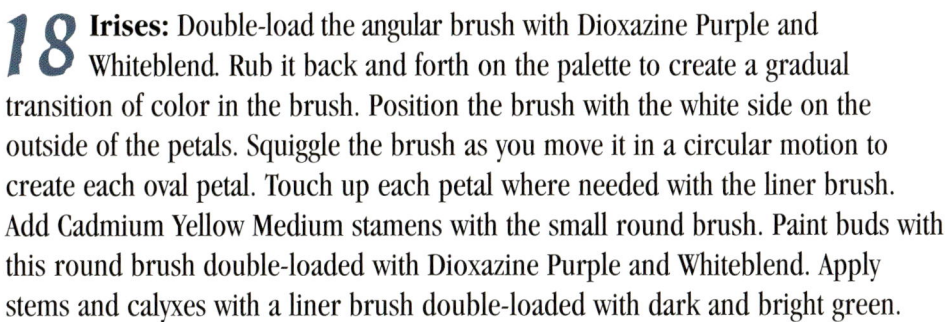

17 **Hollyhocks:** Add blue hollyhocks with the small round brush dipped first in light ultramarine, then in Whiteblend. Starting at the top of a stalk, dab the white and blue to create blooms, making them larger and letting the stalk get wider as you move downward. Add a dot of Payne's Gray here and there to indicate centers in some flowers. Add dashes of bright and medium green leaves around the flowers with the bright detail brush.

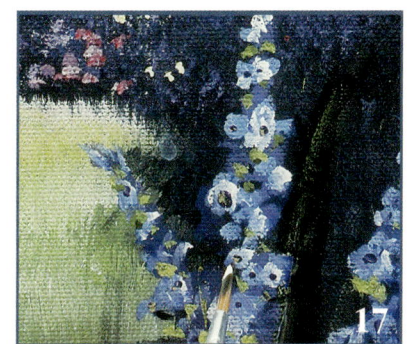

18 **Irises:** Double-load the angular brush with Dioxazine Purple and Whiteblend. Rub it back and forth on the palette to create a gradual transition of color in the brush. Position the brush with the white side on the outside of the petals. Squiggle the brush as you move it in a circular motion to create each oval petal. Touch up each petal where needed with the liner brush. Add Cadmium Yellow Medium stamens with the small round brush. Paint buds with this round brush double-loaded with Dioxazine Purple and Whiteblend. Apply stems and calyxes with a liner brush double-loaded with dark and bright green.

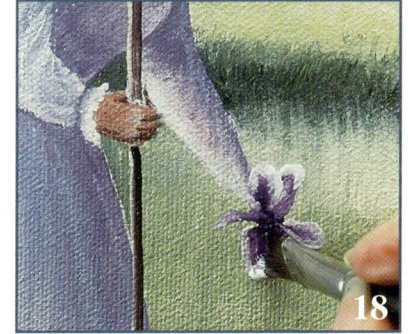

19 **Final details:** Be creative! Paint a variety of sizes, shapes and colors of small flowers in the foreground. Create various values of all the flower colors by adding Titanium White to any tube color you choose, especially Grumbacher Red, Cadmium Yellow Medium, Dioxazine Purple, Ultramarine and Cerulean Blue. Be loose with your strokes and do not paint each flower completely perfect, nor face on. Add a few stems and thin grasses with the liner brush double-loaded with medium green and bright green. Add a variety of leaves with the angular, bright detail or round brush and varying greens from the palette. Lift up a few grasses over the bottom of her dress to settle her into the garden.

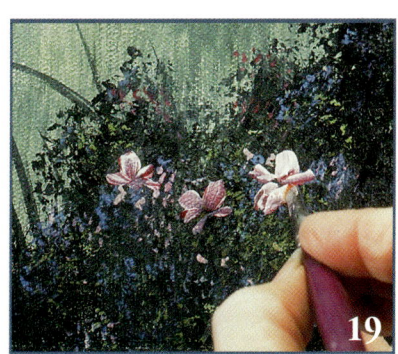

Sign, and pick a bouquet for the table! When your painting is completely dry, spray with Grumbacher Acrylic Painting Varnish to bring out all the glory of the garden!

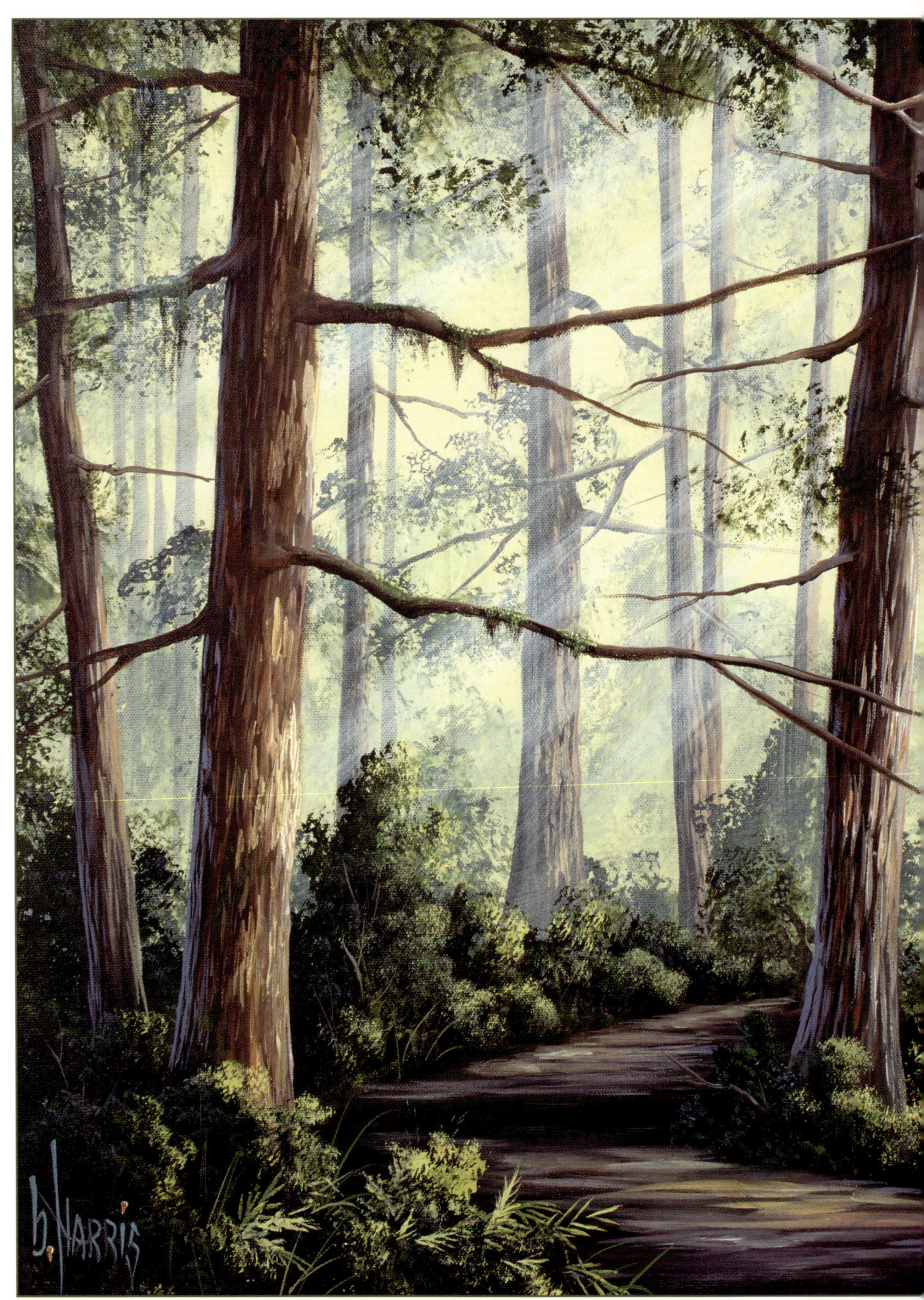

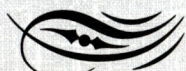

Radiant Forest

Grumbacher Acrylic Colors
Burnt Sienna
Burnt Umber
Cadmium Yellow Medium
Dioxazine Purple
Hooker's Green
Mars Black
Raw Sienna
Titanium White
Ultramarine Blue
Yellow Ochre Light

Brushes
#101 Gesso Brush, Size 2"
#1500 Hake Brush, Size 2"
#4403 Sable Essence® Angular Bright Brush, Size ½"
#4623 Golden Edge® Liner Brush, Size 2
#760F Academy Bristle Flat Brush, Size 6
#1600 Multi-Texture Brush, Size ½"
#582 Eterna Bristle Round Brush, Size 8

Other Supplies
16"x20" Stretched Canvas
Grumbacher Clearblend
Grumbacher Whiteblend
Tapered Painting Knife
Natural Sponge
Wet Palette
Large Water Container
Charcoal Graphite Paper
Stylus
Grumbacher Acrylic Painting Varnish

A visit to Silver Falls, Oregon, provided the perfect subject to demonstrate this unique technique of using layers of glazes to easily create depth and perspective in your paintings.

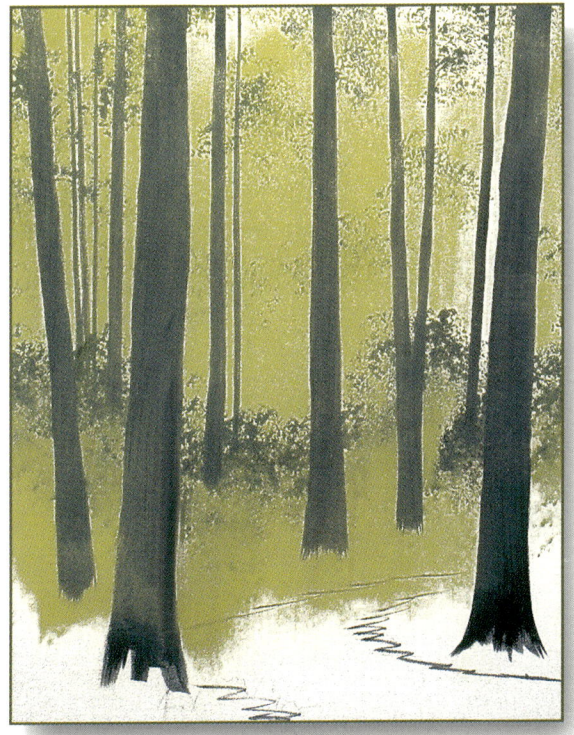

Palette
Before you begin, prepare these color mixtures:

Dark Green—2 parts Hooker's Green, 1 part Burnt Umber

Dark Blue-Green—1 part Ultramarine Blue, 1 part Hooker's Green

Medium Green—1 part Hooker's Green, 1 part Yellow Ocher Light

Yellow-Green—1 part Medium Green, 1 part Yellow Ochre Light, 1 part Titanium White

Light Yellow-Green—1 part Yellow-Green, 1 part Cadmium Yellow Medium, 1 part Titanium White

Bright Yellow—3 parts Titanium White, 1 part Cadmium Yellow Medium

Tan—2 parts Titanium White, 1 part Burnt Umber

Warm Beige—2 parts Titanium White, 1 part Burnt Sienna

Camel—2 parts Titanium White, 1 part Raw Sienna

Violet-Gray—10 parts Whiteblend, 3 parts Ultramarine Blue, 1 part Burnt Umber, 1 part Dioxazine Purple

Glaze Mixtures: (mix each glaze in a separate container)

Yellow Glaze—6 tablespoons Clearblend, 6 teaspoons Whiteblend, 6 pea-sized drops of Cadmium Yellow Medium

Blue-Green Glaze—1¼ tablespoons Clearblend, ¼ tablespoon Dark Blue-Green

Canvas Preparation: Transfer the trees and path to the canvas with charcoal graphite paper.

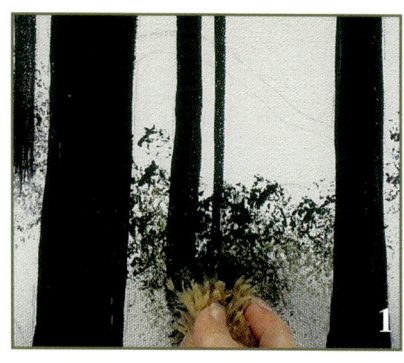

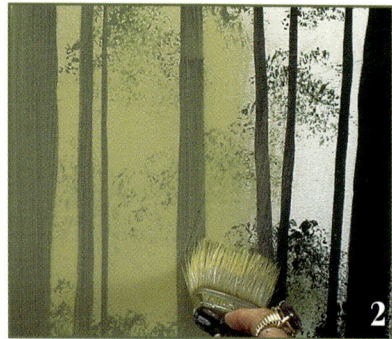

1 **Dark Areas:** Go over the path lines with Mars Black and the angular brush. Paint the tree trunks Mars Black with the liner and angular brushes. Leave them ragged at the bottom. Dry. Sponge sparse foliage around the base of the tree trunks and randomly throughout the background, alternating between dark green and dark blue-green. Dry.

2 **Glaze:** Use the gesso brush to paint a thin coating of yellow glaze over the canvas. Blend away bold streaks in the glaze with a feather touch of a clean, damp Hake brush. Dry.

3 **Tree trunks:** Paint and highlight the middle ground tree trunks one at a time with the angular brush. Apply Burnt Umber on the left and tan on the right, using short choppy

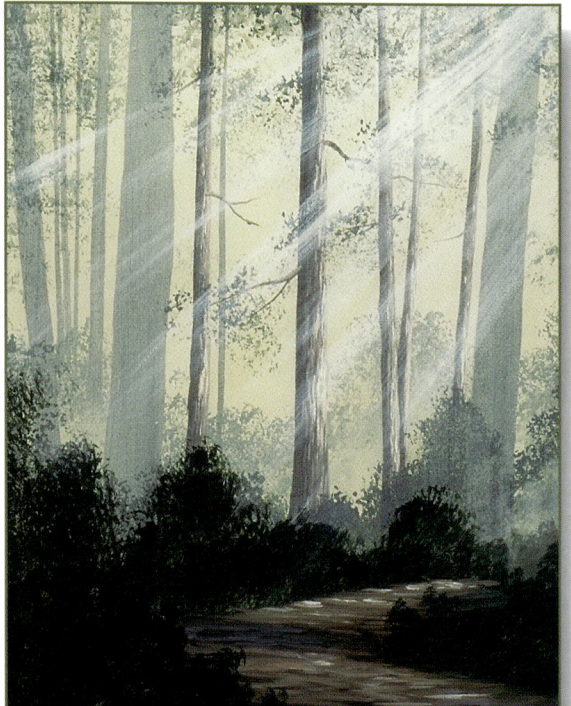

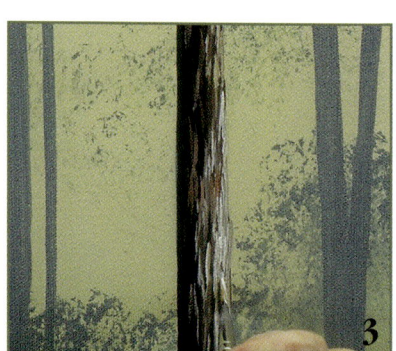

strokes to indicate bark. Create a gradual transition in value from light on the right to dark on the left. Add some Mars Black to the wet burnt umber on the left side of each middle ground tree. Use a clean angular brush to add additional highlights on the right side of each tree with warm beige and camel.

4 **Branches:** Double-load the liner brush with camel and Burnt Umber. Holding the brush with the light side up, refer to the large photo on page 62 and the pattern to paint the branches.

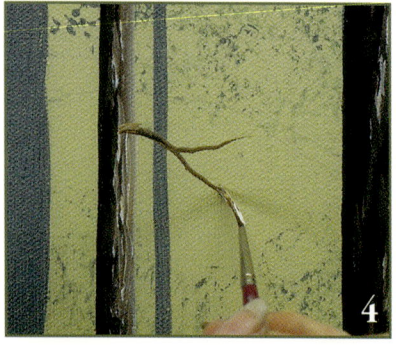

5 **Foliage:** Use the sponge to apply dark green and dark blue-green foliage around the base of the trees. Add sparse leaves on and around the limbs and trunk with the same sponge. Be careful to leave some open background area between the leaves. Dry.

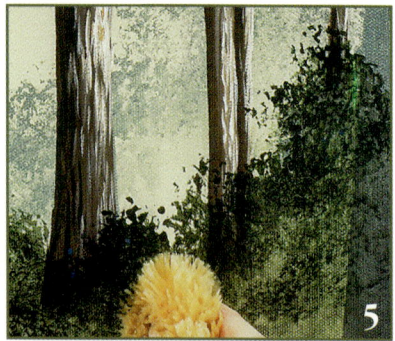

6 Apply a thin coat of the yellow glaze over the canvas again with the gesso brush. If it appears too opaque, remove some glaze with a clean, moist sponge. Blend away unwanted bold streaks with the hake brush. Dry.

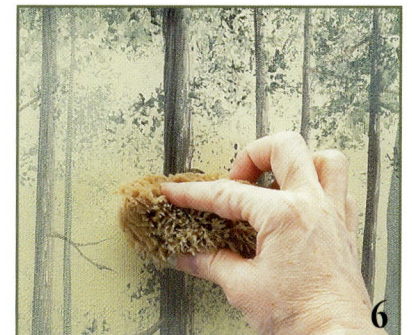

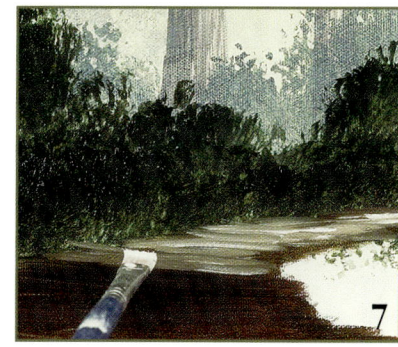

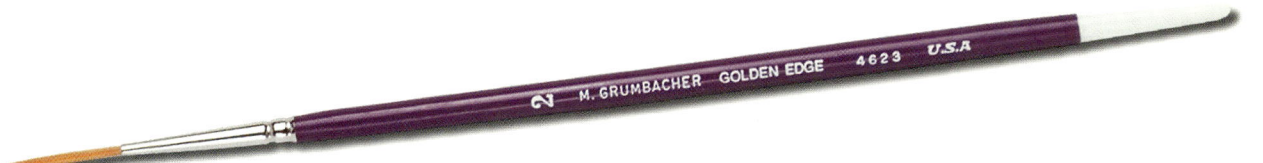

7 **Path:** Use the sponge to tap foliage along the left side of the path, alternating between dark green and dark blue-green. While the foliage paint is still wet, paint the path Burnt Umber using horizontal strokes of the flat bristle brush. Add horizontal streaks of both Dioxazine Purple and Ultramarine Blue in the center of the wet path and along the bottom of the canvas for dark shadows. Use a clean flat bristle brush and both warm beige and camel to apply streaks and spots of light on the back half of the path.

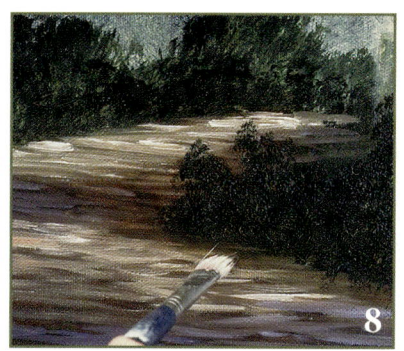

8 **Surrounding bushes:** While the path is wet, use the small round brush to stipple both dark green and blue-green foreground foliage on the right side of the path as shown. While the foliage is wet, swish the flat bristle brush horizontally on the edge of the path and the bottom of the wet foliage to connect them. Use the flat bristle brush to add horizontal streaks and spots of warm beige and camel across the foreground of the path to indicate light. Add a few subtle streaks of violet gray reflected light in the shadowy areas with the uncleaned flat bristle brush. Don't blend the colors; leave the path rough and textured.

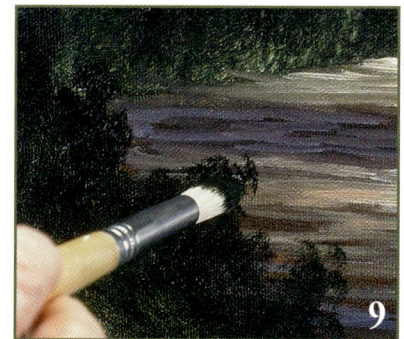

9 Follow step 8 to stipple the foremost ground foliage on the left side of the canvas. Make it stand up and lean over along the left side of and behind the path. Make the edges irregular and lacy. Dry.

10 **Sunbeams:** Pull a clean, moist sponge down from the top right corner, across the canvas to dampen a few streaks in the area where the light beams will be painted. Add Whiteblend and a touch of yellow glaze to the sponge. Tap the sponge on the palette to mix the color, then pull the sponge diagonally from the top right corner across the canvas to apply the beams of radiating light as shown. Dry.

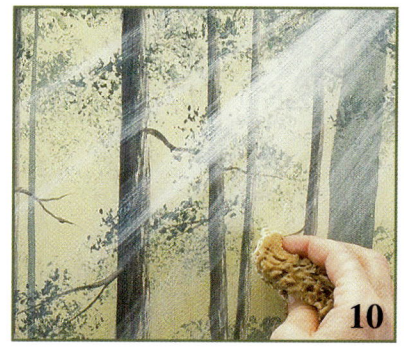

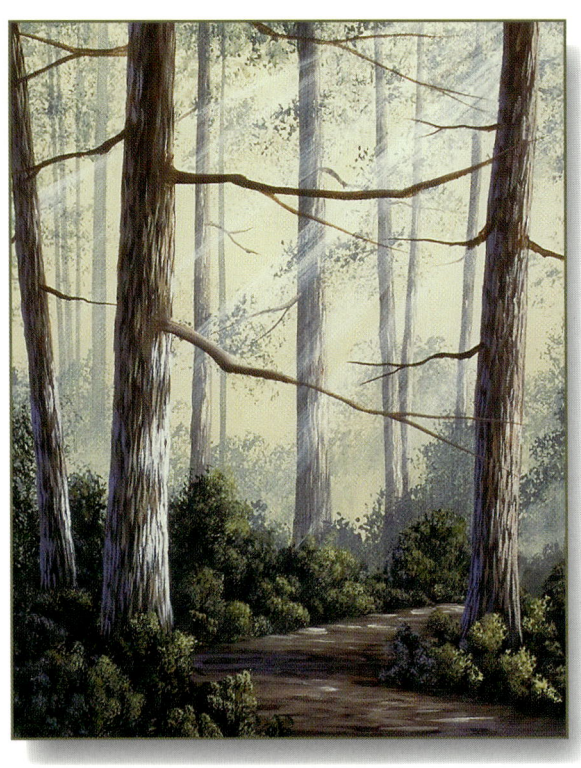

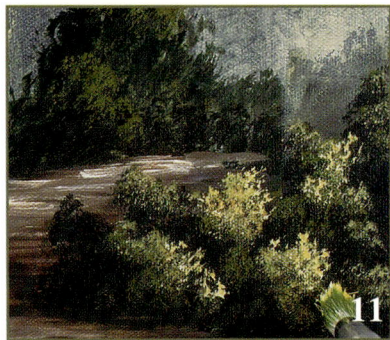

11 **Foliage highlights:** Load the small round bristle brush with medium green and lightly tap randomly in the foreground foliage. Add yellow-green to the uncleaned brush and stipple the top right half of each cluster or bush. Add light yellow-green to the uncleaned brush and tap over the top and right edges of a few bushes.

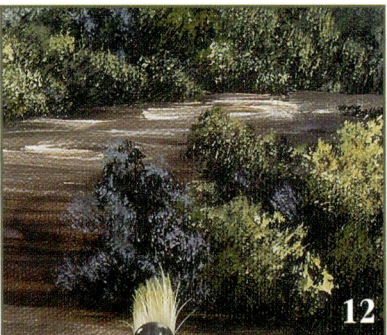

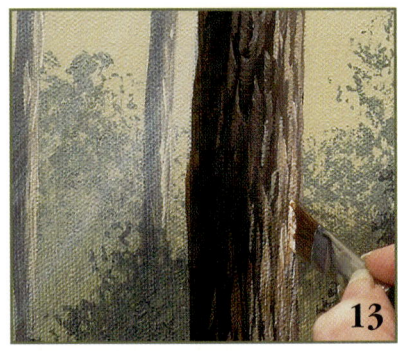

12 **Shadows:** Brush-mix dark blue-green and violet gray on a clean small round bristle brush. Apply sparse reflected light in the shadowy areas of the ground foliage. Dry.

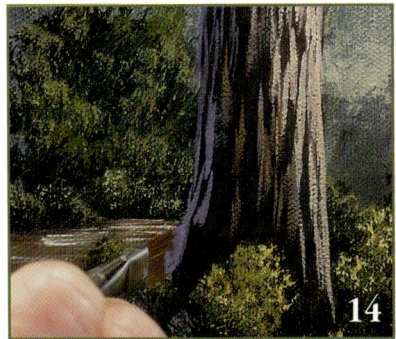

13 **Foreground trees:** Use the flat bristle brush to paint the foremost tree on the right of the canvas burnt umber on the left and tan on the right. Use the angular brush to add Mars Black bark strokes on the left side of the wet tree. With a clean angular brush, add warm beige bark texture and highlights on the center and right side of the tree. Use a clean angular brush to randomly add camel highlights on the right side of the tree, indicating sunny spots.

14 **Reflected light:** Clean the angular brush then apply choppy strokes of violet gray reflected light on the far left side of the tree. Paint short Titanium White strokes to indicate the brightest patches of sun on the bark on the right side. Repeat steps 13 and 14 to paint the other two foreground trees.

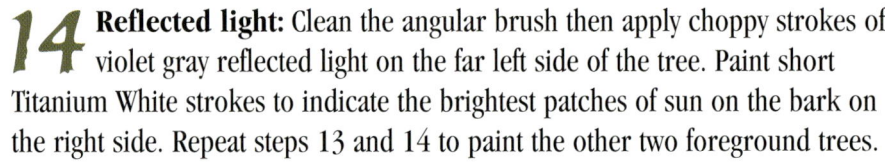

15 **Limbs:** Use a liner brush and Burnt Umber to paint the limbs on the tree on the far left side of the canvas. Use your finger to blot the area where the limb joins the tree with your finger. Double-load the angular brush with Burnt Umber and camel and with the camel side upward, paint the large limbs on the remaining two foreground trees. Repeat for the smaller limbs and twigs in the foreground foliage, using the liner. Dry thoroughly.

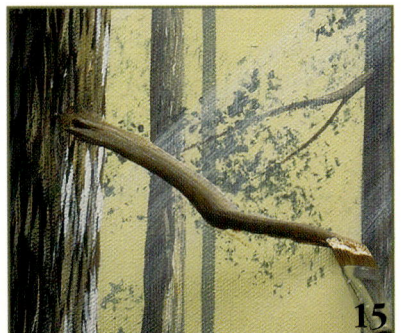

16 Tree accents: Brush-mix a translucent glaze of equal parts Clearblend and Raw Sienna with the angular brush and spread it thinly over the left foreground trees. While the glaze is wet, add sparse Burnt Sienna, Burnt Umber or dark green choppy accents in the dark areas of the trees.

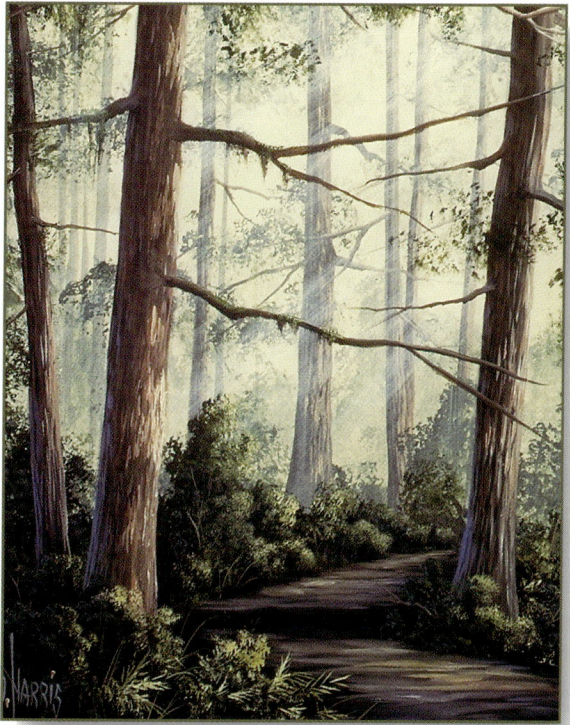

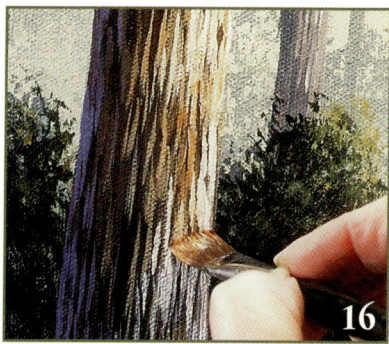

17 Light on foliage: Use a flat bristle brush to scumble a hint of the blue-green translucent glaze over some of the distant foliage that was subdued with the yellow glaze. Tap over the edges of the wet glaze with a clean moist sponge to blend the edges.

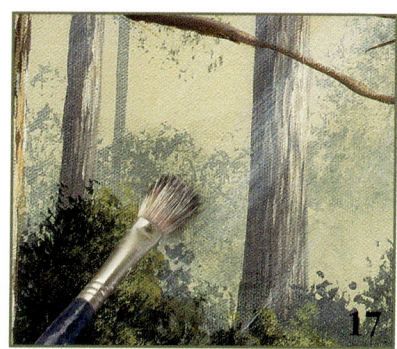

18 Leaves: Use a sponge to tap dark green and dark blue-green foliage near the canvas edges and over parts of some limbs. See the photo on page 62 for placement. Apply the foliage loose and lacy, being careful not to block out all the background color. Use the round bristle brush and any or all of the foliage colors to touch up the ground foliage. Overlap the bases of the tree trunks with some of this ground foliage. Dry.

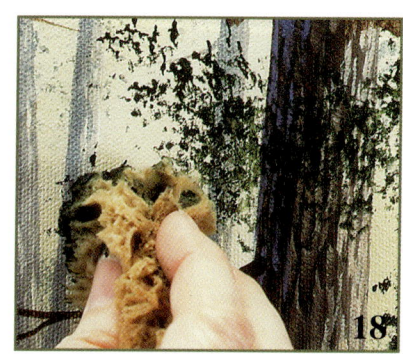

19 Moss: Tap patches of dark green moss randomly on top of some foreground limbs with the multi-texture brush. Drag the brush downward from the patches to create strings of moss dangling from the limbs. Use a clean multi-texture brush and medium green, yellow-green and a hint of light yellow-green to highlight the top edges of the moss.

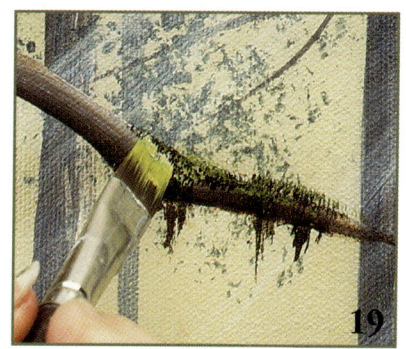

20 Ferns: Use a multi-texture brush and yellow-green and light yellow-green to paint the foreground ferns. Lightly pull the brush tip diagonally as shown to make the fern stems and leaves. Lift up a few wispy grasses with the liner brush and watery yellow-green and light yellow-green. Double-load the liner with Burnt Umber and camel, then add a few twigs and sticks randomly in the foreground.

Sign your painting and take a leisurely stroll through a forest! When your painting is completely dry, spray it with Grumbacher Acrylic Painting Varnish.

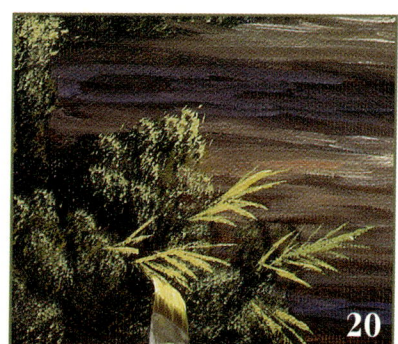

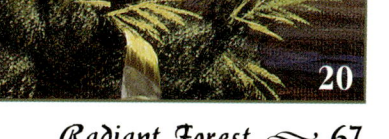

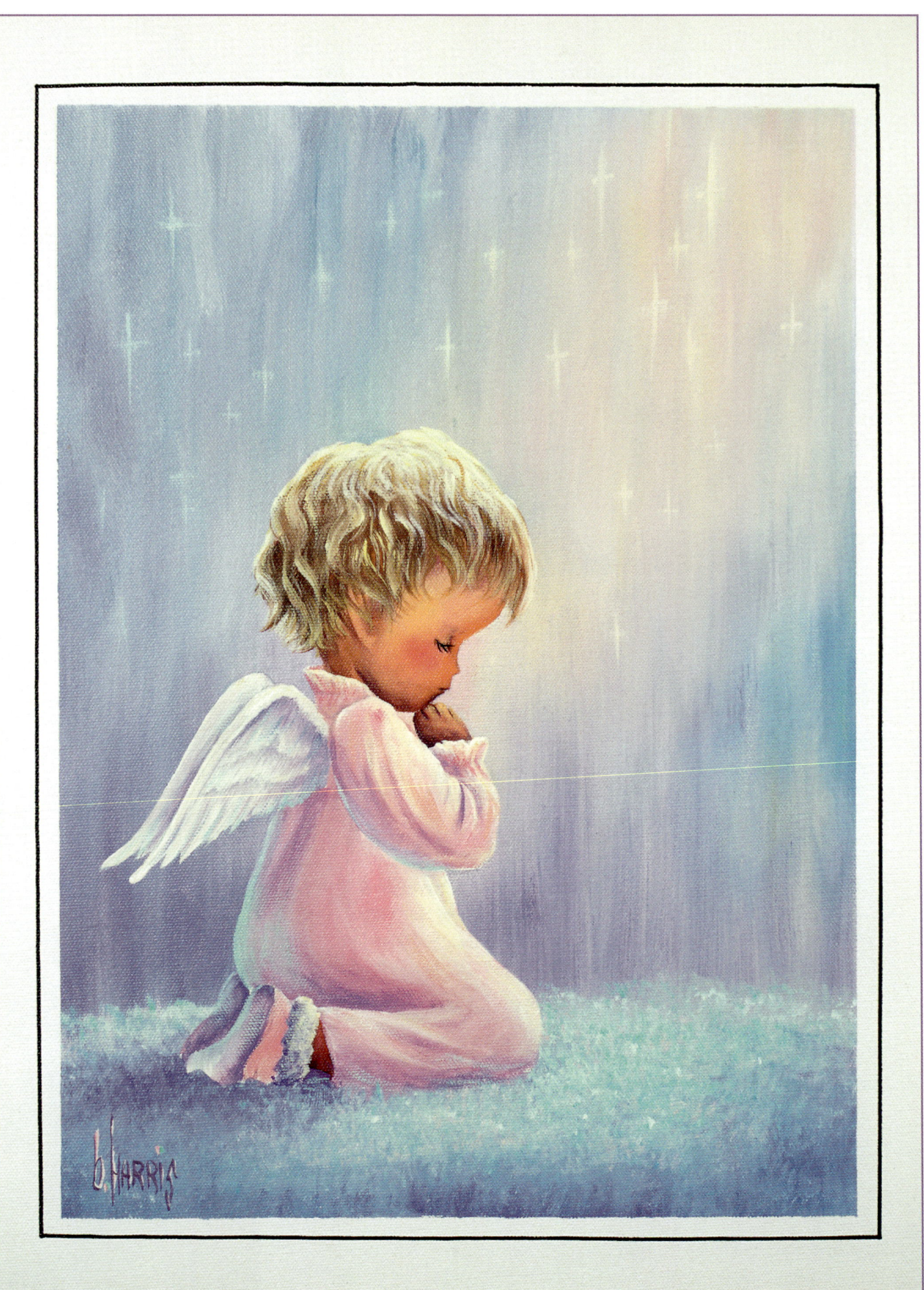

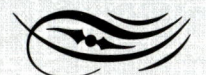

Gramma's Li'l Angel

Grumbacher Acrylic Colors
Burnt Umber
Cadmium Yellow Medium
Grumbacher Gray
Dioxazine Purple
Grumbacher Red
Portrayt
Thalo Green
Titanium White
Ultramarine Blue

Brushes
Two #101 Gesso Brushes, Size 2"
#1060 White Bristle Fan Brush, Size 1
#4403 Sable Essence® Angular Bright Brush, Size ½"
#1600 Multi-Texture Brush, Size ½"
#4623 Golden Edge® Liner Brush, Size 2
#4610B Golden Edge® Bright Brush, Size 6

Other Supplies
16"x20" Stretched Canvas
Grumbacher Clearblend
Grumbacher Whiteblend
Grumbacher Slowblend
Grumbacher Retarder
16"x20" Mat Template (12"x15½" Opening)
Matte Medium
Rapidograph Pen #2.0 and #0.25
Rapidograph Waterproof Ink: Black
Masking Tape
Charcoal Graphite Paper
Tapered Palette Knife
Grumbacher Acrylic Painting Varnish

Recently I have received several requests for a painting of an angel, from viewers, students and friends. My husband and I, as well as two dear friends, are expecting first grandchildren, and we collect angels and cherubs. In celebration of every grandparent's grandchild, I have painted "Gramma's Li'l Angel." Be sure to watch for Book 5 in this series—it includes the companion piece, "Grandpa's Li'l Angel."

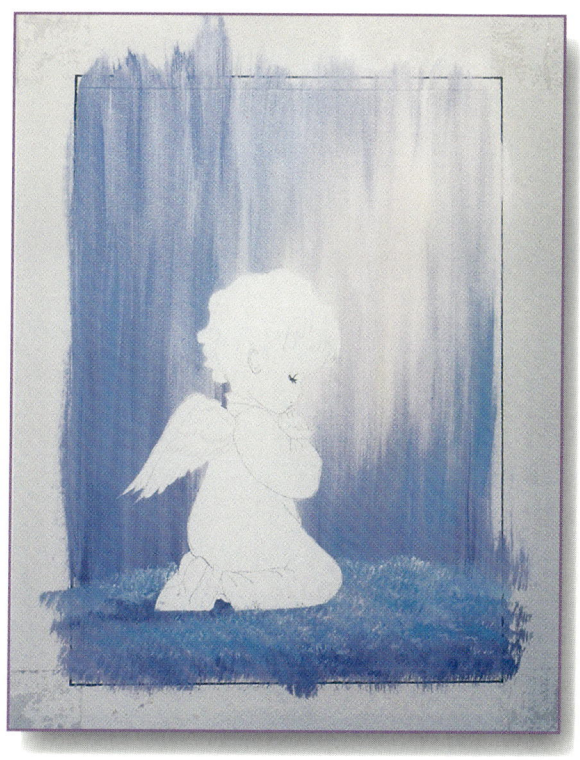

Palette
Before you begin, prepare these color mixtures:

Medium Violet-Gray—15 parts Whiteblend, 5 parts Grumbacher Gray, 1 part Dioxazine Purple

Medium Turquoise—12 parts Whiteblend, 2 parts Ultramarine Blue, 1 part Thalo Green

Light Blue—4 parts Whiteblend, 1 part Ultramarine Blue

Teal—1 part Whiteblend, a touch of Thalo Green

Pale Yellow—1 part Whiteblend, a touch of Cadmium Yellow Medium

Pink—1 part Whiteblend, a touch of Grumbacher Red

Medium Pink—1 part Pink, a touch of Grumbacher Red

Pale Pink—1 part Pink, a touch of Titanium White

Blush—3 parts Titanium White, 1 part Grumbacher Red

Flesh—2 parts Portrayt, 5 parts Titanium White, 1 part Slowblend

Flesh Shadow—12 parts Flesh, 1 part Portrayt, 1 part Dioxazine Purple, 1 part Slowblend

Peach—10 parts Titanium White, 1 part Cadmium Yellow Medium, a touch of Grumbacher Red

Off-White—2 parts Titanium White, 1 part Pale Yellow

Hair Shadow—2 parts Burnt Umber, 2 parts Titanium White, 1 part Portrayt, 1 part Cadmium Yellow Medium

Light Violet-Gray—1 part Whiteblend, 1 part Medium Violet-Gray

Canvas Preparation: Refer to page 2 of the techniques section for instructions on French matting to mat this canvas. Use the #2.0 point Rapidograph pen to draw the mat line. Use the graphite paper to transfer the girl to the canvas, with the bottom tip of her wing 3½" from the left canvas edge and her knees 4½" from the bottom canvas edge. Go over her eyelashes with the small point Rapidograph pen. Dry. Cover the angel with a design protector.

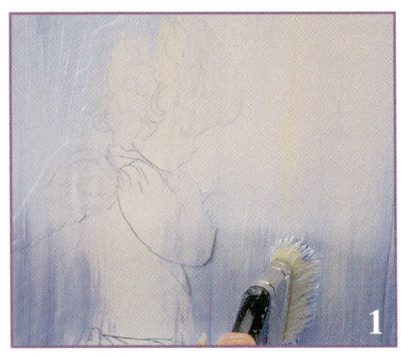

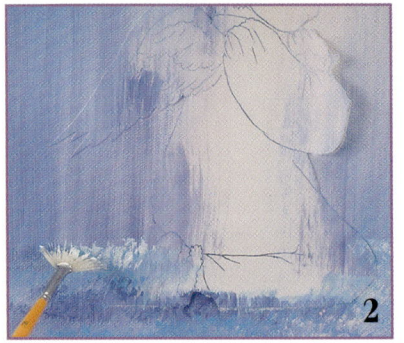

1 **Background:** Apply the background colors with the brush held and stroked vertically. Start in the top right corner and move across the canvas, alternating between pale pink and Whiteblend, ending just behind the angel's head. Add pale yellow to the uncleaned brush and add a few vertical strokes in the pink area. Wipe the excess paint from the brush, then alternate between light blue and Whiteblend to paint the remainder of the background the same way. Add accents of teal, turquoise and medium violet-gray in the blue area while it's still wet. Stroke medium violet-gray up from the canvas bottom to create a shadowy area around the angel. Hold a clean, towel-dried gesso brush vertically and blend the background with vertical strokes. Touch up colors if necessary and blend once more with a hake brush.

2 **Ground:** Stipple the ground area with the same colors used in the background. Hold the gesso brush horizontally with the handle slightly tilted down and tap lightly. Begin with teal along the top edge, then add light blue and end with medium violet-gray at the bottom. Use a fan brush to paint a medium violet-gray shadow beneath the angel. Stipple accents of Whiteblend, pink, pale yellow and medium turquoise randomly around in the wet paint with the fan brush. Dry and touch up any colors if necessary with the fan brush. Dry and remove the design protector.

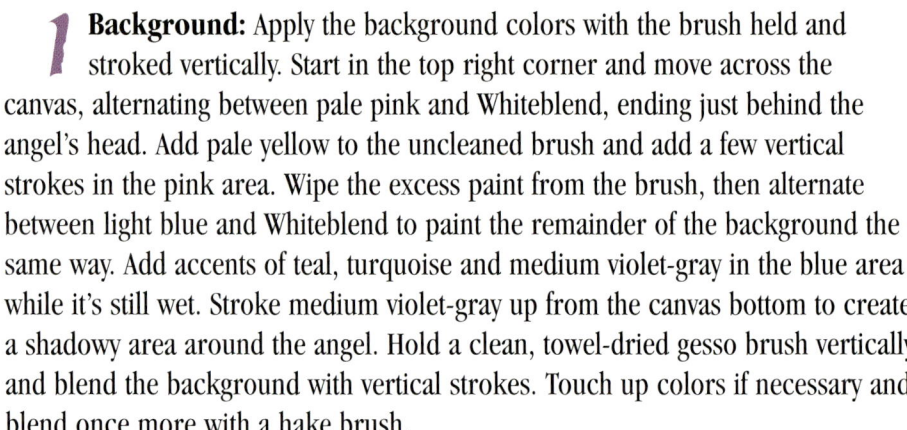

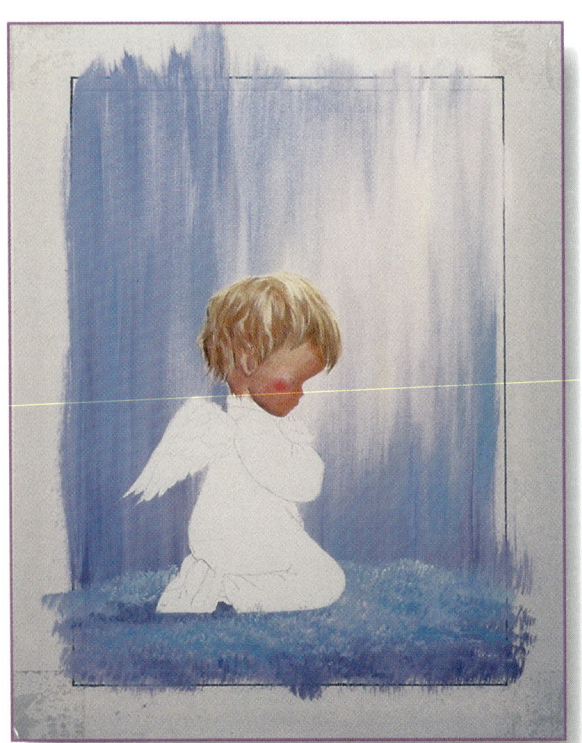

3 **Face:** Paint and blend the face, neck and ear a small section at a time with the bright brush. Starting at the forehead and moving down to the chin, paint a section the width of the bright brush outlining the outside edges of her face with flesh. Apply flesh shadow around the bottom of her chin with the uncleaned bright brush. Blend with a clean, towel-dried bright brush.

4 **Cheek:** Use the bright brush to fill in the cheek with pink and the forehead with peach; blend. Add a dab of blush on the cheek bone and blend. Clean the brush frequently while blending.

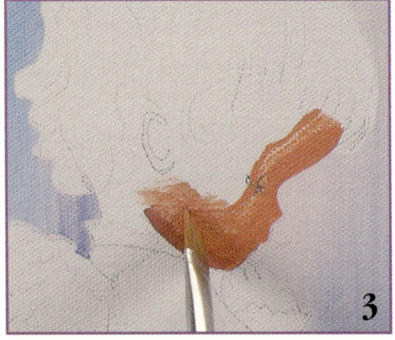

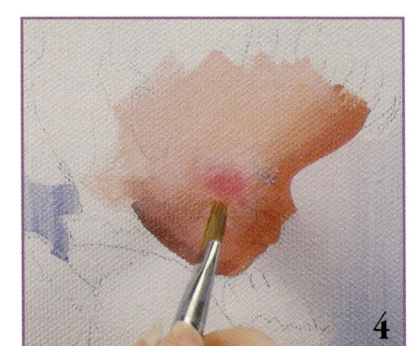

5 **Neck:** Use the angular brush to paint the back of her neck flesh shadow and to paint the area around her ear pink. Blend both areas with a clean, towel-dried angular brush. Use the angular brush to apply flesh shadow inside her ear and blend it toward her face. Repeat with flesh shadow behind her ear, blending toward the back of her head.

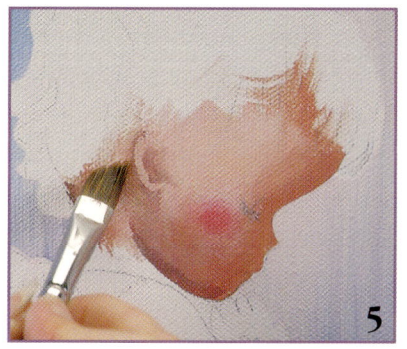

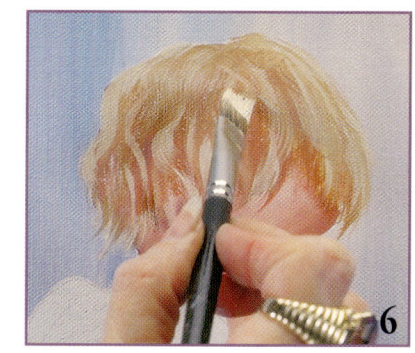

6 **Hair:** Use the multi-texture brush and alternate between flesh, flesh shadow, hair shadow and Burnt umber to create the lower sections of the hair. Add peach to the uncleaned brush and paint the top of the head a value lighter than the bottom as shown. While the hair is still wet, add highlights to it with a clean multi-texture brush and pale yellow.

7 **Hand & Leg:** For her hand, use the bright brush to paint the left and lower area flesh shadow, the center flesh and the right area pink. Use the liner brush to paint a flesh shadow line between each finger; blend slightly with a clean, towel-dried bright brush. Use the liner brush to add a touch of peach highlight on each knuckle, then blend with a clean bright brush. Dry; touch up if necessary. Paint the bottom half of her leg flesh shadow and the top half flesh, then blend between.

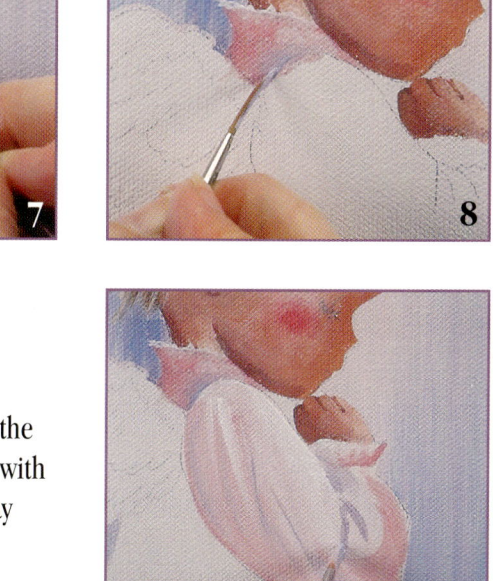

8 **Gown:** Paint and blend a small section at a time. Brush-mix to vary the pink values as you progress by adding more Whiteblend or blush. Paint the collar and back of the gown above the wings pink with the angular brush. Add a touch of blush to the uncleaned brush and shade the back edge of the collar. Use the bright brush to add Whiteblend to the top of the collar and blend. With the liner brush and light violet-gray, add a faint shadow at her shoulder between the collar and sleeve; blend.

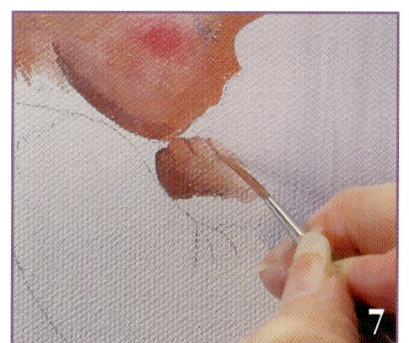

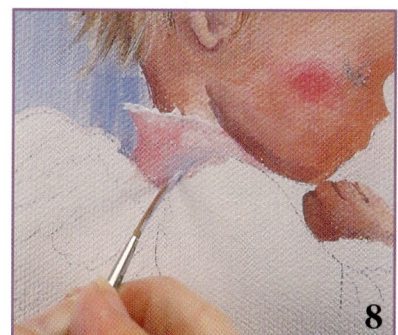

9 **Sleeve:** Use the angular brush to paint the center of the sleeve pink, the lower area medium pink and the upper area pale pink. Blend lightly with a clean angular brush. While wet, use the bright brush to add light violet-gray shadows in the wrinkles and folds as shown; blend lightly.

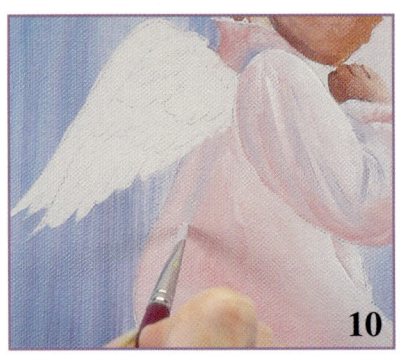

10 **Gown and highlights:** Paint the lower area of her gown a small section at a time. Basecoat her gown pink. Deepen the value of the pink on her hip by blending in some medium pink. Lighten the value on the gown front and over her leg by blending in some pale pink. While the gown is still wet, add light violet-gray shadows on her back, above her leg and in the folds of the fabric under her legs with a detail bright brush. Refer to page the large photo on page 68 for placement. Blend with a clean, towel-dried angular brush.

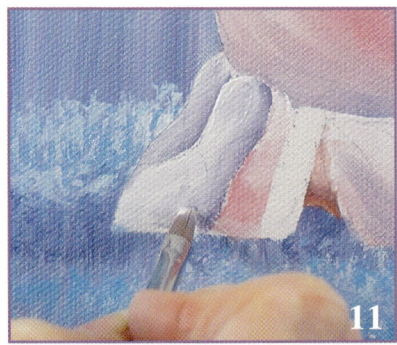

11 **Slippers:** Use the bright brush to paint the side of her slipper medium pink and the heels pale pink; blend. Paint the right sides of the soles medium violet-gray and the left sides Whiteblend with a clean bright brush; blend lightly. While wet, use the liner brush to add light blue and pale pink accents to the soles; blend.

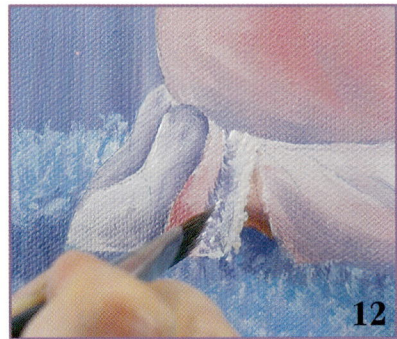

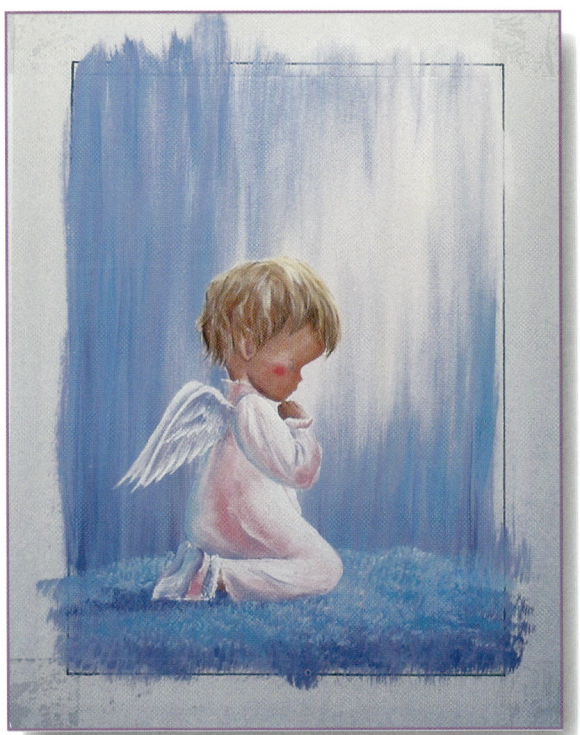

12 **Slipper trim:** Use the multi-texture brush to stipple light violet-gray fuzzy trim around the top of her slipper. Stipple medium violet-gray along the lower edge and Titanium White along the top edge. Accent the white area with hints of pale yellow.

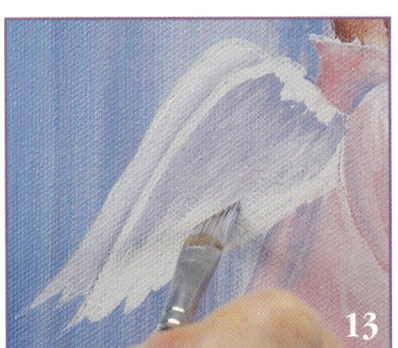

13 **Wings:** Paint one wing at a time, starting at the tip and stroking up. Use the angular brush to paint the bottom edge of her left wing light violet-gray and the top edge Whiteblend; blend. Paint the center of her right wing light violet-gray with the angular brush, then add Whiteblend around the outer edges. While wet, add diagonal feather marks with Whiteblend and the multi-texture brush. Use the angular brush to dab pink on her right wing where it meets her gown and blend. Dry.

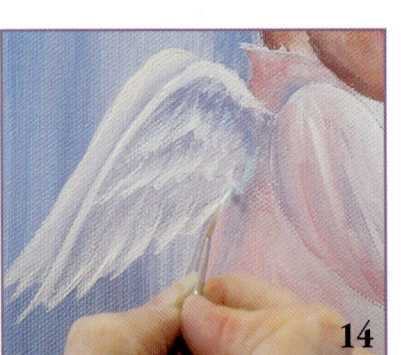

14 **Wing highlights:** Cover her wings with Grumbacher Retarder and add hints of off-white highlights on them. While wet, use a liner brush to add hints of pale pink and teal reflected light in the wings and to touch up the shadows as needed. Blend with a detail bright brush.

15 **Gown Detail:** Cover the sleeve of her gown with Grumbacher Retarder. Use an angular brush to apply off-white highlights on the upper area of the sleeve and blend to the inside. Repeat to highlight her tummy and leg.

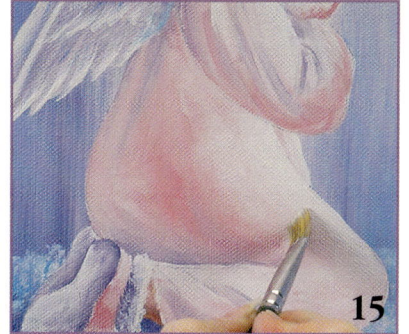

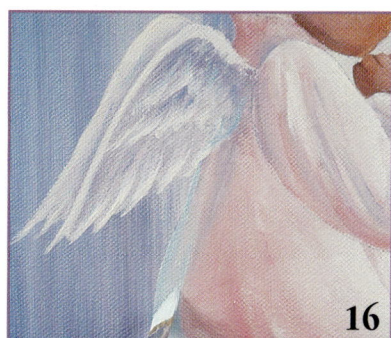

16 Follow step 15 to add reflected light to her back below the wings, on the bottom of her sleeve and on the soles of her slippers. Use teal instead of off-white, working one section at a time. Dry.

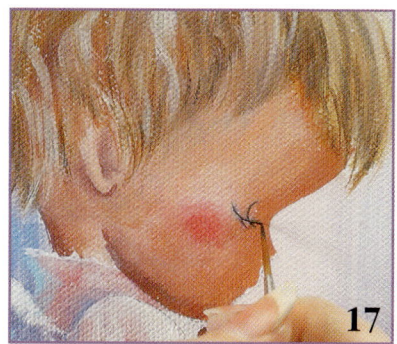

17 **Face detail:** If necessary, cover her face with retarder and touch up. Dry thoroughly. Use a liner brush and a watery brush-mix of Burnt Umber and Ultramarine Blue to go over her lashes, or lay the painting flat and draw over the eyelashes with the fine point Rapidograph pen. To make a mouth, apply flesh shadow under her upper lip with the liner brush.

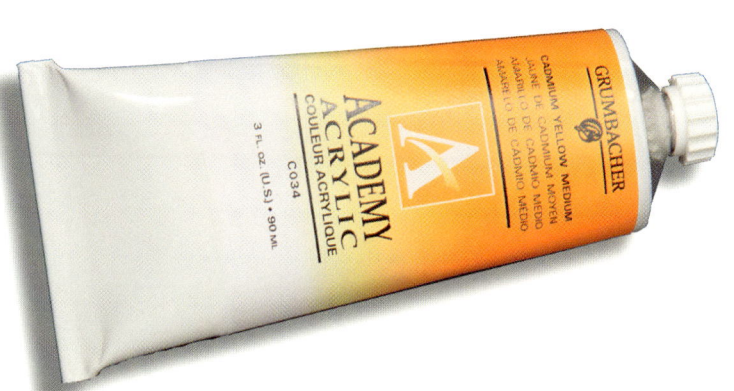

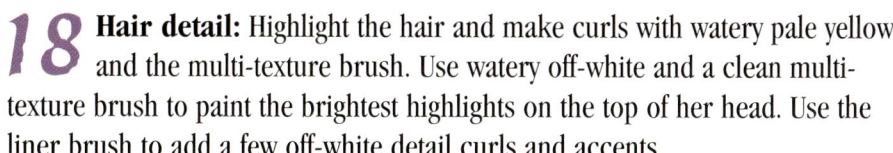

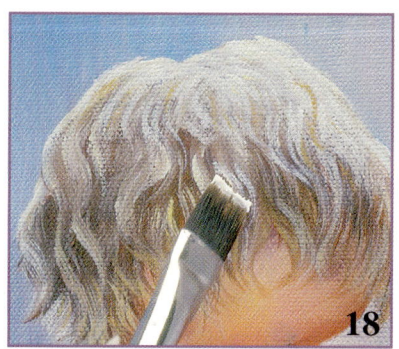

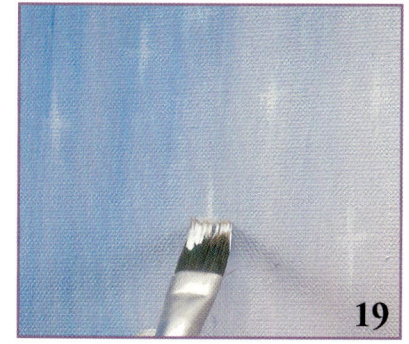

18 **Hair detail:** Highlight the hair and make curls with watery pale yellow and the multi-texture brush. Use watery off-white and a clean multi-texture brush to paint the brightest highlights on the top of her head. Use the liner brush to add a few off-white detail curls and accents.

19 **Stars:** Load the multi-texture brush with Whiteblend, turn the brush vertically to paint the ½"–1¼" vertical stroke. Repeat, turning the brush for the horizontal stroke. Add a touch of blue or teal to the Whiteblend for more subdued stars in the darker areas of the sky, or blot them lightly with your finger while they are wet.

20 Use the liner brush to dab colors from the ground onto her lower gown, slipper and leg in a few places to connect her to the ground.

Sign and "be touched" by your angel. When completely dry, spray your painting with Grumbacher Acrylic Painting Varnish to make your little angel sparkle!

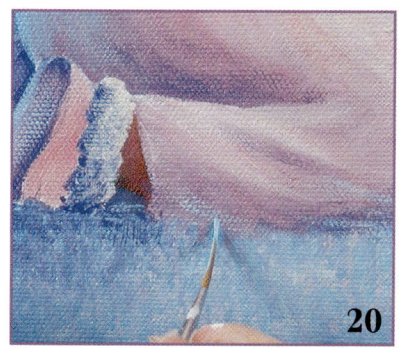

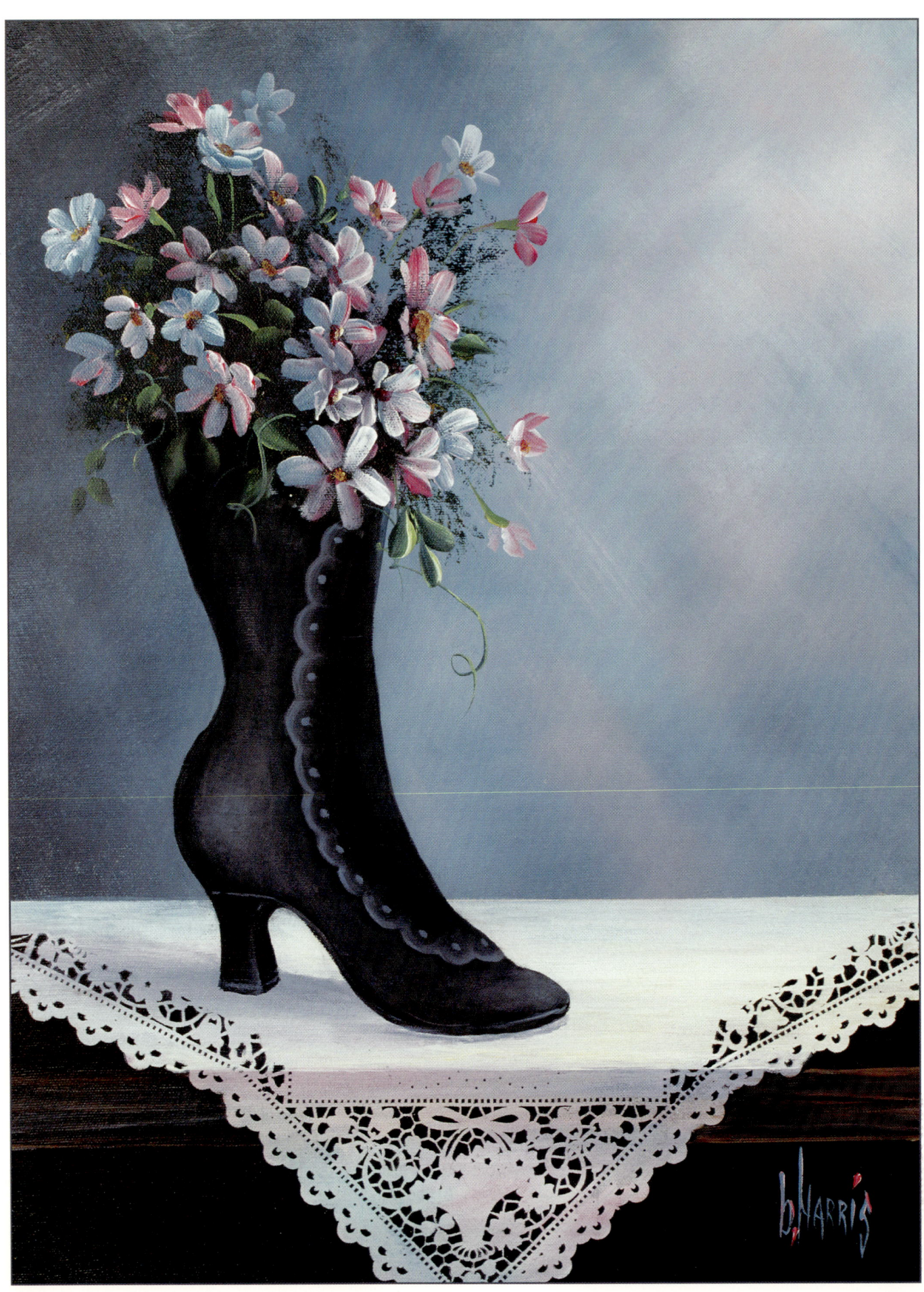

High Steppin'

Grumbacher Acrylic Colors
Burnt Umber
Cadmium Yellow Medium
Payne's Gray
Hooker's Green
Prussian Blue
Thalo Crimson
Ultramarine Blue

Brushes
Two #101 Gesso Brushes, Size 2"
#1060 White Bristle Fan Brush, Size 1
#762 Academy Bristle Filbert Brush, Size 6
#760F Academy Bristle Flat Brush, Size 6
#4623 Golden Edge® Liner, Size 2
#4610B Golden Edge® Bright Brush, Size 6
#4403 Sable Essence® Angular Bright Brush, Size ⅜"
#1600 Multi-Texture Brush, Size ½"
#1500 Hake Brush, Size 2"

Other Supplies
16"x20" Stretched Canvas
Grumbacher Clearblend
Grumbacher Whiteblend
Tapered Painting Knife
Grumbacher Retarder
Natural Sponge
White and Charcoal Graphite Paper
10" Lace Paper Doily
Large Water Container
T-Square or Ruler
Pencil
Masking or Shipping Tape
Scissors
Grumbacher Acrylic Painting Varnish

Arlee Jenkins, a T.E.A.M. Artist and Painting Instructor from Tiverton, RI, created this lovely Victorian composition. "High Steppin'" introduces many new techniques like using a paper doily as a template to create the illusion of lace.

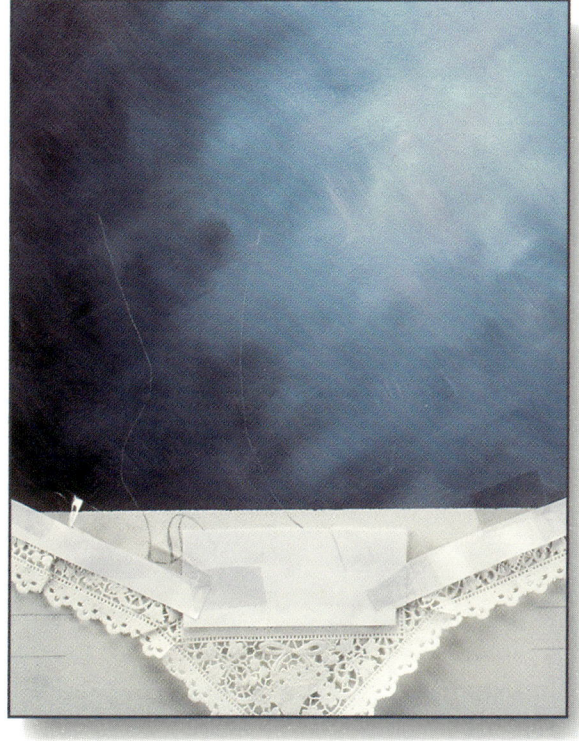

Palette
Before you begin, prepare these color mixtures:

Medium Blue—4 parts Whiteblend, 1 part Prussian Blue, 1 part Payne's Gray

Off-White—1 part Whiteblend, a touch of Cadmium Yellow Medium

Creamy Gray—6 parts Payne's Gray, 1 part Grumbacher Retarder

Bayberry—12 parts Thalo Crimson, 1 part Payne's Gray

Light Prussian—6 parts Whiteblend, 1 part Prussian Blue

Light Pink—6 parts Whiteblend, 1 part Thalo Crimson

Hunter Green—1 part Hooker's Green, 1 part Prussian Blue

Glaze Mixtures: (mix each glaze in a separate container)

Blue Glaze—1 part Clearblend, a touch of Prussian Blue, a touch of Payne's Gray

Blue-Violet Glaze—1 part Clearblend, a touch of Bayberry, a touch of Prussian Blue

Bayberry Glaze—1 part Clearblend, a touch of Bayberry

Gray-Blue Glaze—1 part Medium Blue, 1 part Creamy Gray

Canvas Preparation: Draw a horizontal line 6" from the canvas bottom. Paint the canvas below this line off-white with the gesso brush. Dry. Place a piece of masking or shipping tape below but touching the line. Make a mark on both sides of the canvas 2¼" and 3½" from the bottom to indicate side edge of the table. Use a gesso brush to moisten the area above the tape with water and Grumbacher Retarder. The canvas should be damp, not dripping wet.

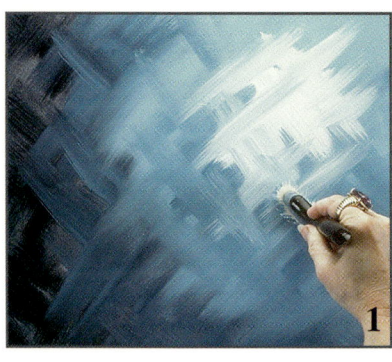

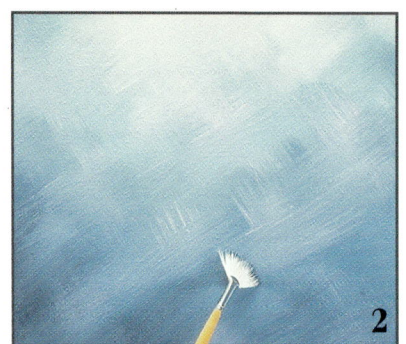

1 **Background:** While the canvas is still damp, apply the background colors with overlapping "X" strokes using the gesso brushes. Apply Payne's Gray in a crescent shape on the left side of the canvas. Apply medium blue inside the Payne's Gray section with the uncleaned brush. Use a clean gesso brush to paint the top right corner light Prussian. Add Whiteblend to the uncleaned brush and apply to the center of the light Prussian section.

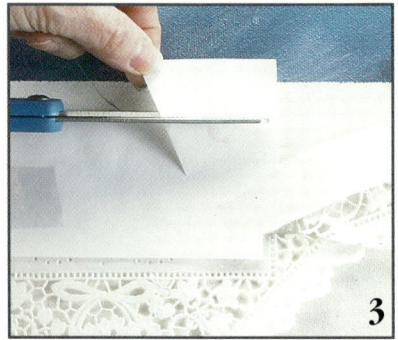

2 Blend the background with a clean, towel-dried gesso brush, starting in the light area and working into the dark and using the same "X" strokes. Don't make all the strokes equal or perfect. Use the fan brush to add light bayberry "X" strokes in the light and medium background areas; blend with a clean, towel-dried gesso or fan brush. Clean the blending brush frequently. Dry.

3 **Doily:** Lay the canvas flat and remove the tape. Transfer the boot, using the white graphite paper in dark areas and the charcoal graphite paper in light areas. The tip of the toe should be 4½" from the canvas bottom and 9¼" from the left edge. Cut a 9½"x4½" corner of the doily. Place the top straight edge along the mark for the upper edge of the table side and tape that edge securely to the canvas. If the doily doesn't have a solid area, cut a piece of writing paper to fit on the top of the doily piece. Tape the doily to the paper, then tape the paper to the canvas. Don't place tape in areas that you want to appear lacy. Repeat for the right and left edges of the tablecloth, using 5"x1½" pieces cut from the doily edges.

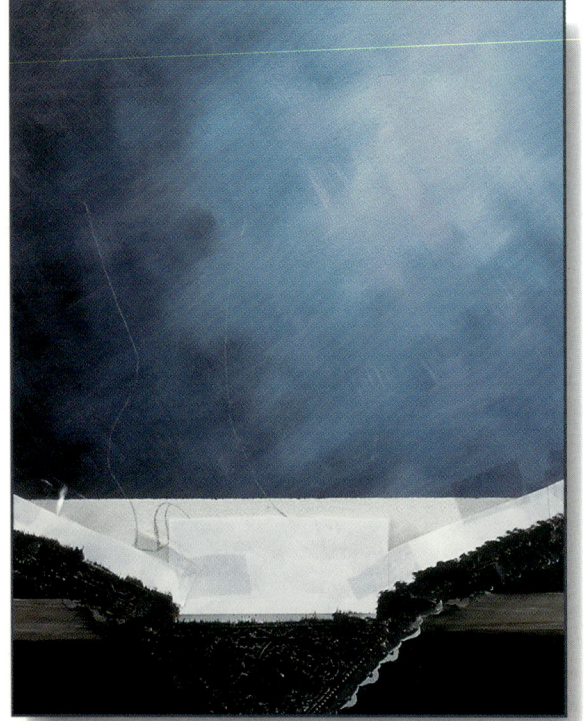

4 Make sure the doily template is taped securely. Place one hand over the bottom edge of the doily to keep it from lifting as you paint with the other. Stipple over the doily holes and along the outside edges of the doily pieces with a flat bristle brush and Burnt Umber. Tap the brush around on the doily pieces, don't drag it. Extend the paint at least 1" outside the doily edges, reloading the brush frequently.

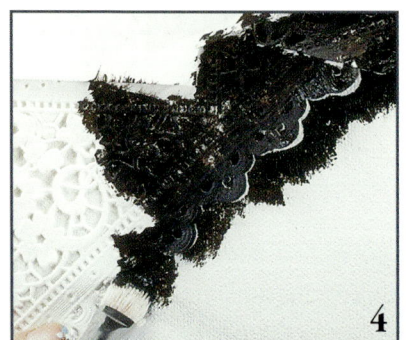

5 **Table top:** Paint the table top by dragging the flat bristle brush horizontally from the doily edges to the canvas edges above the mark indicating the side edge of the table. Add off-white to the uncleaned brush and repeat between the marks indicating the edge of the table top. Clean the brush, then darken below the table edge and in both bottom corners with Burnt Umber and a touch of Payne's Gray. Leave the strokes scruffy.

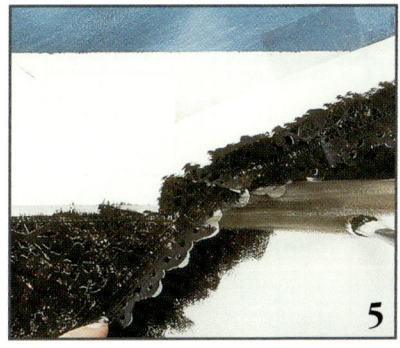

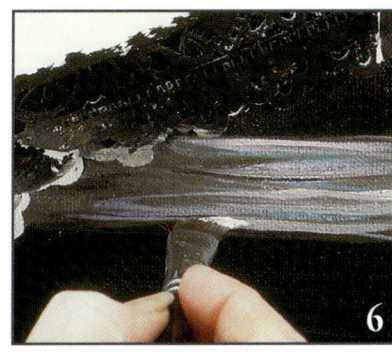

6 Touch up the table edge with the multi-texture brush, alternating among light Prussian, light bayberry and off-white. Dry.

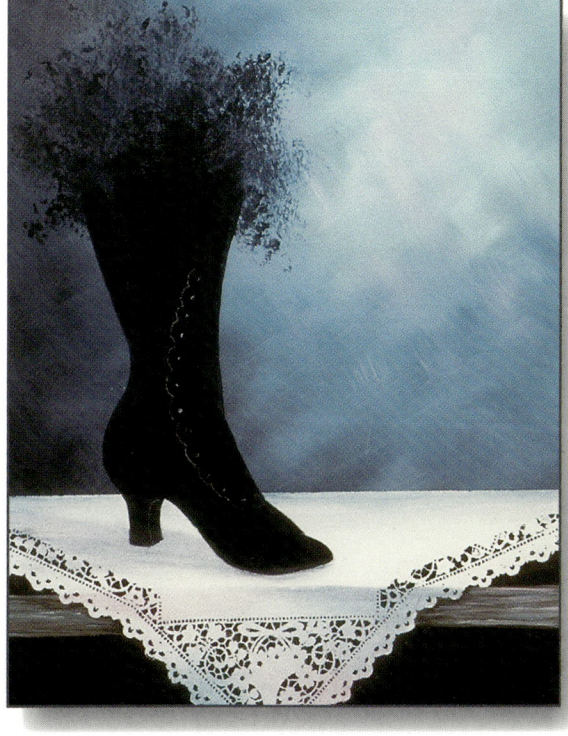

7 **Doily details:** Carefully remove the doily. Use the liner or small round brush to touch up any irregularities around the doily with either Whiteblend or Burnt Umber, depending on the area that needs retouching.

8 Use the angular brush to basecoat the boot Payne's Gray. Stipple "sprinkles" of Payne's Gray coming out of the top of the boot with a clean moist sponge to create a backdrop for the flowers; dry.

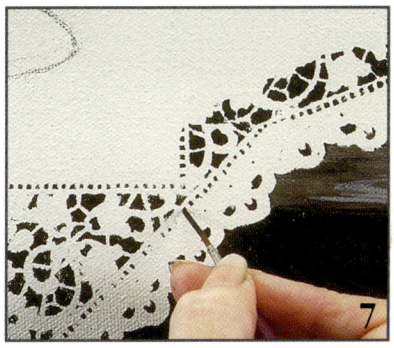

9 **Table shadows:** Use the fan brush to cover the tablecloth with Grumbacher Retarder. While still wet, apply the glaze mixtures on the tablecloth. Apply the blue glaze along the back edge of the cloth, under and behind the boot for a shadow. Apply more blue glaze on the doily near the right table edge for a shadow and on the cloth at the lower left. Add bayberry glaze and blue-violet glaze in the draped area and in the boot shadow. Soften the edges of the glazes with a clean, towel-dried fan brush. Blend away any streaks with the hake brush, then dry.

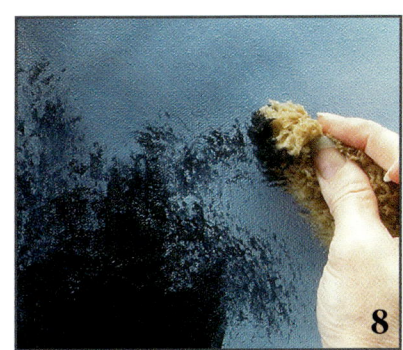

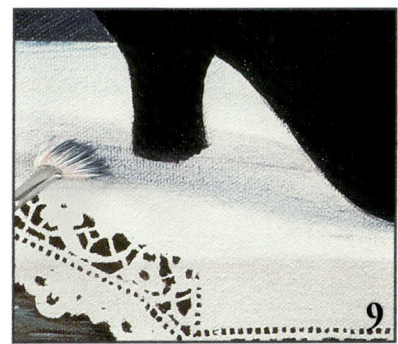

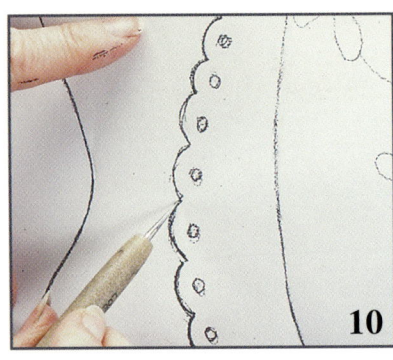

10 Position the boot pattern over the boot and transfer the details and flowers with white graphite paper. If there are white graphite smudges, remove them carefully with a clean moist sponge before adding the details.

11 **Boot details:** Cover the middle of the boot with Clearblend. See the techniques section, page 3, to side-load the angular brush with gray-blue glaze. Holding the brush with the long tip on the left, paint the scalloped edge,

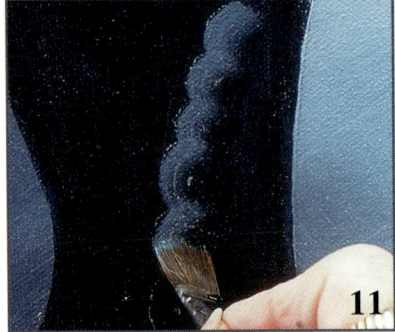

reloading the brush as before when needed. Blend any hard edges from the right side of the scallop with a Clearblend-moistened angular brush. Add dots inside each scallop with the liner brush and gray-blue glaze.

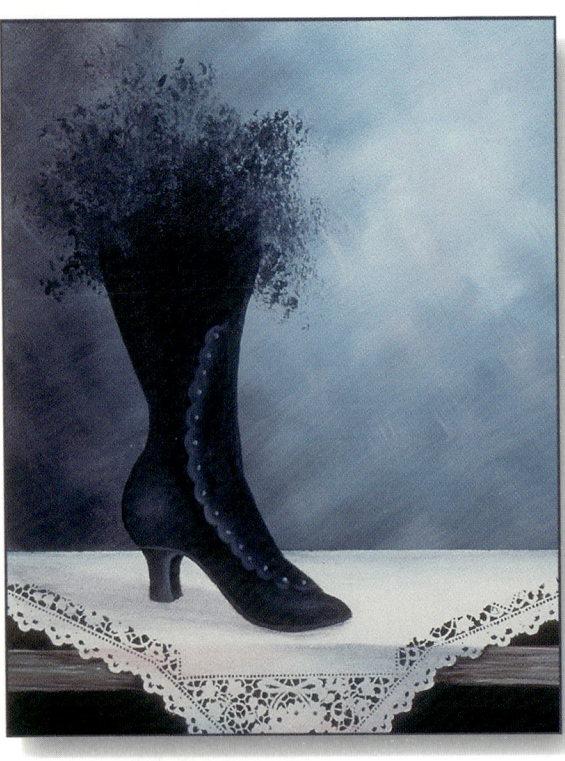

12 **Boot highlights:** Cover the heel with Clearblend. Follow step 11 to load the angular brush with gray-blue glaze and paint the highlight on the front corner of the heel. Blend any hard edges with a Clearblend-moistened angular brush.

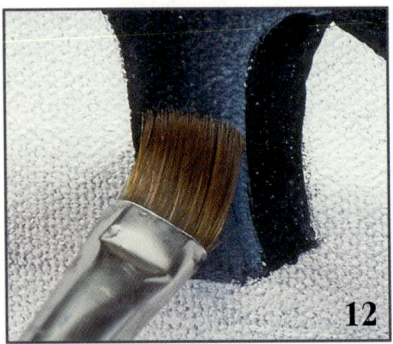

13 Cover the side and toe of the boot with Clearblend. Use the angular brush to paint gray-blue glaze along the side of the boot and to the toe. Tap around the edges of the highlight with a clean angular brush to blend the outer portions, leaving no hard or distinguishable edges. Don't blend smoothly; leave scuff marks.

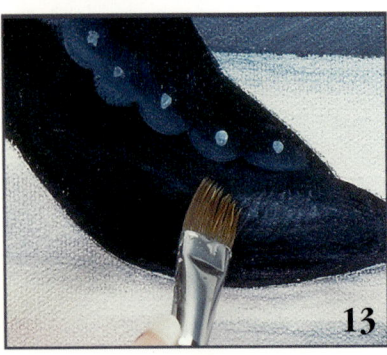

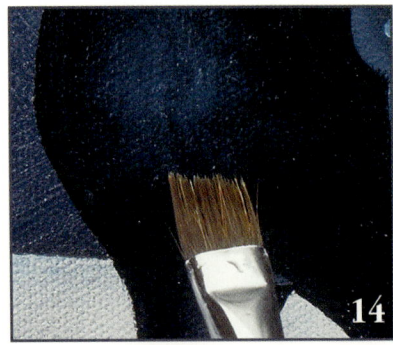

14 Cover the area above the heel with Clearblend. Add a dime-sized dab of gray-blue glaze in the center of this area with the angular brush. Tap around the edges of the patch with a clean angular brush to blend and create a rounded appearance. Keep the spot lighter in the center and blend away any hard edges, but don't blend too smoothly.

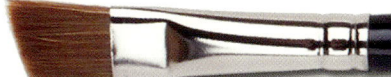

15 Use the liner brush to apply a thin gray-blue glaze line around the sole of the boot as shown; dry.

16 **Flowers:** Sponge hunter green and a touch of medium blue reflected light in the foliage; dry. Apply the larger flowers with the large bristle filbert brush and the smaller ones with the small bristle filbert brush. Use a variety of values of bayberry, light bayberry, light Prussian and Prussian blue. Double-load with a combination of varying pink and blue values to paint some of the flowers. Don't make all the flowers perfect and facing forward. Turn flowers to the side by making the petals shorter on one side of the flower. Make the flowers "cup" by overlapping the front petals over the back petals with a contrasting value.

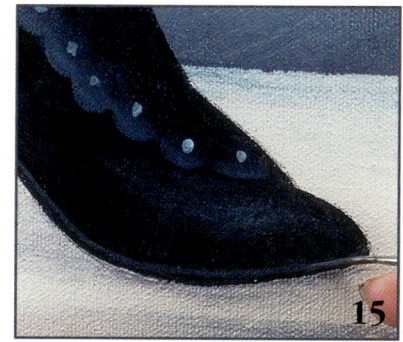

17 **Flower centers:** Use the small filbert brush to tap Burnt Umber centers in some of the flowers. Brush-mix off-white and Cadmium Yellow Medium on a clean angular brush to make bright yellow. Use this to stipple stamens on the Burnt Umber centers, being careful to leave some Burnt Umber showing.

18 **Stems and tendrils:** Brush-mix marbleized bright yellow and hunter green on a liner brush and paint the tendrils and some stems. Double-load the liner brush with hunter green and bright yellow and paint the remaining stems. Refer to the large photo on page 74 for placement of the stems and tendrils.

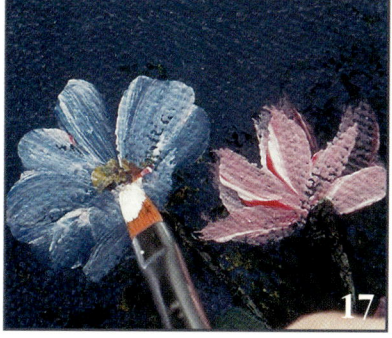

19 **Leaves:** Triple-load the angular brush with hunter green, off-white and bright yellow. Place the long tip of the brush at the top of a leaf. Press the brush down as you pull it gently, then pull it away from the canvas, releasing pressure. Paint different sizes, shapes and values of leaves randomly throughout the bouquet.

Sign your painting. Jump in your boots, go high steppin' to the garden or market and pick a lovely bouquet for a very special person, YOU! When your painting is completely dry, spray it with Grumbacher Acrylic Painting Varnish.

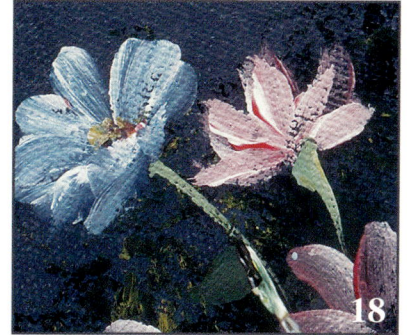

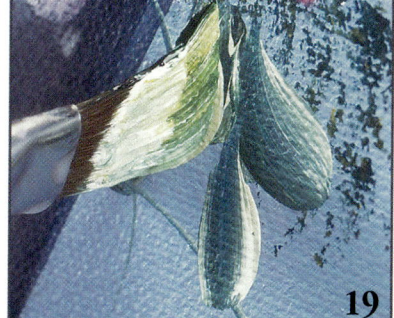

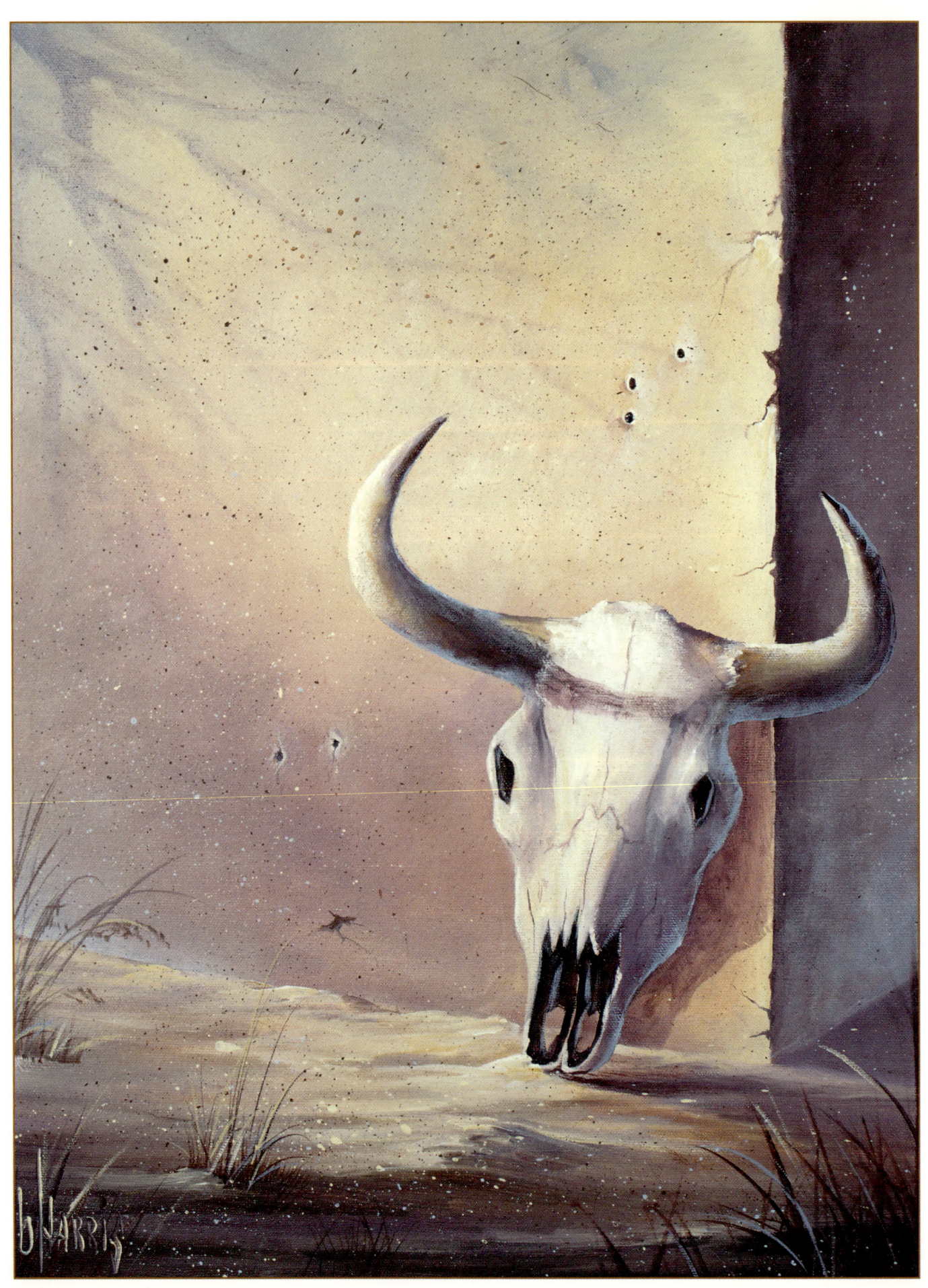

End of the Trail

Grumbacher Acrylic Colors
Burnt Sienna
Burnt Umber
Cerulean Blue
Payne's Gray
Dioxazine Purple
Titanium White
Yellow Ochre Light

Brushes
Two #101 Gesso Brushes, Size 2"
#1500 Hake Brush, Size 2"
#760F Academy Bristle Flat Brush, Size 6
#1060 White Bristle Fan Brush, Size 1
#4403 Sable Essence® Angular Bright Brush, Size ½"
#4623 Golden Edge® Liner Brush, Size 2
#1600 Multi-Texture Brush, Size ½"

Other Supplies
16"x20" Stretched Canvas
Grumbacher Clearblend
Grumbacher Whiteblend
Grumbacher Slowblend
Tapered Painting Knife
Natural Sponge
White and Charcoal Graphite Paper
Toothbrush
Tracing Paper
Stylus
Wet Palette
Grumbacher Acrylic Painting Varnish

"End of the Trail" is a composite of ideas that originated from photographs taken by Estee Rayle, one of our T.E.A.M. Artists from Greensboro, N.C. She is a wonderful teacher and dear friend. Her beautiful photos of the Southwest are truly inspirational. Look through your vacation photos for ideas. Who knows? Maybe your best composition is tucked away there!

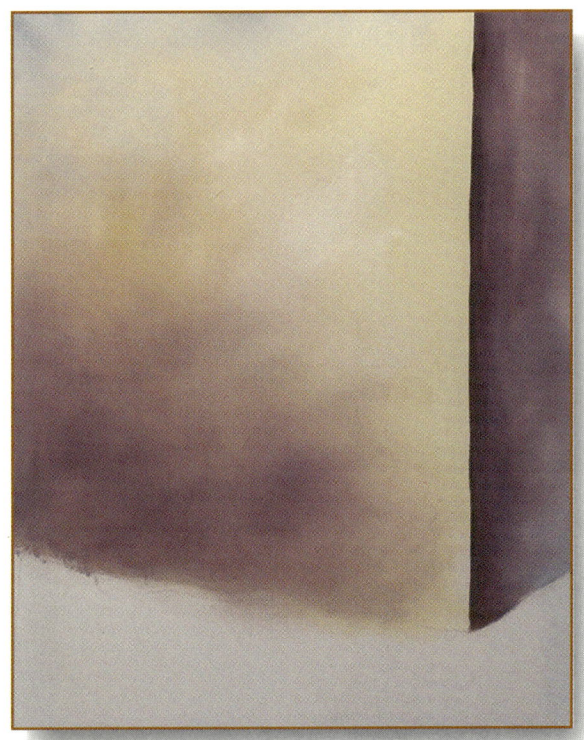

Palette
Before you begin, prepare these color mixtures:

Pale Yellow—1 part Whiteblend, a touch of Yellow Ochre Light, a touch of Slowblend

Maroon—3 parts Burnt Sienna, 1 part Grumbacher Purple, 2 parts Cerulean Blue

Mauve—1 part Maroon, 1 part Pale Yellow

Gray-Green—1 part Cerulean Blue, 1 part Pale Yellow

Mahogany—3 parts Burnt Umber, 1 part Grumbacher Purple, 1 part Cerulean Blue

Taupe—1 part Mahogany, 1 part Pale Yellow

Light Cerulean—2 parts Whiteblend, 1 part Cerulean Blue

Blue-Violet—5 parts Cerulean Blue, a touch of Grumbacher Purple, a touch of Burnt Umber, a touch of Grumbacher Gray, a touch of Clearblend

Raw Sienna—1 part Yellow Ochre Light, 2 parts Whiteblend, 1 part Burnt Sienna

Dusty Violet—6 parts Cerulean Blue, 6 parts Whiteblend, 1 part Burnt Umber, 1 part Grumbacher Purple, 2 parts Slowblend

Canvas preparation: Use charcoal graphite paper to transfer the adobe building pattern to the canvas. Don't transfer the skull pattern yet.

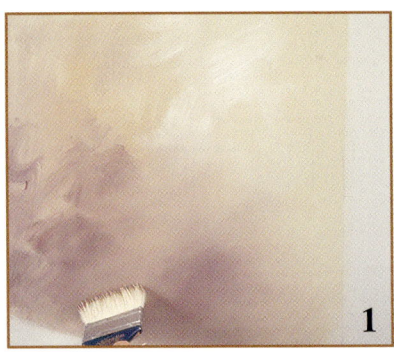

1 **Building front:** The front of the building is applied and blended wet-on-wet. To slow the drying time, use the gesso brush to wet the left side of the building with cool water and a touch of Slowblend. Allow it to soak in a few minutes before applying the paint. The canvas should be barely damp not wet when you apply the paint. Paint the entire front of the building with a generous coat of pale yellow, scrubbing it briskly into the canvas with the gesso brush. Use the uncleaned brush to alternately add Burnt Sienna and Raw Sienna randomly in the central area of the pale yellow. Add mauve and taupe to the same brush and use it to shadow the lower left portion of the wall. Scrub gray-green around the upper left of the wall with the fan brush. Use a clean fan brush and Whiteblend to lighten the area just above the center and toward the top right corner. Blend the wall with erratic strokes of a clean, towel-dried gesso brush, then fluff the brush marks away with the hake brush.

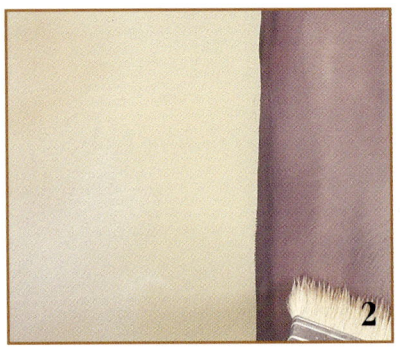

2 **Building side:** Use the flat bristle brush to apply taupe along the edge of the left of the building side, covering about a third of the side. Add pale yellow to the brush and fill in the rest of the wall, adding more pale yellow as you proceed and making the color lighter toward the right edge of the canvas. Follow the large photo on page 80 to add light cerulean and gray-green accents in the lower portion. Blend the wall slightly with the hake brush, keeping this area splotchy.

3 **Ground:** Paint a shadow area on the right side of the building with the flat bristle brush and dusty violet. Add taupe to the brush and darken areas of the shadow. See the photo on this page for color placement when painting the ground in front of the building. Alternate between using the flat bristle brush and the gesso brush to apply mahogany and maroon in the lower portion, mauve and taupe in the center and pale yellow next to the building.

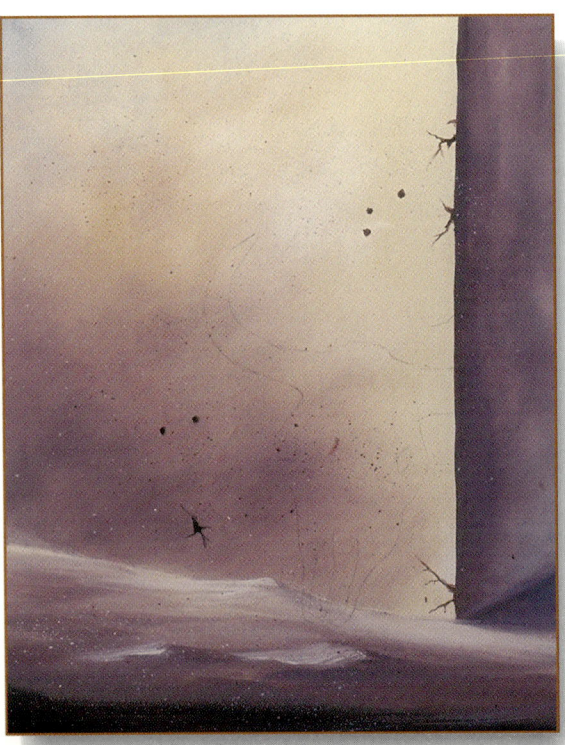

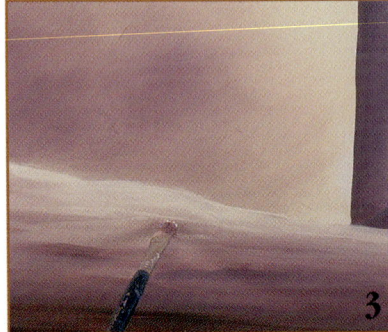

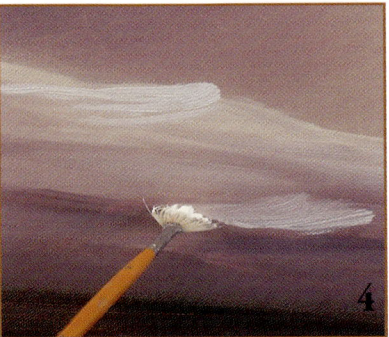

4 Blend the wet colors with a flat bristle brush, pulling light into dark and dark into light; don't overblend. Keep the canvas bottom very dark, creating a deep shadow in the foreground. Add contours with the fan brush and watery pale yellow to create highlighted "hills." Dry.

5 **Speckling:** Use the toothbrush to speckle the ground and the adobe wall with your choice of the colors on the palette mixed with lots of water to create the look of sand. Dry thoroughly. Use charcoal graphite paper to transfer the skull onto the light areas of the building, and white graphite paper to transfer it onto the dark areas of the building. The skull's nose should be 3¼" above the bottom canvas edge and its left horn should be 1½" from the right canvas edge.

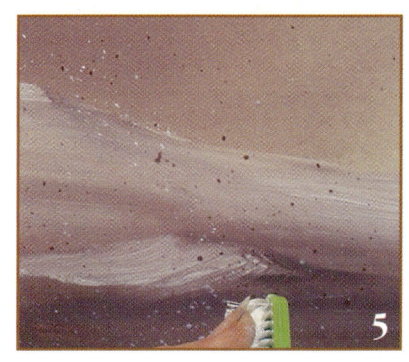

6 **Bullet holes and cracks:** Use the liner brush and mahogany to paint a few bullet holes in the wall. Add a little taupe to some mahogany, then thin it to the consistency of ink. Use the mix to paint the cracks and lines along the edge of the wall. Add a few broken areas of adobe wherever you like.

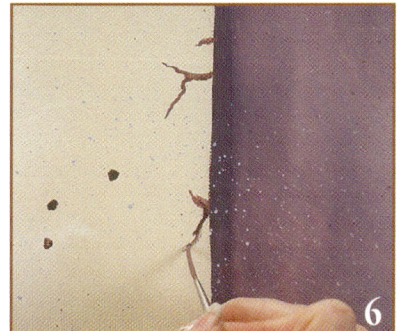

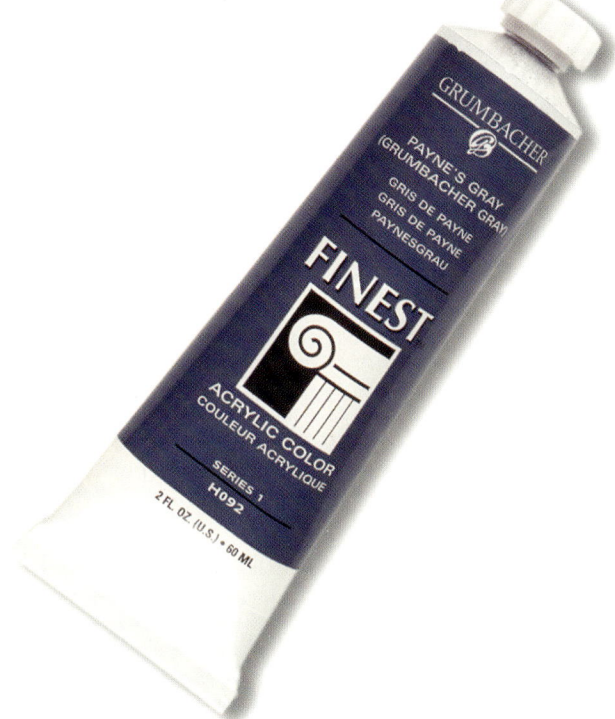

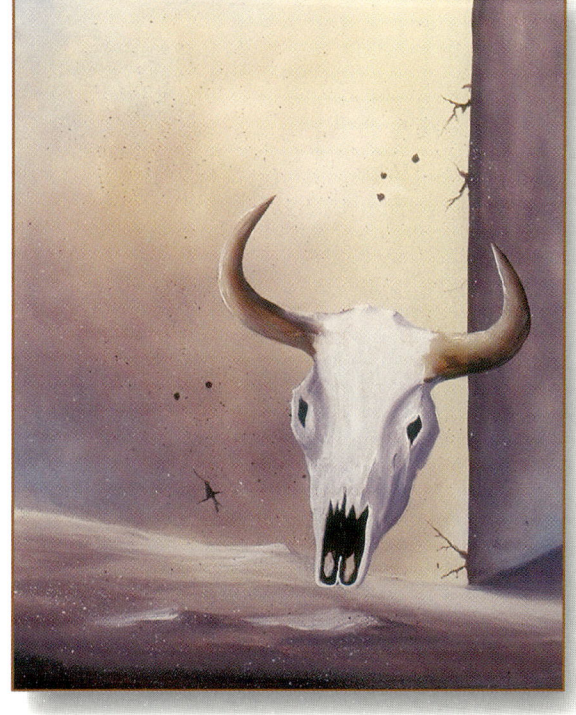

7 **Skull:** Transfer the skull, using the white graphite paper in the dark areas and the charcoal paper in the light areas. Alternate between mahogany and maroon to paint the eye sockets and the nose area with the angular brush.

8 **Horns:** Paint the horns one at a time with the angular brush. See the photo for color placement, alternating between maroon and mahogany in the dark areas. Paint the light areas raw sienna, and blend the two areas while wet. Immediately add Titanium White alternately with pale yellow in the light areas and blend. Apply Whiteblend on the skull where the horns attach and blend.

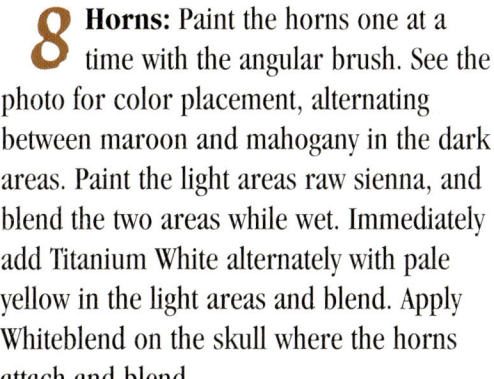

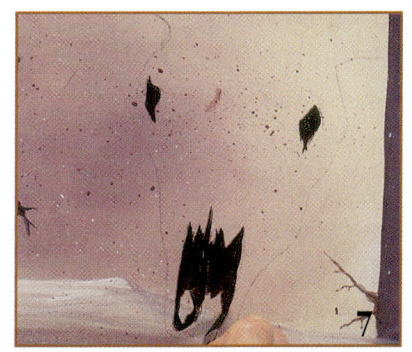

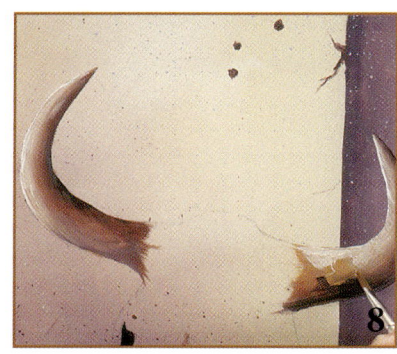

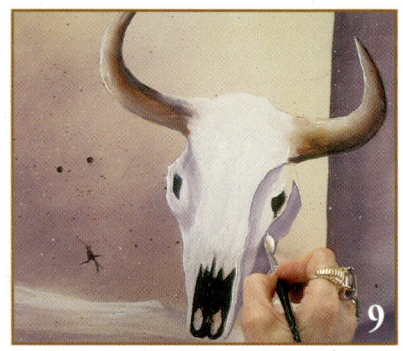

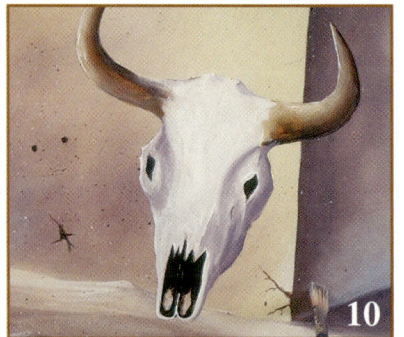

9 Skull shadows: Work the skull wet-on-wet, a small section at a time, blending the shadows into the wet Whiteblend with the angular brush as you work. Check the photo on the previous page often to make sure the shadows and highlights are placed correctly. If the Whiteblend at the base of the horns is dry, wet the area with Clearblend. Fill in the top and center of the skull with Whiteblend, adding dabs of pale yellow occasionally to give it an aged look. Blend it into the wet paint at the base of the horns. Add violet-gray shadows around the crest of the head and blend. Paint the lower left part of the skull with Whiteblend, add the dusty violet shadow by the left eye socket and blend. Repeat for the right side of the skull. While wet, add darker dusty violet accents and lighter Whiteblend accents on the right side and blend any harsh edges.

10 Apply Clearblend to the lower left section of the building front, then scrub light cerulean in this area with the flat bristle brush. Wipe the brush clean and use it to blend the light cerulean into the wet Clearblend, leaving an area of translucent reflected light. Repeat to add reflected light to the bottom of the building side.

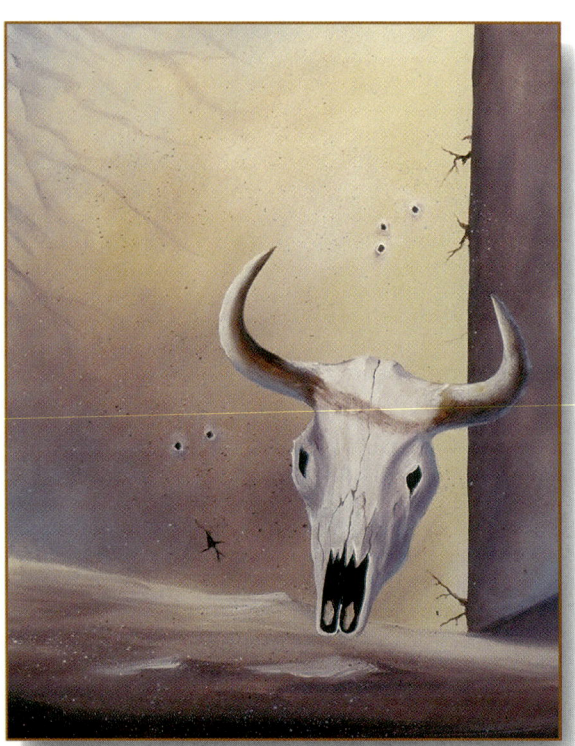

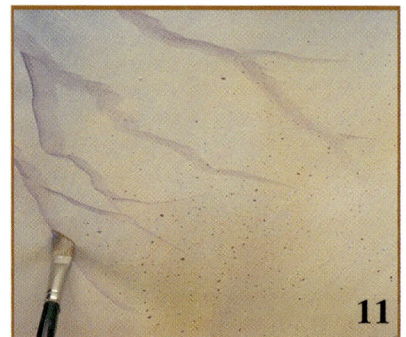

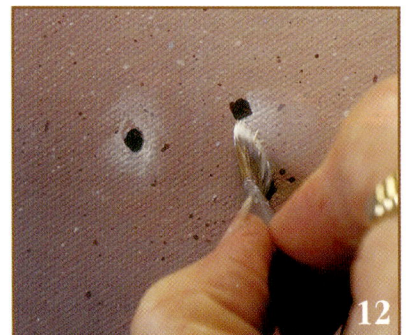

11 Tree shadows: Apply Clearblend to the top two-thirds of the building front. While wet, brush-mix Slowblend and dusty-violet on the angular brush and paint translucent tree shadows across the upper left corner of the building. Tap a clean, damp hake brush lightly over the shadow to blend and soften it.

12 Bullet holes: Brush-mix Clearblend, Whiteblend and pale yellow on the angular brush. Hold the brush with the longer bristles beside the bullet hole and paint the highlight around the hole. Repeat for all the bullet holes.

13 Brush-mix Clearblend and taupe on the angular brush. Hold the brush with the longer bristles next to the highlight around the bullet hole, and randomly add shadows to give the illusion that the hole protrudes from the wall in spots. Repeat for all the holes.

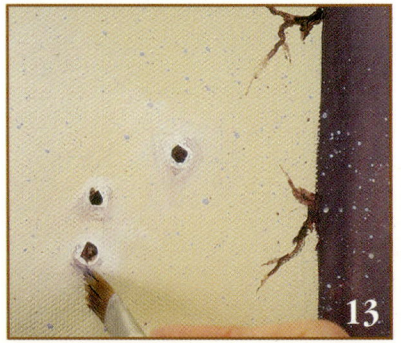